To travel hopefully is a better thing than to arrive.

—Robert Louis Stevenson

CONTENTS

INTRODUCTION

Getting Away From It All

THIS BOOK would not have been possible without your countless hours of hard work. Yes, your work.

We Americans, including the more than seven million of us in the Washington-Baltimore metropolitan area, spend far too much time with our noses to the grindstone. Others know better. Some Europeans, for example, evidently spend about two months less than we do each year toiling at their jobs.[1] Can you imagine working two months less a year? You want to explain that to the boss, or should I?

More likely, you and I will find some extra weekends now and then, maybe even squeeze in a third or fourth day, and head for a hideaway, slow down the engine, remember the rest of life.

Thanks to our long hours, our quick getaways have become precious treasures. In fact, the Washington area is filled with people who, with their equally overworked mates or TV'd-out kids, hunger for effective escape. They are people who work hard but whose weeks are often smoothed and shortened by their hopes or plans for the weekend: to be on a mountaintop, a beach towel or a massage table, to savor a sumptuous meal on plates they won't have to wash, to trek through the rich array of cultures and history surrounding the nation's capital.

I know, because as editor of *The Washington Post's* Wednesday *Escapes* page, I get a lot of their calls and letters and e-mails. Although the requests are remarkably varied, most everyone seems to seek the same thing from those of us at the paper whose work focuses on life after work: *More,* they say. Tell us more about hiking with llamas in Virginia, or about that little Swiss town in West Virginia or the place in New Jersey where you can watch either the birds or the people on the nude beach. And what about that romantic bed and breakfast that makes its own herb sausages and is right next to Whatsit National Forest? What about those Civil War battlefields, Chesapeake Bay historic sites, to-die-for bargain stores, special weekends in New York or Philadelphia, beaches, antique shops, whitewater rafting, the slots of Atlantic City, the Amish of Pennsylvania? People in the Washington area, I've discovered, are exceedingly appreciative of being told where to go.

---

[1] *The Overworked American: The Unexpected Decline of Leisure*, Juliet Schor, Basic Books, 1993.

Escape Plans tells you where—and, even better, *how* and *why*—to go. For all of the Washington area's escape artists, and for anyone else itching to pack a bag and make a swift getaway (meaning one that's generally within an hour to four hours of the Beltway), it is meant to be a useful and wide-ranging palette. Here, in one place, are the details of more than 75 destinations—enough information to chart out years of non-work joy and adventure.

While this guide is based heavily on writings from the *Escapes* pages of the *Post* and regional travel coverage from *Weekend, Travel* and the *Sunday Magazine*, a great deal of new material also has been added—along with nearly 20 maps specially prepared to help you plot your plans. This, of course, is in addition to all the updating, consolidating, rewriting and organizing that's been done to make the book as useful to you as possible.

The escape routes, you will see, are organized into four D.C.-like chapter quadrants—Northwest, Northeast, Southwest and Southeast. Each chapter contains enticing brief essays on different parts of the quadrant, followed by the practical information you need—other attractions, lodgings, restaurants, directions, prices, special packages and the like—to help you choose your own route. Each major destination is followed by still others in that neck of the woods, with each of them also chock-full of details for escape planning.

In general, the listings emphasize smaller or independently owned inns and restaurants over those that are part of big national chains. (You'll also find a ♿ symbol to note establishments that identify their main facilities as handicapped-accessible.) There are phone numbers for every establishment and visitor-information organization listed, plus large numbers of web addresses to use for checking the dates of regional festivals, special performances or details of other attractions that interest you. Before you go anywhere, in fact, it would be wise to call or to browse through web pages for any other information you might desire.

To make it still easier for you to use *Escape Plans*, we have included a section called CROSS-PREFERENCES, which groups destinations by your individual interests or needs. If you're after romantic spots or antiques or the great outdoors—or if you're looking for a place to stay that welcomes pets as well as families—you'll find such options conveniently gathered here.

May it all help make your next escape successful—and one of many to come.

—*Roger Piantadosi*

Chapter 1

Heading South By Southwest

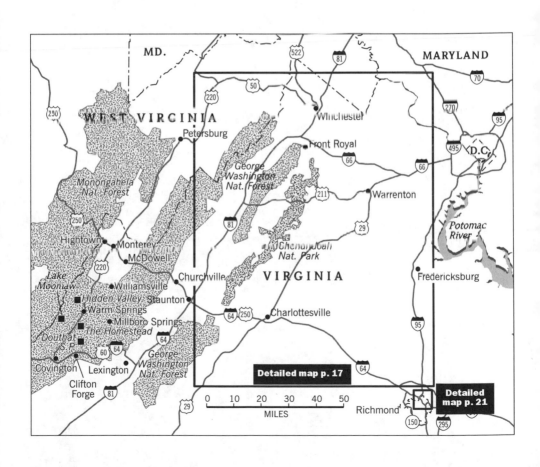

Charlottesville: My Clifton

By Stephanie Mansfield

SOME PEOPLE dream of exotic journeys to far-off places: deserted Tahitian beaches, snow-tipped Tibetan mountains, barging down the Nile. I dream of the perfect country house.

It would be white clapboard, with Tara-like pillars and black shutters. Masses of flowers would border the stone driveway and spill from window boxes and clay pots. I can see it now: The lawn is sloping and impossibly green, with towering oaks and a gazebo for drinks at sundown. There would be a dreamy, romantic "Howard's End" feel, especially standing on the croquet pitch with a glass of Cliquot, the aroma of fresh basil wafting from a nearby herb garden.

In my perfect country house, the sound of cooking would be lyrical: heavy pots clanking and the steady chop of blade against butcher block. There would be a large glass jar, filled with homemade chocolate chip cookies still warm from the oven.

The house would have a spring-fed pool, a clay tennis court and be close to a lake. The rooms would all have fireplaces. And candles. Down pillows and comforters. And oversized fluffy baths towels and white terry robes. There would be hundreds of books, nestled against the wall of a library. Leather wing chairs, overstuffed sofa, Oriental rugs. A chess game would be set up in one corner and Bach would be piped in, barely audible over the popping and cracking of a good fire on a crisp afternoon. Tea would be served afternoons at 4 in the sun-filled morning room: plates of crackers, English Stilton, fresh fruit and a dense square of chocolate cake.

Dinner might be in the cozy dining room, or perhaps on a glassed-in veranda, with fragrant roasted red pepper soup followed by local organic veal, washed down with a good bottle of Cabernet. After-dinner drinks would be served in the hot tub, a short walk from the house. The stars would form a canopy of light, as the rhythmic sound of cicadas pierce the night.

My perfect country house would be free of mortgage and maintenance. After all, a weekend retreat is no escape if the days are spent mowing, caulking, painting and weather-stripping.

So, here I am back at Clifton. Pretending it's mine.

Running my hands lovingly over the worn leather chair in the library, I am deeply envious but equally grateful that somebody—in this case Washington attorney Mitch Willey and his wife, Emily—actually had the foresight to create the perfect country house without my help. And for the last several years, my husband and son have become so enamored of the Charlottesville inn that our presence is becoming slightly embarrassing. The discussion always begins the same way.

Me: "Why don't we see Monticello."

Husband: "Great. Let's go."

Son: "What's Monticello?"

Me: "It's a big house."

Son: "Is it like Clifton?"

Me: "Sort of. Without the hot tub."

So we pack our bags and drive for two hours and pull up to the house. It's our third visit to Clifton, and we have thus far failed each time to muster the energy needed to drive four miles to Thomas Jefferson's house. We seem to like Mitch Willey's better.

"This time, we really mean it," I say as we're being taken to our room. "Is tea being served?"

We decide to go to Monticello the next day. The chocolate cake is even more delicious than I remember. I take two slices and a book to the pool. Swimming and tennis are followed by drinks on the croquet pitch. Friends from Charlottesville have come to join us for dinner. Our nine-year-old is back in our room, watching "Angels in the Outfield" on the portable television delivered to the room along with a gourmet grilled cheese sandwich from the kitchen, where he has free rein. A refrigerator for guests is stocked with wine, beer, sodas and bottled water.

The five-course dinner is stunning. I had watched a young kitchen helper pick the fresh basil only an hour before. The rolls are hot from the oven, and the peaches in the shortcake were gathered earlier in the day by the chef. Guests at Clifton—an 18th Century manor house—are treated to a small cocktail party before dinner, and the aura is one of an English country weekend. Usually, there's a young man playing the baby grand piano. The hokiness factor is certainly a threat, but at Clifton this congeniality doesn't feel forced. And the guests—including, over the years, actors Kevin Costner, Bill Murray and Sissy Spacek and dancer Twyla Tharp—tend to be on the private side. Place cards with our names are set at a table on the veranda. The candles glow. Seconds of shortcake?

The next morning, we sit down to breakfast. This is the day to see Monticello. But after the blueberry pancakes, made with wild berries picked minutes earlier, after the steaming coffee, apple-cinnamon cake and local country sausages, we decide to play tennis. The game lasts until noon. There's a good book by the chaise. The boys take a hike and wind up at the lake, looking for turtles or whatever it is that fathers and sons search for. In the end, the prey is less important than the ritual of basking in the sweet, lazy hours of each other's company. Away from the city, the phone, the fax, the soccer games, homework and video games. In the fall, there are leaves to be gathered, sticks to be examined, snakes to be hunted. In winter, the lake will be frozen, and steaming cups of cocoa will warm us by the fire.

By tea time, we are starving. We have missed Monticello again. We swear we will go next time. The inn's manager appears in the tearoom, just as the first slice of cake is being consumed, before we head off to the croquet pitch. "So how was Monticello?"

Our rueful grins tell the story. "Next time," we all say in unison.

GETTING THERE: Charlottesville is about a 2.5-hour drive from the Beltway. Take I-66 west to U.S. 29 south about 95 miles. At Culpeper, follow U.S. 15 south to Gordonsville. There, get to Route 231/22 south past Keswick and U.S. 250 west at Shadwell. Clifton is around the corner—as is Monticello.

BEING THERE: George Washington may be the father of the country, but Thomas Jefferson—who was born and lived to the age of 83 in what is now Shadwell, Va.—probably comes closest to being its favorite son. (Or, considering how people here in Virginia's Blue Ridge foothills still refer to the revered third president as "Mr. Jefferson," perhaps also its holy spirit.) The enduringly enigmatic Jefferson was an eloquent writer on subjects of liberty who nonetheless took full advantage of enslaved blacks (including in the most intimate way, purportedly, as the debate over his relationship with slave nursemaid Sally Heming continues into its third century). Jefferson was a musician, an astronomer, a studied but brilliantly original architect and philosopher and a dedicated vegetarian and agriculturist (credited with popularizing the lowly tomato and the wine-producing hybrid vines that now flourish throughout the New World). He also was a faithful correspondent who, before and after his best-selling Declaration of Independence was published, wrote more than 20,000 letters— many of them in a recliner he designed with a retractable desk. You can see the recliner, and the glass-enclosed pavilion, the restored gardens—and the concave entrance-hall mirror that greeted guests with an upside-down image of themselves—at his magnificent **Monticello** (804-984-9822, *www.monticello.org* &), the home he started building in 1768 on a mountain overlooking his beloved Virginia piedmont. It's open daily, and it's still possible to avoid long waits by arriving early for the half-hour narrated tours, which are highly recommended. After that you are free to roam the grounds, visit his oak-shaded burial site or just admire the perspective-laden views once enjoyed by a man who would become famous for his own.

In town, Jefferson's eclectic embodiment continues at the lush campus of one offspring he freely admitted fathering: the **University of Virginia** (804-924-3239), with its graceful and functional Rotunda (a scaled-down version of Rome's Pantheon) and the twin colonnades where students still (as Jefferson intended) live and study. Charlottesville itself is a budding cosmopolitan area (novelist John Grisham being its most recent star resident). Much of its downtown is a pedestrian mall of shops and restaurants, many more chic than in years past but still collectively radiating the aura of a pleasantly insulated, upscale Southern campus town. Wedged into a long, narrow storefront at the east end of the Mall, the small **Virginia Discovery Museum** (804-977-1025 ♿) has a 200-year-old log cabin kids can play in. It also has clothes they can dress up in (including U-Va. cheerleader and football player outfits), a daily art project and other exhibits and activities for children. One of the more creative activities hereabouts for grownups is **Sports Car Rentals** (804-823-4442), which rents such restored classic convertibles as a '76 Porsche 911 ($100) and a 1959 TR3 ($80) by the day. That's not a bad way to arrive at the tastings and tours offered by the many wineries nearby, including **Barboursville Vineyards** (540-832-3824 ♿), **Horton Vineyards** (540-832-7440 ♿) and **Jefferson Vineyards** (804-977-3042). It could be considered overkill, though, if you're headed for the elegantly restored homes nearby of Jefferson's friends James Monroe (his **Ash Lawn-Highland**, 804-293-9539, and its 550-acre working farm are a few minutes from Monticello) and James Madison (who domiciled his 5-foot-2 frame in the 77 rooms and 2,700 acres of **Montpelier**, 540-672-2728 ♿). Montpelier is about 25 miles north of Charlottesville in Orange. If you head south of town on Route 20 for about 20 miles, you'll come to the village of winding streets and fine old homes called **Scottsville**. Known as a place for quiet charm and a handful of welcoming restaurants, Scottsville also is a convenient stop on the way upriver a few miles to **Hatton Ferry**, where there is a state-operated historic ferry across the James from April to October. Also here, and significantly busier than the guys poling the ferry, are **James River Runners** (804-286-2338), which offers canoeing, innertubing, kayaking and camping, and **James River Reeling and Rafting** (804-286-4386), which sells bait and fishing equipment and offers rafting, tubing, canoeing and guided expeditions. (Scottsville also is a popular stop in Virginia's James River Bateau Festival. Bateaux are flat-bottomed boats that carried tobacco down the James in the 18th and 19th Centuries. For a week each June, river enthusiasts pilot replicas of original bateaux from Lynchburg to Richmond, spending nights in several river towns—including Scottsville, where they arrive in late afternoon and let bystanders come aboard for a look-see. Crew members dressed in 18th Century costumes camp in old-time tents along the banks. Bateau groupies hawk lanterns, candles, Brunswick stew and fried apples. The whole thing has a nice small-town, old-fashioned feel to it.)

WHERE TO STAY: Mitch Willey and his wife, Emily, obviously saw the potential for a four-star inn when they purchased the 14-room **Clifton** (888-971-1800; doubles $150-$475) in 1983. The Virginia Historic Landmark was the former home of Thomas Mann Randolph, a member of Congress, a governor of Virginia and Thomas Jefferson's son-in-law. Several years ago, the Willeys hired Craig Hartman, a young chef at North Carolina's Pinehurst and Sanderling Inn, to turn up the culinary heat. It worked. In 1995, *Country Inns* magazine named Clifton one of the top 12 in the nation. (Hartman has since been succeeded as manager by European-trained hotelier Keith Halford, whose last Relais & Chateaux property earned AAA's five-diamond rating, and in the kitchen by former sous chef Rachel Greenberg.) Dinner at the inn is prix fixe. A six-course dinner is $58 a person Fridays and Saturdays, a five-course dinner $48 otherwise, excluding wine or drinks. You need not travel far through Virginia horse country from Clifton to find an even pricier spot. That would be **Keswick Hall** (800-274-5391; doubles $215-$575 ♿). This 45-room English manor-style B&B owned by Sir Bernard Ashley has gorgeous public and private rooms, golf and tennis, saunas, a health club and lawn games (but be alert whenever a guest's helicopter is landing at the pad). The **Boar's Head Inn Country Resort** (804-296-2181 or 800-476-1988; doubles $179-$360 ♿), in the rolling hills west of Charlottesville proper, is a full sports resort with three swimming pools, tennis, racquetball, squash, a spa, hot-air ballooning and golf on an adjoining course.

South of town in Scottsville, **High Meadows** (804-286-2218; doubles $189-$275, including breakfast and a six-course Saturday dinner) is another celebrated Virginia Historic Landmark inn with seven rooms and seven suites, wine tastings, nine fireplaces and 50 acres that include its own vineyard and gardens. On a 1732 plantation amid the rolling hills east of town is the veteran country inn **Prospect Hill** (800-277-0844; doubles $280-$365, including breakfast and a highly rated five-course dinner). Of course, all the major chains can be found on Routes 29 and Business 250, and just a block south of where they intersect is the **English Inn** (804-971-9900; doubles $60-$70, including a full breakfast ♿), a pleasant cross between a motel and a B&B. For more nearby lodging options, also see the next section on NELSON COUNTY.

WHERE TO EAT: Charlottesville's college-town status has helped keep the restaurant scene vital and varied—a boon for visitors. Some favorite stops on the historic Downtown Mall include **Hamilton's** (California nouvelle, 804-295-6649 ♿); **Monsoon Cafe** (Thai with an attitude, 804-971-1515 ♿); the boutiquey but must-see **Hardware Store Restaurant** (804-977-1518 ♿); the nouvelle American, kitchen-in the-round **Metropolitain** (804-977-1043 ♿) and the funky, friendly, comfort-food hangout **Southern Culture** (804-979-1990 ♿). Other recommended spots are **Maharaja** (Indian, 804-973-1110 ♿) on Route 29 at Seminole Square and **Michie Tavern** (804-977-1234 ♿), a restored 1765 tavern that's on the way to Monticello, where you can take a tour or just eat authentic colonial fried chicken and apple cobbler in the big cafeteria-style Ordinary. Scottsville's **Caffe Bocce** (804-286-4422) is an unlikely but welcome Italian bistro in the otherwise out-of-the-way hamlet, serving tasty, well-presented fare (the pizzas, pasta and European-style desserts are recommended) at a decent price. And the nearby **Luv N' Oven** (804-286-3830) is a favorite with locals for breakfast, lunch and dinner (chicken livers and gizzards are a specialty).

FOR MORE INFORMATION: The **Charlottesville/Albemarle County Convention and Visitors Center** can be contacted at 804-977-1783 or *www.charlottesvilletourism.org*. There's also useful information to be found at *www.cvillechamber.org/visitor.html* and *www.cjp.com/guide*.

NELSON COUNTY

With 470 square miles and only about 13,000 people, Nelson County welcomes those looking to hike, bike, ski, fish, shop for antiques and much else. Its topography ranges from 4,000-foot peaks in the George Washington National Forest and the Blue Ridge Parkway on its northern boundary to the rolling farmsteads along the James River on the south. The county's best-known attraction (and largest employer) is Wintergreen Resort—see **WHERE TO STAY**, below—but there are many antiques and craft shops along its two or three main (two-lane) roads, including U.S. 29 and Route 151. You also can go on winery tours at **Afton Mountain** (540-456-8667), **Mountain Cove** (804-263-5392) or **Wintergreen Winery and Vineyards** (804-361-2519 ♿). The **Tuckahoe Antique Mall** (804-361-2121 ♿), a collection of 50 stalls of country antiques in Nellysford, is open Thursday through Sunday year round. Up in the national forest area, a memorable half-day hike can be had at **Crabtree Falls** (540-291-2188): a three-mile, 1,200-vertical-foot climb alongside the highest waterfall east of the Mississippi, with a view of the surrounding Tye River Valley that's awesome any time of year. (The trail, past four overlooks and five major cascades, is outfitted with fence-lined switchbacks, resting benches and even stairways for the steepest parts.)

If you spent Thursday nights in the 1970s with a loving, Depression-era TV family that lived in an old farm house on Walton's Mountain in Virginia's Blue Ridge, you might already know that the real-life Hamner family in tiny **Schuyler, Va.**, was the model for the fictional Waltons. Earl Jr., one of the eight Hamner kids (edited to seven for TV), dreamed of becoming a writer and wrote what he knew best—the stories of his family. They eventually became "The Waltons," and Earl became John-Boy. (Earl also became a successful Hollywood scriptwriter.) And Schuyler—mostly a scattering of small houses perched on wooded hillsides and nestled in shady dells, with a cluttered general store, a homey restaurant and picturesque churches, towering trees, wildflowers and singing birds—became the site of the tiny **Walton's Mountain Museum** (804-831-2000; open daily March through November ♿). This converted old schoolhouse has memorabilia, a video to watch, and some lovingly re-created sets. They include John-Boy's bedroom with 1930s furnishings and an old Underwood typewriter like the one on which Earl Jr. began to write; the kitchen with its old pie safe, wood cook stove, butter churn, wooden icebox and long, well-worn table, where the family ate and the kids did their homework under Mama's eagle eye; the homey parlor, etc. A recreated Ike Godsey's country store is the museum's gift shop, which sells high-quality crafts by local artisans. (To get to Schuyler from U.S. 29 west of Charlottesville, turn south on Route 6 and go five miles to a right on Route 800 and another two miles to town.)

GETTING THERE: Most parts of Nelson County are within three hours of the Beltway. Take I-66 to Gainsville and head south on U.S. 29 to Charlottesville. Following U.S. 29 farther south is the fastest way to the central part of the county, while I-64 west is the better route to Wintergreen and other Blue Ridge points.

WHERE TO STAY/EAT: The 10,800-acre, four-season resort of **Wintergreen** (800-325-2200 ♿) is expert at providing city slickers with their

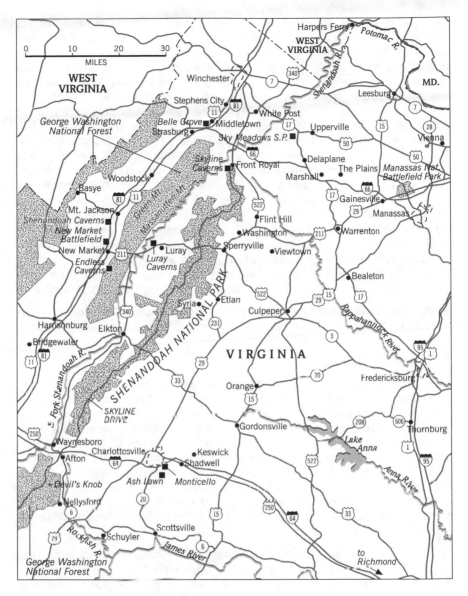

place in the country—whether temporarily, as in a night or two (or four, which they call a "mini-week"), or for a longer stay with a mortgage attached. Besides its well-kept winter ski slopes, tennis courts and restaurants, Wintergreen offers hiking along 30 miles of trails (hikes are led year round by a staff of naturalists); an astonishingly comprehensive outdoors- and ecology-oriented kids camp; 36 holes of year-round golf; five swimming pools and a large spa; horseback riding, and boating and swimming in Lake Monocan. Guests can rent condominiums or homes (or rooms in the main Lodge), most with great views, maid service and amenities ga-

17

lore. Rates start at about $175 in high season (winter) for a studio condo double at the Lodge (or $205 for a one-bedroom condo); golf, ski, family and "romance" packages are available. (A recent family package: $309 a night for a four-night stay in a two-bedroom condo and use of the spa.) You also can arrange to stay at Wintergreen via **Resort Reservations** (540-456-8300), which matches the resort's property owners with renters, almost always for significantly less than the resort would charge. In nearby Afton, there are four rooms with private baths at **Looking Glass House** (800-769-6844; doubles $80-$95), an 1848 Victorian farmhouse that sits on 10 country acres that include a swimming pool open to guests in summer. There are great views all around, and, unlike many small B&Bs, the inn is happy to accommodate families: a complementary rollaway for kids or a twin-bedded second room is $50. In Nellysford, one *Post* contributor and B&B aficionado rates the **Meander Inn** (804-361-1121; doubles $85-$95) a 10 out of 10: "clean, comfortable, handsome, with great beds and good reading lamps and a super breakfast." The inn is a 50-acre working farm of horse-grazed pasture and woods on the Rockfish River, with chickens and horses (you can get up early and help feed them if you want), lots of cats, a hot tub, an old swimming hole and hiking trails.

FOR MORE INFORMATION: Contact the **Nelson County Division of Tourism** at 800-282-8223, *www.virginia.org* or *www.cstone.net/users/nelsonco*.

FREDERICKSBURG

More and more Washingtonians seem to get past the strip of eateries, gas stations, motels and malls just off I-95 to discover the soul of Fredericksburg that is Old Town, the 40-square-block historic district that rests on a serene and lovely bend in the Rappahannock River. Here, five miles from the roar of the interstate, is a pleasant village of small shops, art galleries, restaurants, bed and breakfasts and historic homes resting on some of the most hallowed ground in American history. Fredericksburg outshines Colonial Williamsburg for authentic 18th Century architecture and matches Gettysburg as a memorable Civil War battlefield. It's also a fetching and friendly small town in which hanging out could become habit-forming, especially for those who've grown tired of potholes, polluted air and other signs of advanced civilization.

Capt. John Smith sailed up to the headwaters of the Rappahannock here in 1608 and found a prosperous fishing village of Native Americans—and then he killed a few. By the late 1700s Fredericksburg had become a leading port, welcoming ships from Baltimore, Norfolk and even London. Today it is a celebration of federal-style architecture pre-dating the Revolution and neo-Georgian buildings that survived the Civil War. Home to more than 300 properties built before 1870, the historic district's leading attractions include the **Mary Washington House** (540-373-1569), which George bought for his mother in 1772 and where she lived until her death in 1789. The beautifully restored **Kenmore** mansion (540-373-3381) was the home of Col. Fielding Lewis, who married George Washington's sister, Betty, and retains the original molded plaster ceilings and a diorama of 18th Century Fredericksburg. Around 1760, on Caroline Street,

George's youngest brother, Charles, built a home that was later converted into a stagecoach stop and lively political and social forum. That gathering place, the **Rising Sun Tavern** (540-371-1494), has been restored and welcomes visitors, as does the **Hugh Mercer Apothecary Shop** (540-373-3362), an 18th Century pharmacy and medical office. The **James Monroe Museum** (540-654-1043) houses memorabilia of the fifth president, who practiced law here from 1786 to 1789. When you've finished your historic strolling, take time to visit with the resident tin, pewter, gold, clay and stone artisans at work in their downtown studios. Or buy a Mort Kunstler Civil War print at a gallery. A half dozen quality antique shops are also here, with sticker prices low enough to make Georgetowners blush. Good used bookstores also abound—clustered around **Caroline Street** and the small side streets intersecting it.

The Fredericksburg area was the scene of four major Civil War battles between December 1862 and May 1864. Set in a natural amphitheater created by the hills flanking the river, the city was damaged severely on December 13, 1862, when Robert E. Lee thwarted an assault by Gen. A.E. Burnside—who used Lee's wife's family home, **Chatham** (540-371-0802 ♿), as Union headquarters and a hospital. The loss was such a disaster for the North that "Fredericksburg" later became a Union battle cry at Gettysburg. This battle and others nearby—the Battle of Chancellorsville in 1863 and the Battles of the Wilderness and Spotsylvania Court House in 1864—are remembered at the **Fredericksburg and Spotsylvania National Military Park** (540-373-6122 ♿), an 8,000-acre federal preserve encompassing parts of all four battlefields.

Friends of the Rappahannock (540-373-3448), the local environmental group, provides canoe and rafting trips for kids of all ages. **Clore Bros. Outfitters** (540-786-7749) also puts people on the river for trips of up to 29 miles and carries almost everything needed. Finally, beyond Fredericksburg (geographically and otherwise) in tiny Doswell is **Paramount's King's Dominion** (804-876-5000, *www.kingsdominion.com*), the big-ticket amusement park that in 2001 will launch the HyperSonic XLC. (It's the world's first "compressed air launch coaster." That is, it goes from zero to 80 mph in 1.8 seconds, takes you up 165 feet at 90 degrees and down at the same angle.)

GETTING THERE: Fredericksburg is about 50 miles south of Washington via I-95, about an hour by car unless you run into one of those impromptu rush-hour "Road Warrior" reenactments. (U.S. 1 is the funkier and slower alternative.) Amtrak (800-872-7245) has daily departures; round-trip adult fares are about $42. Virginia Railway Express (703-684-0400) operates commuter trains; round-trip adult tickets are $13.40.

WHERE TO STAY: Many of the national hotel and motel chains offer rooms on the busier outskirts of town. For lodgings more in tune with the surroundings, consider the **Kenmore Inn** (not the historic mansion), a 12-room inn whose original structure dates from the 1700s (540-371-7622; doubles $105-$145 ♿). In the middle of the historic area are the nine rooms of the **Richard Johnston Inn** (540-899-7606; doubles $95-$145), which is in a 209-year-old town house. Inside the battlefield park is the **Braehead Bed & Breakfast** (540-899-3648; doubles $90-$110), a 138-year-old manor house with three guest rooms.

WHERE TO EAT: The **Olde Mudd Tavern** in Thornburg, just south of Fredericksburg (540-582-5250 ♿), serves regional American cuisine in an Early American decor. **La Petite Auberge** (540-371-2727 ♿) offers French cuisine, while the **Smythe's Cottage and Tavern** (540-373-1645 ♿) serves up such colonial fare as peanut soup and ginger beef in a pot. Rest up with a cooling drink at the 130-year-old **Goolrick's Pharmacy** on Caroline Street (540-373-9878 ♿), which claims to have the oldest continuously operating soda fountain in the nation. Or try the vegetarian dishes and inexpensive sandwiches at the friendly, low-key **Sammy T's** (540-371-2008 ♿), which also serves 60 different beers.

FOR MORE INFORMATION: Contact the **Fredericksburg Visitors Center** at 540-373-1776 or 800-678-4748 or *www.fredericksburgva.com*.

RICHMOND

In 1609, Capt. John Smith sailed up the James River to its navigable limit, a series of rapids three miles long. Declaring that there was "no place so strong, so pleasant, and delightful in Virginia" as this spot, he named it None-Such. Luckily, the name didn't stick. In 1737, William Byrd II laid out the city we know today, named for England's Richmond on Thames. A bracing antidote to Washingtonian self-importance, Richmond is relatively small—a town without motorcades—and southern, which is to say courteous, ever mindful of its agrarian roots. (The place was founded upon tobacco, a labor-intensive crop that required even the most fatheaded citizens to shoulder their share of the work.) These things, combined with its nearly 400 years of history, give it a sense of ease that Washington can only envy.

Richmond is so crammed with historical significance and "must see" places that you will run yourself ragged trying to do half of it. The early local architect, for example, was Thomas Jefferson, who modeled the **Virginia State Capitol** (804-698-1788 ♿) after a Roman temple in Nimes, France. The town's leading orator was Patrick Henry, who delivered his "Give me liberty or give me death" speech at **St. John's Church** (804-648-5015 ♿) in the company of Washington, Jefferson and other Colonial eminences. And Richmond not only is the capital of Virginia but also served as the capital of the Confederacy. Indeed, it houses the nation's largest collection of Confederate memorabilia—presented in the most level-headed and absorbing way—in its small but unequaled **Museum of the Confederacy** (804-649-1861 ♿). The exhibits include Civil War weapons and letters, uniforms, photographs and a mockup of General Lee's field tent with his actual table inside. Next door is the **White House of the Confederacy**, Jefferson Davis' official residence until he and the rest of the town fled Grant's advance in 1865 (and the inhabitants, not Union forces, set the city ablaze). Civil War buffs craving more can be sated at the **Richmond National Battlefield Park Visitors Center** (804-226-1981) in Chimborazo Park, which offers exhibits, an audiovisual program, a movie and information on self-guided tours of area battlefields.

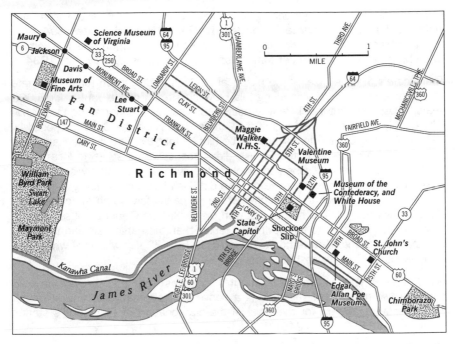

The restored cobblestone streets and alleys of 18th Century Shockoe Bottom and Shockoe Slip—the latter Richmond's earliest commercial district and its answer to Baltimore's Fells Point—are home not only to the **Edgar Allan Poe Museum** (804-648-5523 ♿) and a several-hundred-year-old **farmer's market** but to some of the city's trendiest eateries, music venues and micro-brewery pubs. (The areas take their name from *shacquohocan*, a Native American word for a prominent flat stone at the mouth of a creek that flowed here in the 1600s.) Similarly, in the funky **Carytown** neighborhood you'll find streets enlivened by a social mix to rival Adams Morgan, plus the **Virginia Museum of Fine Arts** (804-340-1400, closed Mondays ♿), whose eclectic collection includes Fabergé eggs, Egyptian sculpture and a few Monets. If it's Saturday night, be sure to take in whatever movie is playing at the 1916 **Byrd Theatre** (804-353-9911), wherein the staff gets up in Roaring '20s outfits and the feature is preceded by an organ performance on an ancient but working Wurlitzer that rises out of the stage. From there it's only a few blocks to **Monument Avenue** and the **Fan district**, which is said to be the largest intact Victorian neighborhood in America. Here also are shrines to Rebel heroes—Lee, Jackson, J.E.B. Stuart, Jefferson Davis and Matthew Fontaine Maury, the father of modern oceanography (whose charts of winds and currents, ironically, helped the Union Navy bottle up the Rebel fleet)—together with one to Arthur Ashe, the first African-American to win at Wimbledon. For families, the **Science Museum of Virginia** (804-367-6552 ♿) offers more than 250 hands-on exhibits, an Imax theater, a planetarium and one of the world's largest Foucault Pendulums (94 feet) in the rotunda, all housed in the enormous former Broad Street Train Station, designed by John Russell Pope. On a much more intimate scale, the **Valentine Museum** (804-649-0711 ♿) is considered the city's "attic," telling the tale of Richmond itself, including the historic relationships, both touching and painful, between blacks and whites. Also worth seeing is the **Maggie L. Walker National Historic Site** (804-771-2017; closed Sundays ♿), where the African-American woman, the first female to found a bank, lived with her family from the turn of the century until 1934.

Then there's the river itself. "The historical plaques in downtown Richmond state that people have been living along this brawling stretch of the James for 5,000 years," *Post* contributor Bill Heavey notes. "But as you wander along the **Canal Walk**, which traces the remains of the James River-Kanawha Canal proposed by George Washington, the text seems to be hinting that the Native Americans liked this for the same reasons the English did: because of its strategic location for water wheels and trade." One good look at the river tells you otherwise, he says. "The Indians liked it here because the fish did. Fish love rapids. You give a small-mouth bass a nice rock to hide under where he can safely watch the cafeteria of life gush by and he thinks he has just won the Publishers Clearing House" prize. If you'd like to get closer to the downtown rapids than the canal walk can take you, see the folks at the **Richmond Raft Co.** (800-540-7238), who take whitewater aficionados on four- to six-hour trips.

GETTING THERE: Richmond is about 105 miles from the Beltway via I-95 south, a two-hour drive. The train is a convenient alternative to driving (about $56 roundtrip), except for the edge-of-the-city location of Richmond's station (Amtrak is at 800-872-7245).

WHERE TO STAY: The **Jefferson Hotel** (804-788-8000 ♿) is a National Historic Landmark originally opened in 1895 by Major Lewis Ginter, a Civil War veteran and inventor of the first mass-produced cigarette. Its winding, 26-step staircase is said to have served as the model for the grand staircase in "Gone With the Wind" (it didn't), and its 274 rooms are done in 19th Century reproduction furnishings. Weekend rates range from $154 to $280, double. The **Berkeley Hotel** in Shockoe Slip (804-780-1300; doubles start at $145 ♿) is an elegant, European-style hotel two blocks from the Capitol. The **Holiday Inn-Historic District** (804-644-9871; doubles from $64 ♿) is a clean, reasonable choice.

WHERE TO EAT: The **Frog and the Redneck** (804-648-3764 ♿) is a hot spot in Richmond whose nouvelle French/New Southern fare includes fresh seafood, pasta and meat entrees. Dinner runs about $50 per person, including wine. (The Frog is Jean Louis Palladin, who is here in name only and under whom the Redneck, Jimmy Sneed, cooked for six years at the Watergate.) The **Tobacco Company** (804-782-9555 ♿), just up the street in a converted tobacco warehouse in Shockoe Slip, is a high-energy bar/restaurant with international and local cuisine. **Mr. Patrick Henry's Inn** (804-644-1322), near the center of town on East Broad Street in two restored 19th Century row houses, offers casual dining, with lighter fare in the English pub. In the Fan district, you'll want to check out the pasta and Southern fare at the popular **Strawberry Street Cafe** (804-353-6860). And the **Third Street Diner** (804-788-4750), open 24 hours a day, seven days a week, will make you breakfast anytime.

FOR MORE INFORMATION: Contact the **Metro Richmond Convention and Visitors Bureau** at 800-365-7272 or 804-782-2777 or check out the Richmond listings at *www.virginia.org*.

THE SHENANDOAH VALLEY

A Letter From Luray

By Linton Weeks

DEAR MOTHER,

Sorry we were out of pocket last week. Life was crazed. We were mad-dashing from home to work to school to sports to church and home again, where the boys mostly begged to watch the Cartoon Network or play Sonic Spinball. Pierre, the dog, kept escaping from the yard, and the gutters needed hanging and the dishwasher was leaking and we just had to get out of Dodge.

I cut an advertisement from the newspaper for Deerlane Cottages, cabins in the Shenandoah woods. The ad said that there was hiking nearby and horse-back riding and canoeing and fishing. And it said dogs were welcome. I called the woman who runs the show. Her name is Quinta Castle, and she made everything easy. She booked us into a cabin called the Spotted Cow.

Maybe it was the way National Public Radio news faded out and Garth Brooks faded in just the other side of Warrenton. Maybe it was the sign "Antique Tables Made Daily" on Highway 211 near Sperryville. Or maybe it was the cold ice cream at the Tastee Freez. But by the time we reached Luray, Va., only two hours or so from Washington, we felt long gone and far away.

On the road, my wife asked several times if Deerlane Cottages provided sheets and towels. I assured her that they did. After all, the cabin cost $125 for each of the first two nights and $85 for the third. For that price, I said, they're bound to. For that price, she countered, they're bound not to. She, of course, was right. So we borrowed linens that we found on a high shelf in the hall closet.

We used a disposal stopper from the kitchen sink as a bathtub plug, and we substituted our shampoo for soap the first night. But there was ample fire-wood and running water and just the right amount of spotted cow what-nots—a potholder, a coffee mug, a refrigerator magnet. It was a fine cabin, just a few miles northwest of Luray.

The bad news: There was a TV. The good news: It received only one-and-a-half networks.

After unloading our luggage, we walked down the hill to the Shenandoah River Outfitters, a country store-looking place that rents kayaks and canoes and sells a modicum of fishing tackle. The shop is run by various members of the Goebel and Sottosanti families. They can tell you just about anything that you want to know about the area.

The river was too high and wild for riding, so we asked about fishing opportunities. They wanted to know where we were staying and, feeling a little sheepish, we told them the Spotted Cow. They didn't bat an eye. Somebody said, "Brooke Shields stayed in the A-frame near there."

One of my sons asked, "Who's Brooke Shields?"

"Princeton," I said. "Class of '86."

They told us that there were several places to fish within walking distance of the store and our cabin. Pointing out the window, Christian Goebel said that the first road to the right led up to a neighborhood lake. We didn't need licenses to fish there.

The first road to the left was a good way to get down to the river in case we wanted to poke around in the mud holes and muck pits. The boys were getting excited. The second road to the left, Goebel said, led around to Bealer's Ferry, a small fishing pond known colloquially as the Handicap Access Lake. To fish there and in the river, he said, we needed licenses. So we bought some.

Before the sun set, we swung by Bill's Guns and Taxidermy shop on Courthouse Road to pick up a mess of night crawlers. The shop was a large, air-conditioned room full of firearms, fishing tackle, stuffed critters and camouflage gear. A young girl knelt at a glass case and declared her love for big pistols. That's something you don't see much in Washington, Mom.

We spent three days in Luray and yet, in a good way, it felt like more.

One morning we walked—Pierre ran—to the neighborhood lake. On the bank, we taught the boys how to rig up a cane pole and bait a hook. We caught a pair of small bluegills and tossed them back, but mostly we just enjoyed being outdoors. Pierre found some friends. They howled and rolled in dirt and manure and had a fine time. The water was black as slate. Clouds passed overhead, and their reflections swam beneath our bobbing corks.

Another morning, I left the family at the breakfast table and drove into town. Luray's Main Street swoops down from a Confederate memorial, past streets with board-game names like Firehouse and Courthouse and signs for Marth-An's Florist shop, The Taxman—a certified public accountant—and River's Bend Cafe, which features live music sometimes and pit barbecue all the time.

You can park your car and investigate the town's antique stores—at last count there were at least three on Main Street. Others wait seductively around nearly every turn. There's also a Visitor's Center on the main drag featuring a blizzard of brochures.

When I stepped into the Super Fresh Sav-A-Center for some soap and other provisions, I eavesdropped on a short conversation between the woman at the cash register and another customer.

"Hear about Bruce?"

"He was a good old guy."

"How's she?"

"Tore up."

Life and death in Luray. Summed up in 13 words.

Late one afternoon we visited Luray Caverns on the edge of town. Though the netherworld was first explored in August 1878, there is still a sense of wonder among every tour group. We had a very good guide who told us fascinating stories about stalactites and stalagmites and answered our most obscure questions. But we also, as a family, enjoyed pointing out formations of our own discovery—the old pirate face and the giant baseball bat.

At night in the cabin we opened the windows to the chilled mountain air. It was cool enough to build a fire. We roasted hot dogs and toasted marshmallows. We played Pictionary and checkers and chess. We read books and talked. No TV, no video games and, most extraordinary of all, no whining.

On our last full day, we really struck gold. We had a fishing experience that cannot be bought. We drove to the lake at Bealer's Ferry, baited the hooks with fat squirming worms, dropped them into the dark waters and—boom!—the bites began.

For the next two hours, nearly every time we lowered a hook we hoisted up a bass or a bluegill. The fish were Lilliputian, but they were fish—20 to 30 of them—and they did bite and they did take the hook and they did stay on the line long enough to haul them in and a few of them were of a respectable size and so we kept four and we slapped them into some cornmeal and fried them up and they were delicious.

We slept well that night, and the next morning we packed up for the trip home. We didn't leave as early as we had planned. In fact, everyone wanted to stay a little longer. Make that a lot longer.

We talked about returning as soon as possible to fish some more, to canoe and kayak on the river, to ride horses in nearby Shenandoah National Park and to visit the Reptile Center and Dinosaur Park near the caverns.

Before I shut the door for the last time, I wrote Quinta a thank you note. I also left a $10 bill, to pay for washing the linens. I tucked them both under a spotted cow sugar jar.

GETTING THERE: Luray, Va., is about two hours from the Beltway. Take I-66 west to I-81 south to Exit 264 (New Market) and follow U.S. 211 east to Luray. (The slightly longer scenic route: Exit I-66 west at U.S. 29 south; at Warrenton, pick up U.S. 211 west over the mountains.)

BEING THERE: Luray has a great location: not far from I-81 on U.S. 211, one of only two east-west routes that pass through Shenandoah National Park, and right between the park's western edge and the eastern slopes of Massanutten Mountain in the George Washington National Forest. It is a serendipitous spot for an overnight, a meal, some low-key, family-oriented sightseeing or just a supply stop. From April through mid-November, **Shenandoah River Outfitters** (800-622-6632) offers canoe, kayak and tube rentals (canoes go for about $48, including shuttle) and will deliver lunch at a stopover on the river or drive you back to their place a few miles west of town for a barbecue dinner with live music. They also can outfit you for tent camping and help you find cabin rentals, the latter mostly at privately owned sites in less-crowded George Washington Forest to the west. Nearby is the century-old **Luray Caverns** (540-743-6551 ♿), where the stalactites, stalagmites and awe-inspiring columns are joined by a unique (and playable) "stalacpipe organ"; a crystal-clear "Wishing Well" (the value of visitors' coins, donated to national health organizations, now approaches $500,000), a state-of-the-art lighting system and no need for air-conditioning. The **Luray Reptile Center and Dinosaur Park** (540-743-4113, closed weekdays November-April ♿) has Virginia's largest live reptile collection and some life-sized dinosaur models. Guided trail rides on horseback (and pony rides for ages 7 or younger) are available at both **Skyland Stables** (540-999-2210, closed December-March) in the national park to the east and, if you're headed west, **TJ Stables** (540-856-8100) at Bryce Resort (see WHERE TO STAY).

In nearby **New Market** is the site of one of the Civil War's most important battlefields, to which young Confederate boys—250 Virginia Military Institute cadets—marched 80 miles in four days to help hold the lines. The **New Market Battlefield Historical Park** (540-740-3102) tells the harrowing story of the Battle of New Market and is the site of the state's longest-running reenactment every May. Also near New Market are **Endless Caverns** (800-544-2283) and **Shenandoah Caverns** (540-477-3115 ♿). For those who've seen enough of the world underground and the War Between the States, try the 11 rooms of the **Bedrooms of America Museum** (540-740-3512), which are authentically furnished in styles from 1650 to 1930. North of Route 11 on the way to Mt. Jackson is the 204-foot **Meems Bottom Bridge,** the longest covered bridge of nine in Virginia and the only one left in the Shenandoah.

Fly fishermen, happy to be almost anywhere in this part of Virginia, are particularly fond of the two northeast-flowing forks of the Shenandoah River. Although the fishable sections of the north and south forks traverse only about 50 and 100 miles of country, respectively, their serpentine courses put the actual number of fishing miles into the high hundreds. For advice on stream conditions and rigs, the place to go is **Murray's Fly Shop** (540-984-4212) in tiny Edinburg. Proprietor Harry Murray is a smallmouth fly-fishing authority of some weight, having written what is believed to be the world's only book on this subject, "Flyfishing for Smallmouth Bass." Murray's shop is inside the local

Peoples Drug, of which he is both owner and pharmacist. "Oh, yeah," he once told *Post* contributor and fly fisherman Bill Heavey. "If I didn't have the drugstore, I couldn't afford the fly shop." Adds Heavey: "It's interesting to watch Murray behind the counter. He'll be talking on the phone to a doctor in his pharmacist voice, then pick up on another line and burst into life. 'I have eight-foot rods, Bob, and I love 'em! But you've got to realize you're not gonna have the drift control you get with a nine-footer, especially if you're throwing a Number 4 streamer. I'd just hate to see you go with anything shorter, Bob, I really would.' " Murray's offers one- and two-day fly-fishing classes for $275; current fishing conditions for smallmouth and trout are updated every Friday on the Web at *www.murraysflyshop.com*.

WHERE TO STAY: Deerlane Cottages (800-696-3337 or 301-567-3036) has eight cottages near the Shenandoah River, just a few miles from Luray. Rates start at $250 for the first two nights and then go down to $85. The most expensive cabin, with three bedrooms and right on the river, is $300 for the first two nights and $95 for subsequent nights. Bring your own linens and towels. Pets are $10 a night extra. On Main Street in town, the **Mimslyn Inn** (540-743-5105) is a 67-year-old grand hotel with summer rates for doubles from $69-$79; suites are $109-$139. The **Luray Caverns Motel East** (540-743-4531) has comfortable, no-frills rooms that start at $70 for doubles and package deals for golf (at nearby Caverns Country Club Resort, also operated by the Luray Caverns folks). There's also a 101-room **Days Inn** (540-743-4521; doubles $65 and up ♿) with a pool and restaurant right on U.S. 211, and, in the national park, **Skyland Lodge** isn't far (800-999-4714; $87-$97 ♿; see the SHENANDOAH NATIONAL PARK section on Page 30). **Jordan Hollow Farm Inn** in Stanley (888-418-7000; doubles $133 to $190, including breakfast) has 20 rooms in two lodges (the four in Mare Meadow Lodge are the nicest) on its 145 acres at the foot of the western slope of the Blue Ridge. Dinner is served in two 200-year-old log-cabin rooms. Near the West Virginia border, about 45 minutes northwest of Luray in Basye, low-key, family-oriented **Bryce Resort** (800-821-1444) offers, among other things, boating, swimming and windsurfing on a 45-acre lake, skiing, hiking, horseback riding and tennis. Lodging options include studio condominiums, town houses and chalets, all privately owned and rented through the resort's real estate agencies. A two-bedroom town house on the golf course rents for $140 nightly (two-night minimum).

WHERE TO EAT: For dinner there's the **Parkhurst** (540-743-6009 ♿) on U.S. 211 and recommended restaurants at both the **Mimslyn Inn** and **Jordan Hollow** (see above). And, in case you were still doubting whether mountain life appeals to the jack-of-all-trades type, **Brookside Restaurant** (800-299-2655 ♿) not only serves three filling and reasonable home-style meals a day but also rents out eight cabins, April through November. (For other options between here and the Beltway, see THIS SIDE OF THE SHENANDOAH on Page 34).

FOR MORE INFORMATION: The **Luray-Page County Chamber of Commerce Visitors Center** (540-743-3915 or *www.luraypage.com*) is open year round, but some attractions are not. Call ahead. Also try the **Shenandoah Valley Travel Association** in New Market (540-740-3132).

FRONT ROYAL/STRASBURG

Two hundred years ago, Front Royal was a hard-drinking frontier outpost with the nickname of "Helltown." Things have changed (despite the ragged look around the Interstate 66 exit). Nowadays, though not quite a suburb of Washington, Front Royal has taken advantage of both its proximity to the Beltway (its revitalized downtown is a pleasantly strollable place of antique shops and boutiques around a village common) and its distance. With the north and south forks of the Shenandoah River converging here, and the northern end of the park's 105-mile backbone, Skyline Drive, a mile from town, Front Royal has become the "gateway to the Shenandoah." Thus there are many places in town to seek provisions for a picnic, a day hike or a full-fledged camping outing. Mid-March through mid-November, you can rent canoes, kayaks, rafts and tubes at **Front Royal Canoe Company** (800-270-8808) or **Downriver Canoe Company** (800-338-1963). Both can outfit anything from a lazy float to a half-day beginning whitewater trip (the Shenandoah rarely musters more than Class II rapids) to a serious 100-mile paddle. If Civil War history is your thing, you can tour **Belle Boyd Cottage** (540-869-2028 ♿), named for the Confederate spy who lived here for two years and passed on what she learned of Union plans. In one case, they say, her reports enabled Gen. Stonewall Jackson to mount a surprise attack that put the hotly contested town of Front Royal back in Confederate hands (at least for a while). A few doors down Chester Street is the memorabilia-filled **Warren Rifles Confederate Museum** (540-636-6982). Not far outside town are the professionally lit anthodites—also known as "cave flowers"—and underground waterfalls of **Skyline Caverns** (800-296-4545).

Just around the northern edge of the Massanutten and Green mountains, **Strasburg** is a busy little commercial center full of small shops, with a main street lined with second-story porches jutting out over the sidewalks. If it feels different from Front Royal, it's because Strasburg was first settled in the mid-1700s by Germans who thought the countryside resembled their native Bavaria, and they built a town (then called Staufferstadt) to prove it. Later, Strasburg also was known as Pot Town because of its six potteries, but for most of the 20th Century it has relied on other sources of income, which today includes auto parts and printing. Strasburg is the site of **Belle Grove** (540-869-2028; open April-October), a mansion built in 1794 and used as Union headquarters during the Battle of Cedar Creek, which is reenacted in a big way every October. Of more than passing interest to Civil War buffs are the **Stonewall Jackson Museum** and **Hupp's Hill Battlefield Park** (540-465-5884 ♿), a solid museum and hands-on learning center on the site where the troops of six different Civil War generals camped or fought. Guided group tours of the battlefield are available by appointment. The collection at Strasburg's **Museum of American Presidents** (540-465-5999) includes a lock of George Washington's hair and the desk at which James Madison drafted the Constitution. Since it's right on "Antiques Alley," *aka* U.S. 11—itself an antique, as the trail between these mountains dates to prehistoric times—Strasburg also is a place that's most welcoming to people with station wagons and checkbooks. The most obvious stop is the **Strasburg Emporium** (540-465-3711 ♿), where more than 100 antiques dealers share a roof and offer merchandise from fine art to architectural antiques to enough knickknacks to make even your grandmother shudder. In summer, there's swimming and scuba diving at Strasburg's **Half Moon Beach** (540-465-5757), with five acres of white sandy beach on a 16-acre private lake. To the north in Middletown, there's live theater at the **Wayside Theatre** (540-869-1776) and, to the east, a large number of wineries, among the closest **Linden** (540-364-1997) and **Oasis Vineyards** (540-635-3103). (For more on vineyards in the Blue Ridge foothills, see THIS SIDE OF THE SHENANDOAH on Page 34).

GETTING THERE: Strasburg is about 90 minutes from the Beltway, Front Royal about 15 minutes less. Take I-66 west to Exit 6 and follow the signs into Front Royal. To get to Strasburg, take I-66 west to I-81 south; at Exit 298, turn left on U.S. 11 for two miles.

WHERE TO STAY: Built last century on a high bluff that reminded its owner of his native Northern Ireland, Front Royal's **Killahevlin** (800-847-6132; $125-$225, double &) is an Edwardian mansion whose four carefully updated rooms (and two suites in the adjacent Tower House) have fireplaces, private baths and whirlpools. After a day of hiking or biking or antiquing or cavern-hopping, this is not a bad place to soak up a Shenandoah sunset. Neither is the **Inn at Vaucluse Spring** (800-869-0525; doubles $135-$250 &) outside Stephens City, about 10 miles north of Strasburg on U.S. 11, where 12 romantic, immaculate rooms are spread over four buildings nestled on more than 100 rolling acres with a spring-fed pond and stream. The inn's 200-year-old hilltop Federal manor house, with its fireplaces and thick stone walls, is spectacularly furnished and offers a lot of privacy. Don't miss the Saturday night dinner. Many romance- or respite-seeking Washingtonians who can't make it to the south of France make do, happily, at the 11-room **L'Auberge Provencale** (540-837-1375; doubles $145-$250) in White Post, Va. Innkeeper/chef Alain Borel, who's originally from Avignon, France, is wont to pluck herbs and vegetables from his garden and ripe fruit from his trees in preparation for his distinctive dinners in the main house, a stone farm building dating to 1753. The inn's newly opened extension, the three-room **Villa La Campagnette** (doubles here are $195-$250), sits on 18 acres about four miles away in Boyce, with a pool and hot tub on the grounds. Strasburg's in-town **Hotel Strasburg** (540-465-9191) has 20 rooms and nine Jacuzzi suites, with rates of $79 to $175, double. Gamely spiffed up with Victoriana (most of it for sale), it retains, to its credit, a funky frontier look, the kind of place where Miss Kitty might have entertained Marshal Dillon. (Until 1915, it was a private hospital, which explains why the rooms have such uncommonly wide doorways.)

WHERE TO EAT: In Front Royal, find good sandwiches and Shenandoah picnic provisions at **Sweet Time Charlies** (540-636-4256; Monday-Thursday, lunch only), hand-tossed pizza at **Castiglia Italian Eatery** (540-635-8815 &) and no-frills fare at the aging but agreeable **Fox Diner** (540-635-3325). Almost all agree that the best food in Strasburg is to be had in the formal Victorian (but bright and accommodating) dining room of the **Hotel Strasburg** (see WHERE TO STAY, above).

FOR MORE INFORMATION: Contact the **Front Royal Visitor Center** at 800-338-2576 or *www.frontroyalchamber.com*, or the **Strasburg Chamber of Commerce** at 540-465-3187.

SHENANDOAH NATIONAL PARK

You can be in Shenandoah National Park, hiking up through forests of oak or pine toward the billion-year-old granite backbone of the Blue Ridge, in less than 1.5 hours from the Beltway. The extraordinary, 196,000-acre park, created by an act of Congress in 1926, straddles a beautiful section of the Blue Ridge, the leading eastern edge of the Appalachian Mountains. (The entry fee for passenger cars, good for a week, is $10. A 12-month pass runs $20.) The better known areas of the park are swamped by fall leaf admirers in mid-October and by others on warm-weather weekends. But if you know where—or when—to go, you can avoid backups on otherwise calming, 105-mile-long Skyline Drive or eating someone else's Gore-Tex dust on the way up to Old Rag Mountain. Including the Appalachian Trail, the park harbors 500 miles of trails, for beginning to advanced hikers. Some suggestions:

❑ **THE SEASON.** Go in the off-season. Winter is anything but dead in the Shenandoah. That's when you'll hear the eerie cronk of the northern raven, a bird seldom seen south of Maine that has begun colonizing these mountains in recent years. You'll see buzzards riding the thin winter thermals and squirrels and deer, their distinctive trails of hoof-ruffled leaves going off in every direction. But other hikers? Hardly.

❑ **THE SIDE TRAILS.** Make use of the PATC's maps and books (see GETTING THERE, Page 32) to find the many side trails which remain, even in peak months, about as literally off-the-beaten-path as you can get (and which the Park Service and PATC work hard to keep debris- and obstacle-free). A good example, about halfway between Luray and Front Royal, is the 4.5-mile **Mathews Arm**. This is a long, gentle arm of a ridge that provides an almost constant gradient up toward the granite spine of Hogback Mountain as well as access to the 93-foot, two-part cascades of **Overall Run**. The cascades are spectacular year round (most folks reach it via the much shorter and wider trail from the Overall Run campground). In its former life, Mathews Arm served as a road to the subsistence farms that dotted the upper reaches of the mountains before the land became a park. Now it's mostly a superior footpath, the kind you can walk at a good clip and not have to watch where you're putting your feet every step. **Directions:** To get to it from U.S. 211 at Skyline Drive, take 211 west to Luray and then head north on Route 340. Turn right on Bentonville-Browntown Road and continue seven-tenths of a mile to a right on Thompson Hollow Road, three-tenths to a left on Carton Ridge, and another seven-tenths to the gate. Another hike that includes waterfalls—but will more likely be a solitary pursuit only in the off-season or on a weekday—is into **White Oak Canyon**, one of the steepest ravines in the park, with six waterfalls, the tallest of which is 86 feet. Park at the White Oak Canyon lot at Milepost 42.6 and follow the White Oak Canyon Trail down through the towering Limberlost hemlocks into the spooky canyon; budget at least four hours. Not far from here is the park's first path accessible to wheelchair-bound visitors: **Limberlost Trail** ♿ is a 1.3-mile, five-foot-wide, hard-packed green stone trail at Milepost 43 that winds through an old-growth hemlock forest, its grade never exceeding 8 percent.

MORE FOLIAGE, LESS TRAFFIC

THE LEE RANGER DISTRICT, the closest-to-D.C. portion of million-acre **George Washington National Forest** (540/984-4101), offers quite a few less-crowded alternatives to the hikes (or drives) past mountains, streams and woodland that bring thousands of city dwellers to Shenandoah National Park every autumn. For hikers and campers (and banned-in-the-park mountain bikers) in particular, two attractive GWNF alternatives easily reached from Luray or Front Royal are the Big Schloss area and Kennedy Peak near the Camp Roosevelt area.

Big Schloss: From the Wolf Gap Campground on the West Virginia boarder, near Woodstock, Va., the Mill Mountain Trail leads north to the summit of Big Schloss, an imposing rock formation that indeed resembles a castle, as the German name implies. Atop Big Schloss you can view valleys and farms in both Virginia and West Virginia. **Directions**: From Front Royal, continue out I-66 west to I-81 south, exiting onto Route 42 west. Turn right onto Route 675 and follow signs to the Wolf Gap Campground.

Kennedy Peak: Farther south, a gently graded trail ascends along the ridgeline of Massanutten Mountain to Kennedy Peak. Once you are at the summit, a trail shelter with a rooftop observation deck presents you with a bird's-eye view of the serpentine bends of the south fork of the Shenandoah River and the town of Luray in the distance to the east. **Directions**: From Front Royal, follow Route 55 west from town, and turn left onto Powell's Fort Road (Route 678). Follow it all the way through the Fort Valley (which George Washington once considered as a federal-forces hideout) to Kings Crossing. There, bear left onto Route 675, and when the road reaches the ridgeline after passing Camp Roosevelt, a public campground, look for a dirt parking area on your right. The trail is across the road from the parking area. (From Luray, you can take Route 675 over the mountains and arrive at the trailhead from the opposite direction.)

Another less-traveled area worth exploring is **Nicholson Hollow**, where the trails give a glimpse into the human history of these mountains. The former inhabitants of Nicholson Hollow—hunters, subsistence farmers and harvesters of chestnut bark for tanneries—were displaced because of a combination of exhausted land, chestnut blight and, finally, establishment of the park. But traces of their homes and their presence are still visible. Some trails lead into the Nicholson Hollow area from Skyline Drive: **the Nicholson Hollow** (Milepost 38.4), **Corbin Cabin Cutoff** (37.9) and the **Hannah Run Trails** (35.1).

You can take a short walk or incorporate several trails into a more ambitious circuit hike. There is parking at the marked trailheads.

❑ **HIKING HELP.** You do the walking—let others do the hard stuff (like meal planning). Among those who'll take you on organized, narrated hikes in the park is **Mountain Memory Walks** (888-811-1379 or *www.mmwalks.com*). Year round, the Plains, Va., outfitter combines easy to moderately strenuous hikes in the Mid-Atlantic area with very unstrenuous stays at local inns and B&Bs. (Weekend excursions start at $350 a person, including meals and lodging. Day hikes start at $30 a person, including lunch.)

GETTING THERE: Shenandoah National Park is about 75 miles from the Beltway. Take I-66 west to Front Royal. Go south on U.S. Route 522 to U.S. Route 211 west, and follow signs to Skyline Drive. The best map of the park's northern area is the Potomac Appalachian Trail Club (PATC) Map of Shenandoah National Park (known as Map No. 9; Maps 10 and 11 cover the central and southern sections, respectively). It's available at most **REI** and **Hudson Trail Outfitter** stores. They also carry books on the park, including the recommended "Circuit Hikes in Shenandoah National Park."

WHERE TO STAY: You can sleep under a roof in the park, April through November, at **Skyland Lodge** (which also offers horseback riding), **Big Meadows Lodge** ♿ or **Lewis Mountain Cabins**. Call 800-999-4714 to reserve a room at any lodge. Six backcountry cabins also are available from the **Potomac Appalachian Trail Club** (703-242-0315). Lodges and cabins fill up fast starting in October, often for the following year. Not in the park but surrounded by it in Syria, Va., the veteran **Graves Mountain Lodge** (540-923-4231; doubles $70-$102 per person, including 3 meals ♿) has many rooms, country houses and rustic cabins, horseback riding, tennis, swimming and some of the most filling, family-style meals you've ever had before falling asleep in a porch rocker. **Camping in the park:** Big Meadows' campground costs $17 a night and requires a reservation from the National Park Service Reservation Service (800-365-2267). Lewis Mountain and Loft Mountain campgrounds don't take reservations and cost $14 a night (call 540-999-3500 for information). Open April through October, each campground has toilets, tables and parking. Serious backcountry campers can rough it almost anywhere in the park (though there are restricted areas; call the number below to check on them). Before hitting the trails, backcountry campers must pick up a free permit at any entrance station, visitor center or park headquarters.

FOR MORE INFORMATION: Contact the **National Park Service** headquarters at 540-999-3500 or check out *www.nps.gov/shen* or the **Potomac Appalachian Trail Club** at 703-242-0315 or *www.patc.net* (an exceptionally wide-ranging web site with details of PATC-sponsored hikes, work trips and other programs).

SPERRYVILLE/RAPPAHANNOCK COUNTY

Rappahannock County sits on the eastern slope of the Blue Ridge, in a comparatively laid-back landscape of meadows and rolling hills. It is close to Old Rag and White Oak Canyon but with a life apart from the national park that takes up so much of its western half. Nowadays the county's population doubles end as respite-seeking city folks arrive (or at least that's what the Sperryville and Washington, Va.). But in the 1960s, a nationwide "back-to-the land" movement lured commune-building hippies and others to this area on a more permanent basis. They seemed to mesh easily with locals, many of whom were mountain people forced to resettle here a generation earlier when the feds started turning their Blue Ridge Mountains into public parkland in the 1920s and 1930s. "The counterculture was tolerated here because the area was already home to a dislocated people," longtime resident Lanise Waites told *Post* contributor Daphne White. Retired military and others with disposable incomes began moving here, disposing of that income and, most importantly, getting involved. Strict land-use ordinances soon were enacted, requiring all lots to have a minimum of 25 acres and thus preserving the county's rural character. Only about 6,600 people live in Rappahannock, and most of them still make their living from the land (besides traditional agriculture, the region has a growing cadre of orchards and vineyards) and ever more from tourism. There is also a notable cultural community in Rappahannock County. "You never know who that person in the overalls is," Waites says. "It could be [former senator] Eugene McCarthy, it could be [columnist] James Kilpatrick, or it could be Lorin Maazel [former director of the Pittsburgh Symphony]." All three own houses in Rappahannock, along with painter Ned Bittinger, sculptor Frederick Hart and other well-known artists.

You can get a sense of the county's recent history at **Mountainside Market** (540-987-9100 &) in tiny Sperryville, where punk looking children of hippie parents now serve gourmet coffees, designer pizzas and spicy soups. Mountainside also carries organic produce, micro-brewed beers and Virginia wines. Nearby are a glassblowing studio, cidery, antiques stores (including the 20,000-square-foot **Sperryville Antique Market**, 540-987-8050), a turn-of-the-century Gothic church that is now a gallery and craft shop, a Faith Mountain Outlet Store and the place whose infamous sign simply says "Antique Tables Made Daily." The nearby town of Washington—surveyed by 17-year-old George Washington in 1749—has since been made more famous by a five-star Relais & Chateaux inn and restaurant whose inside most of the county's residents will never be able to afford to see. There also are two funky theaters: The **Theatre at Washington** (540-675-1253 &), featuring movies, plays, classical music, folk music and other entertainment on selected evenings, and the **Ki Theater** (540-987-3164), with experimental dance, plays and music.

GETTING THERE: Sperryville is under two hours from the Beltway. Take I-66 to Exit 43A (U.S. 29) toward Warrenton. Follow Business 29 around Warrenton and turn right on U.S. 211 toward Skyline Drive. Washington is about 20 miles ahead, Sperryville another six miles.

WHERE TO STAY/EAT: Sperryville's **Belle Meade Bed & Breakfast** (540-987-9748; doubles $130-$160) has four rooms and one cottage with spectacular mountain views on its 137 acres of woods, fields and gardens. A gourmet dinner (as well as a bag lunch) is available with advance reservations. (You also can schedule a massage or more exotic energy-field or spiritual services like Reiki or "channeled readings," to be conducted in your room.) The inn serves breakfasts and dinners that are delicious and wholesome (oatmeal cookies, whole-wheat muffins, brown rice). In a four-story farmhouse outside Sperryville that dates to 1790, **Conyers House Inn and Stable** (540-987-8025) has eclectic rooms with private baths and peerless views of Walton Mountain and beyond for $150 to $300 a night, including breakfast. The inn also offers two-hour trail rides that start at $70. (Fox hunts and more serious riding instruction are available—as is, thoughtfully, massage therapy.) Other choices include **Bleu Rock Inn & Restaurant** (in Washington, 540-987-3190; doubles $125-$195), with five rooms, a restaurant specializing in country French American cuisine and a vineyard, and **Laurel Mills Farm** (in Castleton, 540-937-3600; doubles from $125). Current information about 15 of the Rappahannock County's two dozen bed-and-breakfasts can be found on the web at *www.bnb-n-va.com.*

There are quite a few restaurants to choose from nearby, in addition to the five-star experience of the **Inn at Little Washington** (540-675-3800; fixed-price meals $98 to $138, nine rooms and three suites from $340 to $865, double ⌖). You could have a simple but creative (and most likely organic) lunch or dinner beside the Thornton River at Rae's Place Deli (540-987-9733), or down the road at Sperryville's **Mountainside Market** (see above)—or next door to Mountainside at the **Blue Moon Cafe** (540-987-3162), which also features a bar and an eclectic mix of live music on Friday and Saturday nights. While Sperryville's **Appetite Repair Shop** (540-987-9533) and Washington's **Country Cafe** (540-675-1066) satisfy the locals (and anyone who's just hungry and responds well to a cheerful waitress), the ever-changing new American menu at **Four and Twenty Blackbirds** (540-675-1111; open Wednesday-Sunday only) impresses many who know the route from the Beltway to nearby Flint Hill. And another *Post* contributor and a friend had a memorable brunch at the converted turn-of-the-century schoolhouse known as **Flint Hill Public House** (540-675-1700; closed Wednesdays ⌖).

FOR MORE INFORMATION: Contact the **Washington Town Hall** at 540-675-3128 or *www.town.washington.va.us*, or try the unofficial site at *www.rappguide.com.*

THIS SIDE OF THE SHENANDOAH

Despite ever-encroaching suburbia—for many, Wal-Mart's arrival in Warrenton was an unfortunate milestone—Fauquier County still is a big enough place for much of it to remain prime terrain for the classic family pastime of a generation ago: the Sunday afternoon drive. Sunday or not, ample rewards await those who turn left off of I-66 almost anywhere between Manassas and the Blue Ridge Mountains and are equipped with a good map (the kind that includes roads too narrow or gravelly for white lines). *Post* writer M.J. McAteer, who calls Fauquier County home, notes some of the county's high points:

The **Flying Circus** at Bealeton (540-439-8661; $10 adults, $3 children, open May to October) has been putting its spiffy biplanes in the air for more than 30 years of Sunday afternoon daredevil stunts, wing-walking and precision flying (and, as if to prove it before the show, loudspeakers blare songs and news from radio's golden age). Starting at 11 a.m. (the main show is at 2:30), more daring visitors can opt for an open-cockpit ride for an extra charge. Delaplane, a tiny town formerly called Piedmont Station, once was a busy railroad junction and the place where Stonewall Jackson loaded his troops on a train to head for the first battle of Manassas (see next page). Today the old station and warehouse are occupied by the browser-friendly **Delaplane Store and Antiques Center** (540-364-2754). But Delaplane's greatest asset is the 1,800-acre **Sky Meadows State Park** (540-592-3556). This probably is the closest, most viable alternative to leapfrogging through Shenandoah National Park. If you don't at least take 20 minutes to walk to the top of one of the namesake meadows, you'll be missing one of the prettiest views of the Piedmont Valley, with its ridges of green, its blue hills and tidy barns and silos and its sparkling farm ponds. Except for the reflection of sun off windshields of cars on Route 17, the scene can hardly have changed in a century. In fact, a substantial farmhouse from the 1860s and its outbuildings have been restored here and are accessible without too much effort. Costumed docents give tours of the house, which was home to the doctor who declared abolitionist John Brown dead after he was hanged for his abortive raid at Harpers Ferry, W. Va. Later, when the Civil War began, the doctor's family sided with the Confederates, and you can see where some of John S. Mosby's raiders were hidden in the house when Yankees were abroad in the valley.

Near the tiny, horse-driven town of The Plains, twilight polo games are held on Fridays, June through September, at **Great Meadow** (540-253-5000). In Hume, you can take a 90-minute trail ride at the **Marriott Ranch** (540-364-2627, closed Mondays), a 5,000-acre spread of woods and pastures where you also might mingle with longhorn cattle. The saddles here are Western, the pace is placid, and the level of riding experience needed is zero. The ranch offers moonlight rides, sunset rides, cookouts, cattle drives and river rides. Nearby are tours and tastings at **Oasis Winery** (540-635-7627) and **Linden Vineyards** (540-364-1997). Fauquier has five vineyards in all, including beautifully landscaped **Naked Mountain** in Markham (540-364-1609 ♿) and **Piedmont Vineyards & Winery** (540-687-5528 ♿), which pick up their mail in Middleburg but, truth be told, are in Fauquier.

If your only acquaintance with **Warrenton** is from the collection of chain stores and gas stations along the bypass that takes you toward the mountains, **Old Town** will come as a treat: It has lots of fine old homes and civic buildings, several good restaurants and no parking meters. Warrenton has several horsy shops, where you can try on handsome hunt jackets or, lacking $500 in mad money, spend a couple of bucks on a fox-head bumper sticker. Browsing the town's antique emporiums, be sure to stop in at the delightfully decorated **Sarah Belle's** (540-344-4549). If you're here on a Saturday evening, Warrenton has outdoor concerts downtown as part of the **Bluemont Concert Series** (703-777-6306 ♿). The visitors center has brochures for a self-guided walking tour. It covers, among other things, the courthouse where Supreme Court Justice John Marshall first was licensed to practice and the Warren Green Hotel, which extended hospitality to two notables who had done their part to undermine the British empire: Gen. Lafayette in 1825 and Wallis Simpson some 100 years later. The **Old Jail Museum** (540-347-5525; closed Mondays ♿) near the courthouse dates from 1808 and has displays about Mosby, who practiced law in Warrenton. After bedeviling Union troops throughout the Civil War, the "Gray Ghost" turned around and voted for their commander, Ulysses S. Grant, for president in 1872, not a popular political move here. Indeed, he had to relocate to make a living. He is buried, though, in the Warrenton Cemetery, which also contains the mass grave of 600 Confederate soldiers who died in the battles at Manassas. Though it's closer to the interstate in Prince William County, **Manassas** is not too far from here and is a must for Civil War buffs. The Battle of First Manassas, on July 21, 1861, was the initial test of Northern and Southern military prowess—and the place where Confederate Brig. Gen. Thomas J. Jackson acquired his nickname (as in, "There stands Jackson like a stone wall"). Both sides' troops arrived on these meadows overlooking Bull Run naïve and unprepared for anything but a short and glorious war, and by day's end they left—minus the 900 who never would leave—abruptly versed in the horrors of battle. When the two armies met here again in August of 1862, both were battle-hardened and much larger: Some 23,000 were killed, wounded or reported missing. The Confederates' second Manassas victory opened the way for their first full-scale invasion across the Potomac. All of these tales are told daily in exhibits, self-guided audio-tape tours, regular guided tours and other programs at **Manassas National Battlefield Park** (703-754-1861).

GETTING THERE: Warrenton (like most destinations in Fauquier County) is about 90 minutes from the Beltway via I-66 to U.S. 15/29 south.

WHERE TO STAY/EAT: An overnight stay 1.5 hours from home can be, in itself, an indulgence, so why not pull out all the stops and stay at the **Ashby Inn** (540-592-3900; $145-$180 double, including full breakfast) in Paris, Va.? Magazine magnate Condé Nast called it one of the world's premier inns. In fine weather, many guests pass up the cozy paneled dining room, where the names of steady customers appear on brass plaques, in favor of the patio, where they can take in the sweeping mountain view along with their crab cakes and raspberries. (With wine and tip, dinners run about $75 a person.) The inn itself consists of 10 rooms, eight with private bath. And if a room with wide French doors that open onto a small balcony overlooking the Blue Ridge foothills sounds good to you, ask if the Fan Room is available. The **1763 Inn** in Upperville (540-592-3848; doubles $115-$225 ♿) has 16 rooms with all the modern amenities (including double whirlpools), plus cabins, tennis courts, a pool and a German-style restaurant. On the other hand, if wherever you hang your hat is home and you've come out here mostly to drive, ride, shop or tour, Warrenton's **Comfort Inn** (540-349-8900 ♿) will rent you a large room with two double beds, a large bath, cable TV, microwave and small refrigerator for about $77 a night. In Marshall is **Glascock's Grocery and Middle Eastern Deli** (540-364-1721), a small country store that owner Nick Sarsour stocks with the makings of a great picnic, including homemade sandwiches, moderately priced wines, candy, even pickled eggs. In Warrenton, **Jimmie's Market** (540-347-1942) is also good for gourmet picnics to go, **Earthly Paradise** (540-341-7115 ♿) for a cozy cup of coffee, the **Town Duck** (540-347-7237 ♿) for pâté and the like, **Old Town Cafe** (540-347-4147 ♿) for super soup and **Fantastico's** (540-349-2570 ♿) for first-rate Italian food.

FOR MORE INFORMATION: Contact the **Warrenton-Fauquier County Visitor Center** at 800-820-1021 or 540-347-4414, or *www.fauquierchamber.org*.

Near Warm Springs, The Real Hidden Valley

By Daphne White

"**G**EORGE Washington didn't sleep here," the plaque outside Hidden Valley Bed and Breakfast could read, "but Richard Gere did." Well, Gere didn't exactly sleep here, but he did do love scenes with Jodie Foster for the movie "Sommersby," which should count for something.

I didn't go to Bath County, however, searching for presidents or film stars. I was seeking solitude and had heard of pristine woodlands in which a body could get lost. Then a forest ranger told me of a mansion in the heart of the George Washington National Forest, recently opened as a bed-and-breakfast.

The sun was setting over the mountains that encircle the "hidden" valley as my seven-year-old son and I caught our first glimpse of the Greek Revival building, a distant mirage of red bricks and white columns peeking through a thicket of trees.

Only 240 years ago, this region formed the westernmost outpost of the American frontier. George Washington himself surveyed it in 1754. Even today, entering the secluded valley feels like falling into a time warp. No cars, houses or strip malls are in sight, and wildflowers grow exuberantly by the narrow road: Queen Anne's lace, black-eyed Susans, wild phlox.

The Jackson River was running fast and high when we reached the end of the road, turned left over a small bridge and faced the antebellum building head-on. It is an imposing structure, one that draws several carloads of gawkers every day.

Pam Stidham, who operates the B&B with her husband, came over to greet us and give us a tour. The Stidhams first fell in love with this place in 1978, she told us. The Warwickton Mansion, as it was then known, was exactly the sort of house for which the Stidhams, who'd restored several historic houses in Ohio, had been searching. The hitch was that the U.S. Forest Service owned the building and used it for hay storage. In 1985 the Stidhams put together a proposal to renovate Warwickton at their own expense and operate it as a B&B, in exchange for a 30-year lease. It took the federal government five years to decide, but finally a special-use permit was granted.

It took weeks to drag out the hay and other accumulated trash from the mansion, weeks to convince the resident raccoons, opossums and snakes that their leases were up, and three years to research and renovate the property, which opened for business in July 1993. During this process, a movie producer chanced upon the site, and the Stidhams agreed to allow the filming of "Sommersby"—a film about mistaken identity in the aftermath of the Civil War—in and around the mansion.

We couldn't help feeling that we were on a movie set. The mansion's rooms are large and airy, with ceilings that are almost 11 feet high and lace curtains and damask drapes that descend to "puddle" on polished heart pine floors. Common rooms include a comfortable parlor, a music room with a square grand piano and a formal dining room.

The next morning, Pam wowed us with an extravagant breakfast—individual peach cobblers, cheese strata with salsa, lemon poppy seed muffins—served (I kid you not) by candlelight.

After this introduction to the day, we set off for a hike in the nearby woods. We bumped into a couple of trout fishermen—the Jackson River is reputed to be one of the best native trout streams on the East Coast—but otherwise had the valley to ourselves, except for the wildlife. We spied hundreds of butterflies, hatching in droves after a week of heavy rains. Overhead, birds of prey glided on air currents without a care in the world. We spotted a fawn observing us from across the river and more animal tracks than we could hope to identify.

The George Washington National Forest, denuded after decades of logging, was known as "the land nobody wanted" when the federal government purchased it in 1911. The idea was to protect the damaged watersheds and water supplies. Today the 1 million-acre forest—the largest block of public land in the mid-Atlantic—has recovered nicely, with poplars, maples and oaks providing a diverse habitat for animals and a welcome refuge for humans.

The stunningly pristine Jackson River, shallow and flowing fast at this point, swept across rocks and fallen logs alongside the path. There was an intimacy to its scale and a comforting quality to the sound of the water. We spent hours observing, resting, talking and reading by the banks of the river.

Later that afternoon, we visited the Jefferson Pools (also known as the Warm Springs Baths), about four miles from Hidden Valley and operated by the Homestead Resort folks. There is no need for planning—just drop by, pay $12, and luxuriate in the clear water that gurgles up through the rocks at a constant 98.6 degrees. "Your suit, my suit or God's suit?" the women's attendant asked as I walked into the gazebo-like structure built in 1836. It is painted white and is peeling inside and out. But there is a skylight built into the roofline, and when I floated on my back I could watch the clouds move across the sky. It took some adjustment to realize that there were no lap lanes here and nothing to do but relax.

After the bath, we set out for dinner in sophisticated and bucolic Warm Springs; we ate our desserts on the deck and watched fireflies flash their mating calls across the meadow. Later that night, after everyone else was asleep, I lingered in the parlor to talk with Pam. "You know how people say 'if only walls could talk'?" she remarked. "Well, these walls do talk, if you know how to listen. I believe that buildings have souls—people can't pass through and not leave something behind." Pam, who grew up on a dairy farm in Ohio, is not given to frivolity. But she says she has seen and heard things in this house that can't be explained in broad daylight under scientific conditions.

"People ask us all the time whether this house has ghosts," she continued. "I tell them that it does, but they've been quiet lately. All we hear is footsteps, furniture being moved—little things like that. I think they're happy with what we've done." By the time we finished talking—about the archaeological digs that reveal Native American habitation going back 10,000 years, the history of the families that lived here—I had forgotten what century I was in.

The next morning, after postponing our departure for as long as we could, we decided to head north toward Monterey on U.S. 220, with Jack Mountain on our right, Back Creek Mountain on our left and the Jackson River by our side. It was as beautiful a Sunday drive as I have ever taken. A friend later told me that a Swiss acquaintance broke down in tears on this road, it made her so homesick. We spent the afternoon browsing craft shops as I steeled myself for the interstate and the drive home.

GETTING THERE: Warm Springs is about a four-hour drive from the Beltway. Take I-66 west to I-81 south to I-64 west to Covington. From there, take U.S. 220 north to Warm Springs. (For more scenery and less interstate: Get off I-81 at the Bridgewater exit onto Route 257 west to Route 42 south. At Millboro Springs, take Route 39 west to Warm Springs.) Amtrak's Sunday-Wednesday-Friday Union Station-Chicago trains (800-872-7245) also stop in nearby Clifton Forge.

BEING THERE: Almost 90 percent of Bath County is taken up by forest, including the **George Washington National Forest** (540-839-2521), which has miles of hiking paths, some of the best trout streams in the country and opportunities for biking, mountain climbing, rappelling, caving and wild-food foraging. Among the national forest's more popular sites hereabouts is **Lake Moomaw**, a 15-mile-long Army Corps of Engineers creation with sandy beaches, trout and bass fishing, hiking trails and about 90 camping sites on the ridges overlooking the lake. Around the lake, a scenic drive through the Richardson Gorge on the narrow, gravel Route 603 takes you past an almost tropical, 40-foot vertical garden of moss- and fern-covered rock, over which clear water flows in hundreds of streams. Also nearby is **Douthat State Park** (540-862-8100), which sprawls across nearly 4,500 wooded acres and is traced by 40 miles of well-marked hiking paths around its 40-acre centerpiece, Douthat Lake, where you can swim, boat or canoe. (At the park's Lakeview Restaurant, one of three restaurants in Virginia's state park system, a typical Sunday buffet lunch of fried chicken, mashed potatoes, green beans, a lettuce-and-tomato salad, iced tea and chocolate cake is about $8 a person.) For cabin reservations at Douthat (pronouned *dowth*-at): 800-933-7275. Also highly recommended for outdoors advice and for arranging fly-fishing trips is **The Outpost** (540-839-5442), on the grounds of the Homestead (see **WHERE TO STAY** below). A number of private outfitters offer equipment and guided adventures, including **Highland Adventures** (540-468-2722). On weekend evenings July through Labor Day, the **Garth Newel Music Center** (540-839-5018 ♿) offers chamber music concerts in a converted riding rink. (It also offers fall weekend packages, including room, breakfast, dinner and concert.)

WHERE TO STAY: Bath County is blessed with some of Virginia's most distinctive lodgings. North of Warm Springs, **Hidden Valley Bed and Breakfast** (540-839-3178; doubles $115) has three spacious rooms, each with a private bath. Hour-long tours of the mansion are available to non-guests, by appointment only, for $4 per adult. The six rooms (and two cottages) of the elegant Queen Anne-style **King's Victorian Inn**, (540-839-3134; doubles $85-$150, including breakfast) were built in 1899 by physician Henry Pole, the first person to own an automobile in Bath County. Nowadays, afternoon tea is served to guests in the parlor in the fall and winter and on the veranda in good weather. The **Inn at Gristmill Square** (540-839-2231; doubles $80-$100) has placed its pool conveniently next to the tennis courts; after a searing game, you are only steps from a refreshing plunge. The inn offers 15 rooms and a restaurant (see next page). In Covington, there are five rooms and a suite at **Milton Hall** (540-965-0196; doubles $109-$159, including breakfast and tea), a gabled English country manor built by the Viscountess Milton in 1874. In southeastern Bath County, **Fort Lewis Lodge** (540-925-2314 ♿) is a tasteful and cozy 13-room country inn on an extraordinarily remote and beautiful 3,200 acres of pastures, fields and wooded slopes on the Cowpasture River. From the lodge's deck, the slender river valley stretches into the distance. The river itself tumbles through the property for easygoing tubing, forming a super swimming hole beneath a soaring rocky ledge a brief walk from the lodge. The Hickory Loop Trail, a short hike above the lodge's lands, offers stunning views of the bucolic surroundings. (From October through December, the lodge caters to hunters.) A room for two with dinner and breakfast in the gristmill that has been converted into a restaurant ranges from $140 a night for a lodge bedroom to $195 a night for a cabin.

Finally, one of the Mid-Atlantic's most extensive luxury resorts is nearby in Hot Springs. Rising like a castle above the Scottish highlands, The **Homestead** (800-838-1766; doubles $200-$635, except January to mid-April, when they are $132-$532) is surprisingly friendly and unpretentious inside. The basic room rate includes breakfast and dinner, and the resort package includes more than a dozen planned activities daily (most free). Among these are organized walks past the dozen waterfalls of 300-million-year-old Cascades Gorge, biking, carriage rides and horseback riding, tennis and golf, swimming pool and spa, Ping-Pong, a fitness center, canoeing, swimming and a children's fishing pond. The turn-of-the-century resort even includes an ornate, full-size movie theater that shows both contemporary and classic films (free), plus a bowling alley. The spa, built in 1892 over the 104-degree mineral springs below, offers a dizzying array of hydrotherapy and aromatherapy options, mineral baths, scrubs and herbal wraps. Golf, ski and family packages (including supervised children's activities at the KidsClub) are available.

WHERE TO EAT: Besides the reputable, museum-quality dining rooms of the **Homestead** and the more casual **Fort Lewis Lodge** (see preceding section), other restaurants draw praises. The Inn at Gristmill Square's **Waterwheel Restaurant** (540-839-2231; closed Tuesdays November-April) manages to have an uptown atmosphere in a rustic setting (and a consistent way with local trout). **Michel's** in Clifton Forge (540-862-4119; closed Sundays and Mondays ♿) offers French and American fare from former Homestead chef Michel Galand. In Hot Springs, the venerable **Sam Snead's Tavern** (540-839-7666 ♿), next to the Homestead, serves all-American food and drink in a former bank building converted to a good-natured shrine to the living golf legend (and native son).

FOR MORE INFORMATION: Contact the **Bath County Chamber of Commerce** at 800-628-8092. On the web it's *www.bathcountyva.org.*

MONTEREY, VA.

Highland County (pop. 2,600) often is called "Virginia's Switzerland," but—as its sheep far outnumber its registered voters—it surely could pass for Scotland. Whichever it may remind them of, though, hunters and fishermen and many who simply seek the great outdoors find much to keep them coming back to these mountains and valleys, with their picturesque farmhouses and lush grasses, speckled with gamboling calves and lambs and outcrops of rocks and boulders. Streams and rivulets meander through the pastures to create gentle banks dotted with wildflowers, and Highland County's three main rivers—the Cowpasture, the Bullpasture and the Jackson—are among the best for fishing in the state. Both the crystalline headwaters of the James River and a source of the Potomac emerge in Highland County. Nearby natural areas worth visiting—on foot, bike or car—include **Williamsville Gorge**, which winds past cliffs and through hemlock forests along Route 678 between Williamsville and McDowell. Route 640 through the **Blue Grass Valley** is renowned for its idyllic glimpses of country life, and the **Laurel Fork** area west of Blue Grass has great hiking trails (bring a wildflower book). Strolling past the Victorian homes of **Monterey** and sitting a spell on the porch of the **Highland Inn** (see WHERE TO STAY/EAT on next page) are musts, and you should check out the **Gallery of Mountain Secrets** (540-468-2020) for botanical prints and other works by local artists. Civil War buffs might want to walk the unchanged site of the **Battle of McDowell**, the first Confederate victory of Stonewall Jackson's 1862 valley campaign (get directions from the Chamber of Commerce, (next page). Families with kids might be interested in the **Virginia Trout Company's** (540-468-2280) self-guided tours of its large fishery. Highland County also is renowned for its **March Maple Festival**, featuring maple

Rejoice Cautiously at Black Bears

THE SECRETS OF RAMSEY'S DRAFT

IN A LITTLE-KNOWN valley not far from Staunton lies **Ramsey's Draft Wilderness,** a 6,500-acre, congressionally designated tract carved from the middle reaches of George Washington National Forest. A nearly pristine vale that's like an open-air museum of Old Appalachia, Ramsey's Draft somehow escaped the wholesale timbering that razed the eastern half of the continent. Thus, along the banks of the serpentine creek that gives the area its name, you can walk beneath stands of giant hemlocks, some of which sprouted in the first half of the millennium now coming to a close.

The heart of a web of side trails, the five-mile **Ramsey's Draft Trail** hopscotches the rocky stream bed all the way to the creek's trickling headwaters at the peak of **Hardscrabble Knob** (4,282 feet). Its first two miles follow an ancient lumber road. About three miles in it meets a smaller creek called Jerry's Run, and the trail up the run to the left leads to a narrow hollow that feels like a Hobbit forest, gnarled old trees clinging to mossy, sometimes sheer cliffs. It's an enchanting route.

If you're going in for the day, as *Post* contributor Steve Hendrix did, pack a picnic and water. But he cautions: "Hiking here can be difficult—the trail requires numerous and sometimes tricky stream crossings. If a tree has fallen across the path, you'll have to climb or go around; trail

products, clogging, a maple queen and tours of the sugar camps. It's the one time of year the county actually gets crowded.

GETTING THERE: Highland County is about a 3.5-hour drive from the Beltway. Take I-66 west to I-81 south to U.S. 250 west, which will lead you to McDowell and Monterey.

WHERE TO STAY/EAT: In Monterey, the **Highland Inn** (888-466-4682; doubles $55-$85) has 17 rooms, a two-story porch with rockers and a friendly, country elegance—plus a restaurant and tavern. Other options include a few smaller B&Bs (contact the Chamber of Commerce, below) and, in Hightown, the **Endless Mountain Retreat Center** (540-468-2700; doubles $65 plus $15 for kitchen access), for a mountain setting and outdoor recreation programs. For other nearby choices, see the previous section on **WARM SPRINGS**.

FOR MORE INFORMATION: Contact the **Highland County Chamber of Commerce** at 540-468-2550 or *www.virginia.org*.

maintenance is minimal to nonexistent. If you're staying overnight, be prepared for classic primitive camping. (And if you're so lucky as to see a black bear, rejoice cautiously. If a bear sees you, it will surely bolt, unless you surprise it. If it's heading away from you, just be still and watch. But if it looks like your paths might cross, give an early shout to let it know you're there, and it will run the other way. In camp, keep your food and garbage packed tightly away.)"

The same common-sense approach applies in the **St. Mary's Wilderness,** a 10,000-acre chunk of GW Forest farther south and west, between the Blue Ridge Parkway and I-81 in Augusta County. It lacks Ramsey's Draft Wilderness' old-growth forest, but it has some seasonally spectacular falls.

GETTING THERE: Ramsey's Draft is under three hours from the Beltway. Take I-66 west to I-81 south. At Staunton, pick up U.S. 250 west, and a few miles past West Augusta, go right at a sign for "Mountain House Recreation Area." Trailhead parking is across the small bridge and to the rear.

WHERE TO STAY/EAT: See section below on **STAUNTON**.

FOR MORE INFORMATION: Permits are not needed to camp in Ramsey's Draft, but information is. Maps are available at area outfitters such as **REI** and **Hudson Trail Outfitters,** and substantial help (including history, a discussion of bears and a map that can be downloaded) are on the excellent **Potomac Appalachian Trail Club** web site (*http://patc.simplenet.com*). For current trail conditions, check with the **George Washington National Forest** Deerfield ranger district at 540-885-8028.

AROUND STAUNTON

People unfamiliar with the lower Shenandoah Valley usually are pleasantly surprised by Staunton, a bustling patchwork of hills and history originally settled in the early 1700s and kept more or less freshly painted ever since. (The people of Staunton, who appreciate it if you correctly pronounce it STAN-ton, seem genuinely happy to fill in us outlanders.) The birthplace of both Woodrow Wilson and the Statler Brothers, Staunton has, of course, museums for both. Downtown, walks are rewarding: You could compile a veritable encyclopedia of architectural styles just from the classical, beaux arts, Victorian, Romanesque revival and Venetian revival buildings along Beverley Street. Staunton's five separate historic districts give the city a more solid, commercial feel than many along the Blue Ridge. The reason might have to do with the town's early role as the capital of a vast region called Augusta County (which in the early 1700s encompassed what is now Ohio, Illinois, Kentucky, West Virginia, Indiana and some of Pittsburgh). When Virginia's General Assembly fled the British during the Revolutionary War, Staunton also served briefly as the state capital. Location is a key to understanding Staunton—not so much its location today, which could be described as remote, but its strategic position during the Civil War. The Central Virginia Railroad reached Staunton in 1854, transforming the town and making it a vital link between the Confederate South and "the breadbasket of the Confederacy": the Shenandoah Valley. Union troops eventually destroyed the original train station, factories, foundries, stables and mills, and by the end of the war 1,777 Confederate soldiers had been buried at **Thornrose Cemetery.** (Many of them died at the Virginia Institute for the Deaf & Blind, which had been converted into a military hospital.) But the town suffered much less damage than most in the valley.

Just southeast of downtown, the living-history **Museum of American Frontier Culture** (540-332-7850 ♿) offers a unique perspective. Three old European farmsteads were dismantled and reassembled on this 78-acre tract to show the evolution, through early transatlantic migration, of American farms. There's a tiny German house (lived in from 1688 until 1983) with a handsome barn; a 19th Century farmhouse from Northern Ireland with a dirt floor, outbuildings and a blacksmith forge; a pink, half-timbered English house dating from the early 17th Century, and an 1830s Virginia farm. Each has costumed interpreters and still functions as a working farm, using distinct national techniques. The museum is staffed with dedicated history buffs. In summer, **Shenandoah Acres Resort** (540-337-1911) in Stuarts Draft has a sandy swimming beach on a lake and horseback riding, miniature golf, tennis, camping and cottages (starting at $81, double) and an arcade at the beach. **Sherando Lake Recreation Area** (540-291-2188), near Waynesboro, is at one of two adjacent mountain-ringed lakes built by the Civilian Conservation Corps. The **James River Basin Canoe Livery** (540-261-7334) can help get you around some other national forest areas.

GETTING THERE: Staunton is about a 3.5-hour drive from the Beltway. Take I-66 west to I-81 south to Exit 222. Pick up Route 250 west, which leads into downtown Staunton. Amtrak's Union Station-to-Chicago runs on Sundays, Wednesdays and Fridays also stop in Staunton (800-872-7245); round-trip fares start at about $44.

WHERE TO STAY: Staunton has a number of historic inns, and the surrounding area offers several more modern (and predictable) accommodations. The **Thornrose House** (800-861-4338; doubles $60-$80, including breakfast), a 1912 Georgian house, has a wrap-around veranda and a beautiful garden, across the street from Gypsy Hill Park. The **Belle Grae Inn** (888-541-5151; doubles $95-$245, including breakfast and in some cases dinner ♿) is an elegant, four-diamond Victorian B&B. The fetching Antebellum **Sampson Eagon Inn** (800-597-9722; doubles $95-$115, including breakfast) lives up to a rare mix of adjectives: elegant, friendly, well equipped and not overpriced. Out in the country nearby, **Pennmerryl Farm** (800-455-2864; doubles start at $80, including continental breakfast and a light lunch) offers motel-like lodging, but if you're a horse person who'd like to do more than a guided walk, this is your place. You can work on cross-country jumps in the field ($50 for a 60-minute lesson), or walk, trot or canter on escorted rides through 300-plus acres of meadows and woods for $30 to $50. Cabins for two to eight people also are available, with rates adjusted for those who bring their own horses.

WHERE TO EAT: Staunton has a surprising variety of cuisines and prices, but your first stop should be **Rowe's Family Restaurant** (540-886-1833). This is an old-fashioned eatery offering hearty meat-and-two-vegetable lunches accompanied by freshly baked rolls, plus homemade pies for dessert. At **L'Italia** (540-885-0102), excellent pasta entrees and pastries are the norm, while the **Pampered Palate** (540-886-9463) is known for its sandwiches, vegetarian selections, coffees and wines. In the restored Wharf Area, on a stretch of dramatically curved tracks at the foot of a cliff, the **Pullman Restaurant** (540-885-6612; closed Monday) has a great lunch buffet and huge windows facing the tracks and the rocky cliff, plus a virtual archive of authentic Victorian furnishings. (The original owner outbid both the Smithsonian Institution and the Walt Disney Co. to purchase the wooden, floor-to-ceiling pharmacy cabinets. The chandeliers come from the passenger lobby of a now-defunct Milwaukee train station, and the ornate Victorian backboard bar is itself worthy of a Historic Landmark designation.) At **MJ's Cafe** (540-337-6427; closed Sunday) in Churchville, between Staunton and Ramsey's Draft Wilderness (see box on Page 42), hikers can count on a country-style carbohydrate festival followed by excellent pie.

FOR MORE INFORMATION: Contact the **Staunton-Augusta Travel Information Office** at 800-332-5219.

Chapter 2

Fleeing North
By Northeast

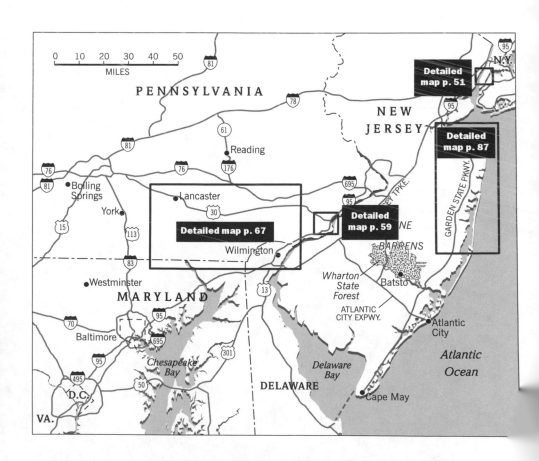

Never Mind Paris—It's April in New York

By Nancy Lewis

I T WAS LIKE this little no-brand hotel where we stay in Paris: a hardware store on the corner, a supermarket in the middle of the block, fish and meat markets across the street and pocket-sized cafes everywhere. The view from the room was of lush rooftop gardens and a wedding cake confection of an apartment building that would be right at home facing the beach at Nice. But the street below wasn't Rue Monge in the Latin Quarter. It was Broadway on the Upper West Side.

In the spring we did France in the Big Apple.

My husband, Gene, and I dined at grande dame French restaurants, a flower-filled auberge and a noisy bistro. We strolled through lush city parks, down well-manicured residential streets and along wide boulevards, their sidewalks brimming with young couples pushing baby carriages. We roamed through markets filled with mouth-watering displays of foie gras and caviar and past masses of seductive-smelling flowers. We slept late and spent our afternoons in art galleries with the impressionist paintings of textbooks and coffee table tomes. And we heard opera, opera and more opera. All without jet lag or sticker shock.

We are mostly off-season travelers. That way we avoid crowds and save money on airfares and accommodations, so we can spend it on things that matter more to us, like fine food and music.

The enticement for our New York escape arrived last fall in one of the Metropolitan Opera's never-ending promotion brochures: a trio of classic operas—"La Traviata," "Der Rosenkavalier" and "La Boheme"—on a single weekend, no price break but preference in seating. We succumbed and ended up with tickets to die for. Our original intention was to do just this wonderful weekend in one of the world's great cities. Then we decided to splurge on some extra days.

A couple of months in advance, we bought too many books, as always, and began wading through them, trying to pin down the details of a five-day fling in a city with a year's worth of interesting things to do.

Sticking to our rule-of-thumb mandate of keeping nightly hotel costs as close to $150 as we can get, we chose the Beacon, a residential hotel on Broadway at 75th, because it was just a short way from the Met but still in the middle of a real neighborhood.

About a month in advance, we winnowed the restaurant possibilities to four prime choices, all of which happened to be French and where last-minute reservations were said to be impossible—and then easily booked tables for exactly the dates and times we wanted.

It was raining hard when we left Washington a few Wednesdays later, but by the time we pulled up in front of the Beacon, the skies were dappled blue. It was rush hour for New Yorkers but vacation time for us, and the activities along Broadway that day were as foreign to our everyday Washington lives as the happenings along Rue Monge.

Next door was the Beacon Theater, where live performances are mounted several days a week. Across the street, sidewalk display counters were laden with lush red strawberries, vivid green asparagus and a dozen types of oranges. At the Italian deli and fish market, a saleswoman was handing out fresh ravioli—just turned out by a massive and complex machine in the front window—as fishmongers hawked lobsters and turbot and salmon and ceviche in the background.

At a Paris-sized supermarket (tiny, and tucked between specialty markets), we stocked up on yogurt, Perrier, Cokes and crackers for breakfasts and late-night snacks. We added a bottle of wine from a liquor store next door to make our settling-in complete.

We had expected our dinner that night, at the famed Lutece with owner/chef Andre Soltner still in command, to be the most memorable. Lutece was one of the first premiere French restaurants in New York, and for more than 25 years it had been considered the standard by which others were judged. It has changed hands since, and the new regime headed by former Le Bernardin chef Eberhard Muller has since earned a three-star rating from the *New York Times*.

The cab ride down Central Park West and across the park in a drenching rain seemed magical as lights of cars and buildings blurred into bright streaks. We alighted to find a waiter, clad in a long white apron, French-style, standing at the entrance to greet us with an umbrella. Things went downhill from there—the elegant upstairs dining room was closed, the poorly disguised Quonset hut "Garden Room" sprang a leak during the deluge, the service was poor, the chairs uncomfortable . . . Let's just say that we're sorry we got to Lutece before Muller began his much-applauded makeover.

But the next day was perfect. Our destination for a late lunch was Restaurant Daniel, whose owner, Daniel Boulud, has braved David Letterman's antics to cook on "Late Night" and written a cookbook filled with dazzling, if complicated, recipes. The restaurant, in a small hotel on the Upper East Side, was almost directly across Central Park from our hotel, so we decided to walk.

The sunshine was brilliant, and the air had the sweet smell that follows a rainstorm. Central Park was mostly deserted. A few Japanese tourists snapped photos of the Strawberry Fields, a couple embraced on the sidewalk, a little boy rode by on a bike with training wheels, his nanny in tow.

The quiet elegance of Daniel was like a warm embrace. Flowers filled the corners of the dining room in spectacular arrays, imaginative bouquets adorned each table, the chairs invited lingering, the service was expert, the food was stunningly creative and wonderfully flavored. Chef Daniel stopped by for a chat. The bill was under $90.

A few hours later, we were practically in the middle of the grand ball in the opening act of "Traviata." Our seats were dead center, third row. We didn't need opera glasses to see the expressions on singers' faces; we could almost feel their breath on ours. The experience was almost overwhelming. But then there was lunch Friday followed by "Der Rosenkavalier," and "La Boheme" Saturday followed by a late night dinner at Cafe des Artistes and . . .

GETTING THERE: Planes: Most major airlines fly between airports in the Washington and New York areas, but which ones go where is a bit complicated. In early 2001, the cheapest fares (about $125 roundtrip) were for Saturday and Sunday travel on the Delta and US Airways shuttles from Reagan National to LaGuardia and on United from Dulles to LaGuardia. But all three Washington airports also have scheduled flights on American to JFK and on Continental to Newark. United flies from Dulles to all three New York airports, and US Air and Delta have other scheduled flights to LaGuardia and JFK. **Trains:** From Union Station to New York's Penn Station, regular one-way Amtrak service Monday through Thursday and on Saturday is $68 unreserved. On Friday and Sunday from 11 a.m. to 11 p.m., one-way fares start at $85. On the faster Metroliner (reservations required), Monday through Friday, the one-way fare is $124, but on weekends it drops to $105 either way. The new high-speed Acela Express, which gets you there 15 to 30 minutes faster but in significantly more comfort, is $143 one way weekdays, $122 weekends. **Autos**: For two or more people it may be cheapest and more convenient to drive, even if you simply park the car in a garage in New York (many hotels offer special parking rates). Round-trip tolls are about $25, and the 230-mile drive requires no more than a tank of gas each way.

BEING THERE: New York can daunt even the most experienced trip-planner, so we sought counsel from friends in New York—not on the city's endless sights or shopping or shows but simply on things to do on the Upper East and Upper West sides before or after (or instead of) the opera. Some of their recommendations:

By all means visit the **Metropolitan Museum of Art** (5th Ave. and 82nd St.; 212-535-7710 &), but not just for the paintings, sculpture and artifacts—for the evening concerts as well. "It's the setting," says one friend. "It's so beautiful. They have such a variety of quality performers: Billy Taylor does a series, and the Musicians From Marlboro. Most performances are in an auditorium, but sometimes they hold performances right in the galleries." Tickets are $15-$60; reservations suggested (concert information: 212-570-3949). Another friend likes to hang out at the **Frick Collection** (70th and 5th Ave.; 212-288-0700 &), a mansion filled with Old Masters and period furniture (no children under 10), because it's also one of the city's quietest museums. A third says that many people miss the lively **Museum of the City of New York** (Fifth Ave. at 103rd Street; 212-534-1672 &), which celebrates New York's past, but "gives a wonderful perspective in terms of architecture, fashion, etc." Lots of videos and other interactive playthings. Similarly little known, one source notes, is the **Conservatory Garden** (Fifth Avenue at 105th Street, at the top of Museum Mile; 212-860-1382 &), an area of Central Park that offers "a beautiful garden, especially in spring, during tulip time and lilac time." The **Community Garden** at 111th Street and Riverside Park, created and managed by neighborhood people, is an excellent corner to escape the bustle, put up your feet and appreciate the fact that real people live in New York City. For shopping, **Maxilla & Mandible** (212-724-6173), near the Museum of Natural History is great for fossils and bugs and mounted butterflies. **Black Orchid** on 81st between First and Second (212-734-5980) is a little bookstore specializing in crime and mystery and also functions as a hangout for the whodunit set. **Shanghai Tang** (61st St. and Madison Ave.; 212-888-0111 &) is a Hong Kong-style department store that's "hot right now," one source says. "A lot of New Yorkers are dressing Asian, with a lot of silks and fine fabrics. This is the place to go for beautiful, high-end Asian clothes." Friend Constance Martin, a publishing executive who knows the neighborhood well, offers a sample strolling/shopping itinerary: "Start at Columbus Circle (66th Street), with the **Metropolitan Opera House** and my favorite **Barnes & Noble**—the Lincoln Center branch—on your left, and head uptown on Columbus. **Cafe Mozart** (154 W. 70th St.; 212-505-9797) has millions of different types of cheesecakes and pastries, just to die for. **Isabella's** (359 Columbus Ave. at 77th Street; 212-724-2100) is a big people-watching place, with tables on the sidewalk—great for Sunday brunch. Stop in at **April Cornell** (487 Columbus at 84th Street; 212-799-4342 ♿)—they have beautiful linens and hand-blocked pillows. And **Nice Price** (493 Columbus Ave. at 84th Street; 212-362-1020) has very, very discounted women's clothing—some stuff for as low as $10. **Merchants** (521 Columbus Ave. between 85th and 86th streets; 212-721-3689 ♿) is a good place to stop for a drink. When you get to 86th, go west a block to Amsterdam Avenue and the **Popover Cafe** (551 Amsterdam Ave. between 86th and 87th streets; 212-595-8555 ♿)—you can eat in or get a popover to go. **Drip** (489 Amsterdam Ave. between 83rd and 84th streets; 212-875-1032 ♿) is a new coffee hangout—like the one on 'Friends' but darker. And don't forget **Krispy Kreme** (141 W. 72nd Street between Columbus and Broadway; 212-724-1100 ♿). It's not an official hangout, but it's becoming more and more popular."

WHERE TO STAY: The **Hotel Beacon** (Broadway at 75th Street; 800-572-4969 or 212-787-1100; standard doubles start at $195 ♿) is a residential hotel that caters to musicians and other performers. It has an arrangement with a small garage a block away for hotel guests to park for $20 for each 24-hour period, one in-and-out a day permitted. Two other nearby hotels are the **Radisson Empire,** directly across from Lincoln Center (800-333-3333 or 212-265-7400; doubles $200 and up ♿), and the **Mayflower Hotel** at 15 Central Park West (800-223-4164 or 212-265-0060, doubles from $185 ♿). All three of these hotels periodically offer special lower rates. Another good neighborhood choice is the **Amsterdam Court** at 50th St. between Broadway and 8th Ave. (212-459-1000; doubles $130 and up, weekend parking $20). It's worth noting that a recent $125-a-night stay at this hotel—and at others in New York and in other major cities—came through a hotel discounter, **Quick Book** (800-789-9887).

WHERE TO EAT: After two separate quests to dine well (and, as it happened, French) author Lewis provides the following notes. "For a lunch at **Restaurant Daniel** (212-288-0033 ♿), we ordered two appetizers each, shared a dessert, added wine and coffee, for a total bill (with tip) of less than $100. (Daniel also offers a $35, three-course, fixed-price luncheon menu.) A post-opera dinner near Lincoln Center at the **Cafe des Artistes** (212-877-3500 ♿) featured impeccably hearty bistro food amid landmark-designated murals of decorous nude ingenues frolicking in flowered meadows. The bill for three, including drinks and wine, came to about $150. For dinner at **Lutece** (212-752-2225 ♿), which has a $72-a-person fixed-price menu, the bill ballooned to more than twice that with supplemental charges, ranging from $7 a person for asparagus to $14 a person for Grand Marnier souffles. **Jean Georges** (212-299-3900 ♿), a sleek, spare restaurant in the latest Trump-ed corner of Central Park, is beautiful not just in décor but in food and presentation. I had the best salmon I have eaten (since I eat it out often, that's saying a lot), and my husband had a perfect squab stuffed with foie gras. The service is serious and seemingly effortless, and the $100 price tag for lunch for two makes it just about perfect. **Le Bernardin** (212-489-1515 ♿) is considered New York's top serious fish restaurant, a place where the powerful lunch, not just to be seen but for the food. The room is luscious, literally filled with flowers. The fish is superb. The chocolate tart is sublime. **Les Celebrités** (212-484-5113 ♿) is tucked on the back side of the Essex House/Nikko Hotel on Central Park South and seats only about 40 in a room that whispers of Old World elegance. The food is just as refined. This is one expensive restaurant where there are good buys on the wine list and the sommelier doesn't turn up his nose at by-the-glass requests."

Our New York friends offered additional choices. The **Latin Quarter** (2551 Broadway at 96th Street; 212-864-7600) is a dance club for the elegant set. **Senor Swanky's** (287 Columbus Ave. between 73rd and 74th streets; 212-501-7000 ♿), a Mexican cafe where you can savor fancy cigars with your margaritas, is "definitely for an older crowd," one friend warned (then again, she's 19).

FOR MORE INFORMATION: Contact the **New York Convention and Visitors Bureau** at 212-484-1237, 800-693-7291 or *www.nycvisit.com*

FELLS POINT, BALTIMORE

Washington Post contributor Jeannette Belliveau has lived for a decade in Baltimore's Fells Point, a maritime district dating from 1726 (older than the city proper) and birthplace (circa 1850) of the clipper ships. While some Washingtonians already know the neighborhood's rowdy waterfront bars, Belliveau says Fells Point offers much more than that. "Fells Point provides a window on East Baltimore. You may see streetwalkers or a senator, trash pickers or cart horses. Where the literal-minded will see lingering seediness amid the gentrification, others will recognize the vitality of one of America's most entertaining neighborhoods—the wellspring for the humanist and comic visions of writer Anne Tyler and film directors Barry Levinson and John Waters."

Her recommendation is to start with a walk down to the waterfront via **Ann Street** and to be sure to pay attention to the little things. On Ann Street, these include the red stars embedded in the sidewalk (which formerly indicated the location of broth-els) or maybe a jingling sound—the harness bells of a pony pulling the cart of a man selling produce the turn-of-the-century way. A few blocks down is a humble row house, giving no clue that a U.S. senator lives in this unlikely milieu. Maryland sent Barbara A. Mikulski to Capitol Hill after she led efforts in the late 1960s to prevent Fells Point, her home, from being turned into a spur of Interstate 95. She still commutes every day to the Senate. From time to time, she steps out into the neighborhood with her shopping bags, buying tea from Deb at **Fells Point Coffee** in the **Broadway Market**.

In summertime, Fells Point's row houses sizzle, and the action moves outside. Right on the sidewalk, families eat steamed crabs off newspapers, and children make chalk drawings or splash in kiddie pools. If the Orioles are playing, you'll know it—radio coverage issues forth in all directions from windows and stoops. The windows and doors of Fells Point are worth studying for such details as screen paintings (usually of rural farms) in the doors and basement windows, original stained-glass house numbers (circa 1850), and bricolage, the practice of erecting statuary displays in windows. (Samples: Elvis and the Virgin Mary, penguin families, leprechauns—and, at least during Desert Storm, full-size store mannequins in combat fatigues. Elderly Polish and Ukrainian residents, who spend their days at the windows, keeping eagle eyes on the streets, preserve these traditions.)

Down by the water, Belliveau suggests you turn right on cobblestoned Thames Street, past the Nighthawk clipper ship and the bulk of **Recreation Pier** (often featured in Levinson's TV series "Homicide: Life on the Street"). Here you can look for the **Moran Towing** tugboats, at least if they are not out elsewhere. If it's morning, go up Broadway a block to **Jimmy's Restaurant** (410-327-3273 &), the official and very crowded Place to Go for breakfast in these parts. You will be called "hon" here, you will pay very little, and your coffee, pancakes or waffles will arrive lickety-split on your red-checked table-cloth. At the next table may be a tug crew, a film company or even the First Lady. (In 1993, Hillary Clinton stopped by to solicit views on health care and learned that most of Jimmy's tireless waitresses simply cannot afford it.) If you'd prefer to experience other people's lives from a darkened row of seats, nearby are the funky **Fells Point Corner Theater** (410-276-7837), where the talented house troupe will shine—if the play itself does— and the **Orpheum** (410-732-4614), where creaking seats and scratchy prints fail to detract from this homey spot for repertory and revival films. Books can be found at a number of neighborhood spots, including **Adrian's Book Cafe** (410-732-1048), a coffeehouse and bookstore with frequent readings and live music. Of other Fells Point hangouts offering drinks made with caffeine rather than alcohol, **Daily Grind** (410-558-0399) has art on the wall and cobblestones on the floor, and Richard Belzer sometimes stops in for java between takes of "Homicide." **Funk's Democratic Coffee Spot** (1818 Eastern Ave.; 410-276-3865) is small and smells great and most nights features multicultural performances: jazz, readings, hip-hop poetry, singer-songwriters with acoustic guitars. **Jabali** (Bond and Lancaster 410-276-1737) is a tiny space taken up mostly by couches. It serves coffee, etc., and has an impressive display of cigars and cigar paraphernalia for sale as well. For bargain hunting around Fells Point, **Scratch and Dent Liquidators** (423 S. Broadway; 410-732-7702 &) is an Aladdin's cave of cheap merchandise stacked to the roof, and **H&S Bakery Outlet** at 1616 Fleet St. (410-522-9323 &) always has marked-down bagels, potato chips and pumpernickel bread.

On **Brown's Wharf**, you can stroll along the brick promenade featured in "Sleepless in Seattle," where Baltimore-bound Meg Ryan stares out at the wide vista and wonders if she should pursue the appealing radio voice of Tom Hanks. Here you can hop the **harbor shuttle** (410-685-4288; every half hour, 11-5:30, Memorial Day-Labor Day) to **Fort McHenry** (where, during 1814's Battle of Baltimore, Francis Scott Key was to immortalize those broad stripes and bright stars). On the way you'll pass another film landmark: the warehouse where the fire scene in "Avalon" was shot.

If you're looking for more of a sightseeing tour of the Inner Harbor and other Baltimore destinations, check in with the **Baltimore Tickets** kiosk, outside the visitors' center in the Inner Harbor, which often offers family-friendly package

THE WONDROUS WORLD OF C-MART

SHOPPING can be a grind—but "when the destination is C-Mart, an idiosyncratic discount store in nondescript Forest Hill, Md., it's an adrenaline-filled rush," reports *Post* contributor Margaret Engel.

"This place has everything—women's, kids' and men's clothes, shoes, sports equipment, towels, toiletries—whatever brand-name goods the owner can get cheap. Twice a year, I drop the kids off for school, head for Baltimore with a friend, spend the day at C-Mart, pausing only for a Greek salad at Manny's Family Restaurant in the adjoining strip mall. Then it's back through the Fort McHenry Tunnel and home for school pickup with enough bargains to avoid gift or clothes shopping indefinitely. Now, that's one day of pure escape with lasting, time-saving benefits."

Engel grew up in Cleveland, which she says gives her a natural affinity for Baltimore, the city of FormStone, marble steps and sheds selling flavored snowballs (one is across from C-Mart). "So when I learned that savvy New Yorkers, not to mention Philadelphians, were hot-footing it to C-Mart, it smelled like an adventure in bargain-hunting."

To get in the C-Mart spirit, she says, you should read the owner's hand-written ads every Thursday in the Baltimore Sun. (True mavens like her sign up for the store's weekly fax hotline.) In the ads, owner Doug Carton, whose parents opened C-Mart almost 30 years ago, describes his stupendous luck in persuading insurance companies to part with prime goods.

"C-Mart bought over 7,000 pieces of all holiday '97 goodies after the shipment arrived from Europe too late for two big fancy dept. stores," reads one. Another tale of ladies sportswear notes: "They flew this huge load into JFK from the Orient. When they unloaded the plane it started to rain (that's good for you) and the outer cartons got wet (that's good for us) and we bought the whole thing." A load of Nikes, TVs, VCRs, tea and

deals. A recent "Weekender" package cost $131 for a family of four and included admissions to the **National Aquarium**, **Baltimore Zoo**, **B&O Railroad Museum**, a sailing on the **Clipper City** boat and two days of water taxi trips.

GETTING THERE: Baltimore's Fells Point is less than an hour from the Beltway. You can exit at the Baltimore-Washington Parkway and follow that until it becomes Russell Street, or take I-95 and exit at Russell Street. On Russell, turn right at the Inner Harbor; go a bit more than a mile, past Little Italy, and you're there.

fishing rods comes to C-Mart because "someone stole a truckload of freight. The insurance co. paid off, the police caught the bad guys (yea), then the insurance co. sold the whole load to C-Mart (double yea)." Insurance companies are the key to Carton's ability to bring shoppers such buys as $60 Bruno Magli shoes, $71 Emanuel Ungaro lined wool pants and a $131 Linda Allard-for-Ellen Tracy ski jacket (tagged at $465). A size 12 Dolce & Gabbana black crepe, long-sleeved, ankle-length dress is $345 instead of $2,300. A black quilted Dana Buchman jacket is $105, instead of $348, a $1,050 Searle coat priced at $248.

The important thing about C-Mart, Engel says, is that the stock turns over daily and there's lots of sales help, making sure that clothes and shoes are hung and arranged neatly, by size. "You don't have to excavate here, and you won't find items with broken zippers or other blemishes. If they're seconds, they're marked. But most of the shipments are top-drawer merchandise. The downside is that C-Mart might not have what you're interested in the day you visit. But when your interests and Carton's insurance gods are smiling, it's nirvana. How about an entire department store stock of Keds, in every size, shape and description, for $5 each? That was one memorable score that avoided the painful $45 sticker shock for kids' tennis shoes. Or the time the California earthquake emptied out Bullock's full hosiery inventory, so our savings went off the Richter scale with Donna Karan stockings, in every color and size (C-Mart buys entire lots), for $2 a pair."

GETTING THERE: From I-95 north of Baltimore, take Exit 77-B and follow Route 24 toward Bel Air. About eight miles out, bear right, following the signs for Philadelphia, and take the exit a mile later for Route 24 north. The store is a block down on the right at 1503 Rock Spring Rd.

FOR MORE INFORMATION: Contact **C-Mart** ♿ at 410-879-7858 or *www.cmartdiscount.com*. It is open 10 a.m. to 9 p.m. weekdays, 10 a.m. to 6 p.m. Saturdays, 11 a.m. to 5 p.m. Sundays. **Manny's Family Restaurant** (410-879-6976), in the middle of the strip mall behind C-Mart, offers inexpensive Greek and Italian fast food. The $5.20 Greek salad has sufficient feta and greens for two. Ditto on the drinks—go for a small. The gyros, pizza and broiled crab cake are fine.

Amtrak has daily departures, $25 round-trip excursion fares. MARC commuter trains to Penn or Camden stations (weekdays only) are $9.50 round trip.

WHERE TO STAY: The founder of the 80-room **Admiral Fell Inn** (410-522-7377 or 800-292-4667; doubles starting at $125, packages available ♿) was recruited in the mid-'80s by then-Mayor William Donald Schaefer to create a B&B inn for Fells Point. He—and the inn—succeeded. **Ann Street Bed & Breakfast** (410-342-5883; doubles $100-$110) has three rooms. A local couple renovated the property (it was the husband's childhood home). **Celie's Water-front B&B** (410-522-2323 or 800-432-0184; doubles $132-$242 ♿) has seven rooms, a romantic rooftop deck and corporate amenities (meeting room, modem, fax). The **Inn at Henderson's Wharf** (410-522-7777; doubles $139-$259 ♿) has 38 rooms in a converted 1894 tobacco warehouse with a land-scaped courtyard and rooms with harbor views.

WHERE TO EAT: Piccolo's of Fells Point at Brown's Wharf (410-522-6600 ♿) has a fantastic view and *buona cucina*, Tuscany style. Also at Brown's Wharf, busy **Lista's** (410-327-0040 ♿) has good New Mexican food; re-serve on weekends. **Henninger's Tavern** (410-342-2172) is a century-old neighborhood tavern with stellar nouvelle cuisine and atmosphere; allow time to linger. At **Pierpont** (410-675-2080), chef Nancy Longo creates nouvelle Maryland cuisine (smoked crab cakes, corn soup). **M. Gettier** (410-823-0384) serves up sophisticated French food in a funky location, and **Obrycki's** (410-732-6399 ♿) is the place for crabs on brown paper. The legendary **Bertha's** (410-327-5795) is still dishing up plates of steaming mussels in a boisterous and crowded space hung with maritime junk, musical instruments and cool signs, and you can listen to live Dixieland jazz (and other easy-on-the-ear styles) Tuesday through Thursday. At another local legend, next door in Little Italy, a family of four can fill up on huge plates of pasta for about $40 at **Sabatino's** (410-727-9414 ♿).

FOR MORE INFORMATION: Contact the **Baltimore Area Convention and Visitors Association** at 800-282-6632 or *www.baltimore.org*, or **Baltimore Tickets** at 410-752-8427.

PHILADELPHIA

So diverse and so much closer than the Big Diverse Apple, Philadelphia has long been an appealing place for quick-escape artists. You can have wonderful week-ends here, especially if you organize your visits around particular interests and you carefully pick a few not-so-obvious things to do. You want Colonial Philly? Ethnic Philly? Pop-Music Philly? Real-life Philly? Shopping Philly? Philly With Kids? Con-sider the following:

COLONIAL PHILLY: Most visitors wind up filing through **Independence Hall** and the **Liberty Bell** pavilion. But escapees who are truly intrigued by colonial history should consider visiting **Christ Church** (215-922-1695 ♿), towering over South Second Street in the Old City neighborhood for more than 250 years, a place where 15 signers of the Declaration of Independence worshiped. Today you can sit in pews once occupied by George Washington, Benjamin Franklin and Betsy Ross. The interior is elegant and largely unadorned—no stained glass or gilded whatnots. The church, the birthplace of the Protestant Episcopal Church in America, is still home to an active Episcopal congregation. A small burial ground sits outside its doors, but its official cemetery, with the penny-strewn grave of Benjamin Franklin, is at Fifth and Arch. **Society Hill**, a brick-paved, cherry tree-lined residential area, has rows of red brick houses dating from the mid-1700s stretching from about Front to Seventh and Walnut to Lombard streets. But despite the quaint homes, elegant churches, and charming walkways and gardens, it fell into decline early in this century and stayed there until the 1950s. A remarkable story of urban renewal, Society Hill is now one of the city's poshest neighborhoods, with the greatest collection of 18th Century vernacular architecture in America. Concentrate your walk on Pine, Delancey and Spruce streets. Along the way, make time for visits to several public buildings: at 244 S. Third, **Powel House** (215-627-0364) and **Physick House** (321 S. Fourth, 215-925-7866), once home to the father of American surgery. A splendid Palladian window, serene graveyard and huge old trees make **St. Peter's Church** (Third and Pine, 215-925-5968 ♿), one of Society Hill's most evocative sites. **FOOD/LODGING:** A meticulous re-creation of the original 1773 eatery that stood on the same spot, **City Tavern** (215-413-1443 ♿) is washed in pale blues and lit by candlelight, and its many dining rooms offer a romantic experience stressing Colonial-inspired entrees like turkey pot pie presented in a round pewter bowl. Servers in breeches and bonnets may be a bit precious, but everything else is done just right. And though George Washington didn't sleep here, **Thomas Bond House** (800-845-2663; doubles $95-$175) was built in 1769 and has been a B&B since 1988. Extras include gourmet weekend brunches and complimentary wine and cheese nightly.

ETHNIC FOOD PHILLY: Philadelphia is parsed into ethnic neighborhoods, but the one that has most influenced the city's image is Italian-dominated South Philly. Though it has become more eclectic in recent years, its style and manner have remained reassuringly constant. On a Saturday afternoon, the **Italian Market**—a five-

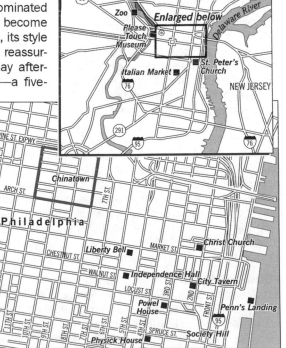

block stretch on Ninth Street from Christian to Wharton streets—hums as people pile into family-owned shops to sample and buy. By 11 a.m., the queue outside **L. Sarcone & Sons** bakery is a half-block long. By 2, the shelves are bare. At **DiBruno Bros.**, known for its cheese spreads, artisan cheeses and barrels of olives, people slink through the narrow shop, while down the street at the **Spice Corner**, they sniff multi-colored, fragrant containers. Wild game carcasses and slabs of meat hang in butchery windows, while in bakeries cannoli, biscotti and classic cookies are stacked daintily. On the street, the air smells of fresh-baked bread, espresso, cheese, fresh fish and live seafood. Restaurants here are among the best values in town, with pasta entrees starting under $8 and few entrees topping $20. The oldest is **Ralph's** (215-627-6011), a classic Neapolitan restaurant that opened in 1900 and has a National Historic Landmark post outside its doors. The maitre d' wears a tux, though most patrons dress informally. Nearby you'll find North America's fourth largest **Chinatown**—bounded by North Eighth and North 11th streets, Filbert and Callowhill. Most visitors experience only the restaurants, but other layers reveal a more authentic reality. Inconspicuous **Chinatown Mall** on 11th Street is an underground market where locals shop for products from their homeland and grab a quick, cheap meal at the **Tasty Place** (215-593-8990 ♿). For classic Chinese pastries, try the **Asia** bakery at 10th and Cherry. For an unusual meal, check out the kosher **Cherry Street Chinese Vegetarian** (215-923-3663 ♿); chef Raymond Fong trained in the kitchen of a Buddhist monastery. **LODGING:** The **Shippen Way Inn** (800-245-4873) is a nine-room B&B in a nifty neo-Colonial stone building five blocks north of the Italian Market. Rates are $90-$110 and include breakfast and afternoon tea in the garden. Rooms are small but, like the Italian Market, they have plenty of character.

POP-MUSIC PHILLY: For visitors seeking the pop sounds of Philadelphia, Old City's cozy club scene has become an attractive alternative to the Generation X post-punk that dominates the South Street area and the pounding, canned disco of Delaware Avenue's dance clubs. Along the narrow streets of this urbane extension of Society Hill, you'll find live blues, jazz, singer-songwriters, swing and Latin dancing. Folks go to **Warmdaddy's** (215-627-2500) to hear blues spiced with funk and jazz. Like most clubs in this former industrial zone, Warmdaddy's is a deep, narrow space where the band sets up in back. If you want to talk, sit near the door; the bar goes on for miles. The swing era is enjoying a comeback at the **Five Spot** (215-574-0070), a showcase for jitterbug aficionados located down a cobbled side street. You'll spot it by the line that forms on weekends. Sip martinis at candlelit tables that ascend in tiers from the dance floor. Bands perform against glittery red-lit drapes and include regulars like Ronnie James and the Jez Hot Swing Club. They dress like Humphrey Bogart in "Casablanca" and deliver a running patter of vintage jive-talk between Tommy Dorsey covers and songs like "Chattanooga Choo-Choo." To join the Lindy-Hoppers on the dance floor, come back on Sunday; dance lessons are given at 8 p.m. while a big band plays.

FOOD/LODGING: Both clubs offer dinner—Southern fare at Warmdaddy's, meat, potatoes and seafood at the Five Spot. But better eating can be had at **Serrano** (215-928-0770), where Asian respins—satays, wild-mushroom mu shu and chili pepper-crusted yellowfin on sugarcane—are delicious and reasonably priced. Acts like Rosanne Cash and Jeffrey Gaines play upstairs at the **Tin Angel**. If you stay in one of the 40 small but spiffy rooms at the 1828 landmark **Penn's View Hotel** (800-331-7634, doubles start at $145 &), you'll be steps away from Warmdaddy's. At the wine bar downstairs at **Ristorante Panorama,** 120 different wines are served by the glass, including splits of five tasters.

REAL PHILLY: While others descend on the tourist hubs, you could be ferreting out real Philadelphians—plumbers, cabbies, toll takers—by joining them in their natural habitats. You might, for example, try your hand at a cheesesteak taste-off at **Pat's King of Steaks** (215-468-1546 &) and **Geno's** (215-338-3360 &), which stare down each other at Ninth Street and Passyunk Avenue in South Philly. Both are open 24 hours a day. Or you could grab breakfast at the **Famous Fourth Street Delicatessen** (215-922-3274 &), a crowded corner eatery that's been owned by the Auspitz family since 1923 and whose patrons all seem to know each other. Don't expect the Ritz—or even IHOP: Food arrives on foam plates, cutlery is plastic, coffee comes in plastic cups. When there recently, *Washington Post* reporter John Deiner dug into cheese blintzes and an omelet the size of a hubcap, and then started making plans to get back to try the fried matzos and potato pancakes. Breakfast for two was $16. Bonus: the homemade chocolate chip cookies the waiter delivered at meal's end. **LODGING:** Spend the night at the **Holiday Inn Independence Mall** (215-923-8660 &), a genial Joe-and-Jane-Tourist headquarters a hop from just about everything. Deiner was quoted a weekend rate of $169 on his trip—not an Average Joe rate—but when he asked about AAA discounts, the clerk lopped $74 off the price.

SHOPPING PHILLY: Rittenhouse Row, a district encompassing Broad to 21st and Pine to Market streets, is home to plenty of the usual suspects in upmarket retail, including Tiffany, Polo, Brooks Brothers and Burberry's. But you'll also find a few nuggets of individuality, including the no-frills, library-like **How-to-Do-It Book Shop** (1608 Sansom St., 215-563-1516 &). **Urban Objects** (1724 Sansom St., 215-557-9474) offers artful housewares in an environment of high-toned designerese: a $50 yellow-and-green earthenware pitcher with a grape-vine motif, a $14 silverplate and black Lucite candle snuffer, a $7.50 cube of glycerin soap that encases the classic bath accompaniment, a rubber ducky. Northwest of Center City, the canal-side mill town of **Manayunk** supports a number of imaginative independent retailers along Main Street. Among them: **Palais Royal** (215-508-1288), where Francophiles shop for Provencal-patterned place mats, lace-trimmed pillowcases and other French country housewares; **American Pie** (215-922-2226 &), a crafts emporium with a large collection of handcrafted menorahs, along with a well-edited selection of artisan-created glass, ceramics, jewelry and metalwork; and, for funky-but-chic women's wear, **Ma Jolie** (215-483-8850), set in a former bank building. **FOOD/LODGING:** A few blocks south of Rittenhouse Square, a tiny, bring-your-own-booze, no-reservations, no-credit-cards restaurant called **Audrey Claire** (20th and Spruce, 215-731-1222 &) is a real find. A modern rustic aesthetic reigns. It mixes the simplicity of Shaker design (a long communal bench, wide-planked floors and tables, bowls filled with Granny Smiths or white tulips) with urban minimalism (exposed duct work, bare white walls). Food stresses farm-fresh ingredients and skews toward the Mediterranean. Entrees fall in the $15 range. Try the grilled sea bass with citrus scallion salsa. If you're here to shop, and if you're flush, stay at the

Philadelphia grande dame, the **Park Hyatt at the Bellevue** (215-893-1776; weekend doubles $179-$300 ♿), a 1904, amenity-laden showpiece that has retained most of its charm.

PHILLY WITH KIDS: Thanks to its walkability, wealth of museums and vast park system, Philly is a good place to take youngsters. The **Please Touch Museum** (215-963-0666 ♿) was the nation's first children's museum, the **Franklin Institute Science Museum** (215-448-1200 ♿) the granddaddy of science museums for children. But if you've been there/done the kids' museum thing, here are suggestions unique to Philadelphia. A real local haunt, **Smith Memorial Playground** (215-765-4325 ♿) is an old-fashioned, six-acre gift from wealthy Philadelphians Richard and Sarah Smith. In sweeping Fairmount Park, it features a huge outdoor area with colorfully painted swings, merry-go-rounds and wading pools. Its 12-foot wide, 60-foot long slide can accommodate 10 children side by side. Members of the preschool set are welcome to explore a toy-laden, three-story playhouse/mansion to their heart's content. In the basement, "Smithville" is a kid-scaled village with a working traffic light, a mock gas pump and parking meters, where kids can drive pedal-push cars. It's free. The playground is open 9-4:45, the playhouse 10-3:30 (closed Sundays). In early 1998, the **Academy of Natural Sciences** (215-299-1000 ♿) unveiled a revamped, 15,000-square-foot gallery dedicated to the task of making dino-appreciation more dynamic. **Dinosaur Hall** attempts to go beyond mere skeletons and create a better understanding of how the creatures moved, ate and lived. It's also designed to give kids a behind-the-scenes peek at fossil hunting and paleontology. It does that best with a re-created dig site that gives little ones the chance to dirty their hands in search of real fossils. **FOOD/LODGING:** The **Reading Terminal Market** (12th and Arch streets; 215-922-2317 ♿), a lively Philadelphia institution in a former railroad terminal, has a multiethnic smorgasbord that will astonish your kids. Tucked in among the farmers' stands, fishmongers, butchers, flower stalls, bakers and brewers is a section of Amish purveyors. Kids love watching the pretzel makers who knead, twist and butter their exquisite creations. The market closes at 6 p.m., but the funky **Down Home Diner** serves up burgers, grilled cheese sandwiches and the like until 9 p.m. The **Embassy Suites Hotel** (215-561-1776 ♿) is nicely situated across from the Academy of Natural Sciences and on the way to Fairmount Park. Family touches include a children's playroom next to the exercise facilities, complimentary buffet breakfasts and complimentary evening snacks. Rates from $90 to $200.

GETTING THERE: Philadelphia is a 2.5-hour drive from the Beltway. Take I-95 north and follow the signs into town. Amtrak offers daily service between Union Station and Philadelphia; fares start at $34.

FOR MORE INFORMATION: Contact the **Philadelphia Convention & Visitors Bureau** at 800-537-7676 or *www.libertynet.org/phila-visitor*.

An English Lesson

By Roger Piantadosi

I LOVE DRIVING. My wife, who has many times proven to have more grace and endurance behind the wheel than I do, *tolerates* driving—much as I tolerated, say, the third and final hour of "The English Patient." So when we headed for a recent weekend among the horse-drawn lives and slanting, silo-defined skylines of Lancaster County, Pa., I drove.

The region's waves of majestic green and gold farmland have always made it a great place for driving. And you could pass the time by describing the complex function, origin and dimensions of various farm outbuildings and equipment, or explaining why this Amish farmer's hat was wide-rimmed and black and that one was straw. You couldn't possibly know any of this but would make it up as you went along.

But then they changed things. Off the main roads, it's still breathtakingly beautiful, even (or, to me, especially) in winter, and there are still lots of guys in untamed, mustache-less beards and muddy boots leading horses and mule teams around and waving back when you pass. What they did was add a bunch of reasons for . . . stopping.

For designated drivers like me, "Stopping" is way down there with "Shopping" on the priorities list. As in this exchange, which occurred as we approached Bird-In-Hand on Route 272, a two-lane road that winds diagonally through some of the prettiest parts of the county:

"That place looks interesting, let's stop here," says Charmaine.

"Sorry, what?"

"Slow down! Let's stop in there."

"What, there? Stop? Jeez, look at how full the parking lot is! What do we want with Amish furniture? Quilts? Do we have to—"

"You never want to do anything fun. Okay, don't stop."

I don't know about your car, but ours is equipped with a special guilt-activated braking system. We stopped. When we drove off 45 minutes later, two wrought-iron votive candleholders were in our back seat.

Of course, now that we've been there once together (I returned another time alone), I'm forced to admit that the most memorable moments—not to mention the durable and/or cheap goods—were collected while we were . . . you know, stopped.

Stopping, or at least slowing down, seems to be the main point of Lancaster County, the best-known home of the open-handed and close-ranked Amish religious community (though there is actually a larger Amish settlement in Ohio). The Amish share the county with the somewhat less ascetic Mennonites and a good number of others who do drive cars and pay electric and phone bills.

With beliefs meant to allow them to be "in this world but not of it," the 30,000 or so Amish are mostly farmers. But as their ranks continue to expand, they are running out of farmland, so many have become carpenters, cabinetmakers and even factory workers.

If all you wanted was to move among the slower, season-bound rhythms of a fertile valley, you could drive 90 minutes up the Potomac from Washington to western Loudoun County, Va. But there is something more uplifting about this part of Pennsylvania. It is not simply the sense of achievement in finding, say, a handmade oak leaf table that seats 10 for $1,600 (including the chairs) or cantaloupes for $1.25, in most cases directly from the man or woman who grew it. It has more to do with the feel of driving at 15 mph for a mile behind a gray Amish horse-drawn buggy, not really wanting to pass.

The other large segment of Lancaster County's population, especially on weekends and in warmer weather, is "the English," as the Amish call anyone whose society, like it or not, includes Weird Al Yankovic. Busloads of tourists visit— as much to see Amish country as to partake of the many outlet shopping centers between here and Reading. This can make for some interesting cultural contrasts.

From among the ticky-tack "country" gift shops, fast-foodish "Amish" restaurants and prefab "historic villages" along Route 340 in Intercourse, for instance, we chose to stop at the People's Place. This small complex includes a good bookstore and a Mennonite-related artists' gallery, a hands-on but disappointing "museum" and a half-hour slide documentary on Amish history and lifestyles. After the show, which strengthened our admiration for a people who do without TV and baptize only young adults who choose to join the church, we stood out on the porch facing Route 340, waiting out a light drizzle.

Milling crowds of Englishers were crisscrossing the highway from quilt shop to country store in jackets and shirts advertising such modern deities as Nike and Budweiser and the New York Giants. A dozen Amish carriages passed in 20 minutes, Route 340 having a wide shoulder whose brown cast clearly denoted usage by one-horsepower vehicles. Each time a buggy approached, the tourists would stop and stare. The carriage occupants, in hats and bonnets reflecting mostly a belief in simplicity, did not stare. Occasionally they would smile, shyly and uncomfortably. Primarily, though, they kept their eyes on the road and drove back to their self-contained lives.

GETTING THERE: From the Beltway, central Lancaster County is about a three-hour drive. Take I-95 north to 83 north to York. There, pick up Route 30 east into the bustling farm-country city of Lancaster, from which well-marked roads lead throughout the county.

BEING THERE: In colder months, Pennsylvania Dutch country is a more sparse (and, I think, more friendly) place than in the April-October tourist boom—though you should respect, on a year-round basis, Amish people's objection to having their pictures taken. The nicest way to meet the locals is to do business with them. This is possible at any of the county's year-round farmers' markets. The best is a Tuesday-only affair, but it's worth the effort to get to **Roots Farmers Market** (Route 72 south of Manheim; 717-898-7811 ♿). The **Green Dragon Farmers Market** (Route 272 north of Ephrata; 717-738-1117 ♿) is an all-day Friday market that is larger but a bit more touristy. For perspective on the Amish and Mennonite peoples (both before and after the 1985 movie "Witness" again focused popular attention on them), try the **People's Place** (Route 340, Intercourse; 717-768-7171). Its three-screen slide documentary ($4, $2 for 2-11) is smart and fair. Or there's **Plain & Fancy Farm** (717-768-8281 ♿), whose roadside complex includes a restaurant, stores, tours, buggy rides by an Amish family and daily screenings of the well-regarded film "Jacob's Choice" ($6.75, $3.75 for 4-11; 717-768-4400). The most vivid and gentle perspective on Pennsylvania farm life is presented daily in exhibits and living-history demonstrations in the recreated village of 23 buildings at the **Landis Valley Museum** in Lancaster (717-569-0401, closed January-February ♿). For eclectic browsing and a good selection of places to stay, head seven miles north of Lancaster onto the tidy, sweet-smelling streets of Lititz. This was once a Moravian religious enclave and now is better known as the home of one of the nation's best small-town Independence Day celebrations—as well as of more original 18th Century buildings than Williamsburg. Try the **Julius Sturgis Pretzel House** (717-626-4354 ♿), the oldest pretzel bakery in the country, which offers daily tours ($2), and the aromatic **Wilbur Chocolate Factory** (717-626-1131) and its small free museum and very fattening gift shop. If you have time, visit the towns of **Marietta** (Routes 441 and 743), **Mount Joy** (Routes 722 and 230) and **Manheim** (Routes 772 and 72), any of which could have served as the model for Disney World's Main Street U.S.A. All three are home to lovely 19th and early 20th Century homes as well as to some fine antique shops.

For organized tours of the countryside hereabouts, there are three options. First, try the **Amish Experience** (717-768-3600), which offers a two-hour Farmlands Tour twice a day Monday through Saturday and once on Sunday ($17.95, $10.95 4-11). The **Mennonite Information Center** (717-299-0954) puts an on-call Mennonite or even Amish guide in your car; a two-hour tour is $26 a car, each additional hour $9.50. **Old Order Amish Tours** (717-

299-6535) promises an insider's tour by appointment only. A two-hour tour for three persons is $30, and no cameras are permitted.

Not everything in Pennsylvania Dutch country relates to the Amish. The steam trains of the **Strasburg Railroad** (Route 741 in Strasburg; 717-687-7522 ♿) make many trips each day from Strasburg to Paradise and back, passing through the area's fertile farmland. And there are more than 50 locomotives and other rolling stock at the adjacent **Railroad Museum of Pennsylvania** (717-687-8628 ♿). Antique lovers will discover their vision of heaven in **Adamstown** (Route 272 northeast of the Pennsylvania Turnpike), where more than 1,000 dealers peddle their wares on weekends.

WHERE TO STAY: In Lititz, there are a number of choices. The Victorian landmark **General Sutter Inn** (doubles $83-$105; 717-626-2115) has 12 uniquely furnished rooms, a comfortably odd lobby with three exotic singing birds, and a restaurant that serves three sturdy meals a day. The **Alden House** (717-627-3363; $90-$120 double) is a redone, Victorian-casual B&B with three suites and two rooms, all with private bath, color TV and queen beds. Three miles north of town on a lakeside hill is the **Swiss Woods Bed & Breakfast** (800-594-8018; $105-$175); it offers remarkable breakfasts, a common room with a wall-wide fireplace, an unbeatable location (especially if you come to hike) and seven spacious rooms with private baths—two with Jacuzzis. Other off-the-beaten-path options include **Clearview Farm Bed & Breakfast** (717-733-6333; doubles $95-$115), an Ephrata farmhouse built in 1814, and the **Historic Strasburg Inn** (717-687-7691; doubles $119-$159 ♿). The inn, which actually is quite new, offers 101 rooms in five buildings surrounded by lush farmland. All of the major hotel chains also have locations in Lancaster County, most often on or near the busy Route 30 corridor. And there are a few resorts with pools, game rooms and other diversions for families with young children. In centrally located Lancaster itself, these include the **Best Western Eden Resort Inn** (717-569-6444; doubles $99 to $169 ♿), **Continental Inn** (717-299-0421; doubles start at $73 ♿) and **Holiday Inn Lancaster Host Hotel** (800-233-0121; doubles $139 and up ♿).

WHERE TO EAT: You should sample the Amish fare at **Groff's Farm Inn** (717-653-2048 ♿); this Mount Joy restaurant, which is in an old stone farmhouse next to a pond, serves authentic Pennsylvania Dutch food that includes some of owner Betty Groff's own creations, such as Chicken Stoltzfus, chunks of chicken in a cream sauce on a bed of light pastry, and black raspberry tarts. **Haydn Zug's** in East Petersburg (717-569-5746 ♿), serves continental fare in a 1756 farmhouse. The aptly named **Good 'N Plenty** in Smoketown (717-394-7111 ♿) offers thousands of family-style, Amish-fare meals (fried chicken, mashed potatoes, noodles, fruit pies, roast beef and the ever-popular ham loaf), and across the street is a working Amish farm. If you go there, you might see horse-drawn farm wagons at work.

FOR MORE INFORMATION: For a map and hotel and restaurant information, call the **Pennsylvania Dutch Convention and Visitors Bureau** at 717-299-8901 or 800-723-8824.

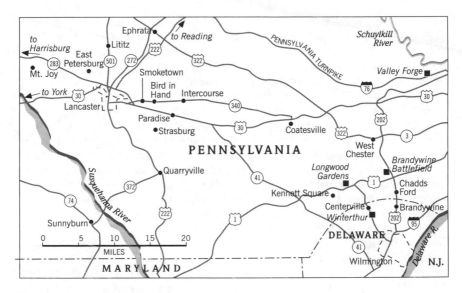

BRANDYWINE VALLEY

Near where southeastern Pennsylvania meets northern Delaware is a small river valley whose vistas alone are enough to cheer most visitors. Originally the territory of the Lenni Lenape tribe, the Brandywine Valley was consecutively overtaken by the Dutch, the Swedes, the English and finally by armies of du Ponts and Wyeths. Today it is home to magnificent mansions, elegant gardens and grand museums of art and industry. In late summer, the hills here are a landscape of soft, subdued colors, a palette that decades ago attracted illustrator N.C. Wyeth, famous for his portraits of pirates, Indians and frontiersmen in children's books. Son Andrew (known for "Christina's World" and the "Helga" series) and grandson Jamie (perhaps best known for his painting of a pig) also have drawn inspiration from the land. The first du Pont was lured here, too, by nature: The Brandywine River offered enough water to run the first du Pont gunpowder and explosives factory, the foundation for today's worldwide industrial colossus. In early autumn, though, it is difficult for man-made wonders to compete with the valley's spectacular scenery.

The valley, with its long list of things to do and see, rewards repeat visits. Some would start the list with **Winterthur Museum, Gardens and Library** (800-448-3883 or 302-888-4600 ⏦) on Route 52 between Wilmington, Del., and Chadds Ford, Pa. The creation of the late Henry Francis du Pont, the nine-story, palace-like chateau's 175 rooms display an unequaled, 89,000-piece collection of American antiques and decorative arts dating from 1640 to 1860. The museum also maintains 200 acres of landscaped gardens. Others might like the **Hagley Museum** (302-658-2400 ⏦), three miles north of Wilmington on the Brandywine River, where the du Ponts founded that gunpowder factory in the early 19th Century—a sprawling and oddly peaceful place. Its combination of multimedia exhibits, live demonstrations and restored buildings and equipment brings to life the significant role of the region in the American Industrial Revolution. On the grounds is **Eleutherian Mills**, the mansion built by the first E.I. du

Pont, a French nobleman and son of Louis XVI's finance minister, and home to five generations of du Ponts. At **Nemours Mansion and Gardens** (302-651-6912), the 102-room Louis XVI-style estate and gardens of Alfred I. du Pont displays rare antiques, Oriental rugs and paintings and tapestries dating back to the 15th Century. **Longwood Gardens** in Kennett Square, Pa., (610-388-1000 ♿) is a 1,050-acre creation of Pierre S. du Pont. It has gardens of roses, peonies, waterlilies, topiaries and more, plus more than three acres of conservatories: gardens under glass, with orchids, bonsai, daffodils, jonquils, tulips, primroses and hyacinths. There's a tropical greenhouse and a special kid-sized topiary maze. (May is the month of "maximum outdoor spring bloom" at Longwood, when 50,000 bulbs, mostly tulips, bloom in the 600-foot-long beds of the garden walk as close to 17,000 gallons a minute spurt from the multitude of fountains.) A few miles to the east, the **Brandywine River Museum** (610-388-2700 ♿), a Civil War-era gristmill renovated into a light-filled modern gallery, exhibits the most comprehensive collection of art works created by three generations of Wyeths. Before you even enter, the wildflower garden, full of local species planted with precise abandon by the Brandywine Conservancy, is likely to take your breath away. The **Brandywine Battlefield** (610-459-3342 ♿) is where the Battle of Brandywine was fought during the Revolutionary War. Still there are the Marquis de Lafayette's quarters and the place where General Washington made his headquarters—before rounding up his badly beaten troops and retreating to the painful winter at Valley Forge.

Other sites worth a stop include **Chaddsford Winery** (610-388-6221; closed January-April), where the tour is free and wine tasting costs $5 (including a souvenir wineglass). In Franklin Center, check out the **Franklin Mint Museum** (610-459-6168 ♿), the world's largest private mint. And when you produce almost half of the nation's mushrooms, as Pennsylvania does, you're bound to come up with some novel uses for your product. Most of these can be found at the gift shop of the modest **Phillips Mushroom Museum** (610-388-6082 ♿) in Kennett Square, Pa., including wild mushroom caviar and mushroom fettuccine, mushroom-motif ties, lamps, key chains, chocolates, mobiles and birthday cards. Fungal fanatics can buy "I ♥ mushrooms" buttons or watch a video on making "mushroom surprise meatloaf"—but the item to note is that the shop sells mushrooms, year-round, at great prices: plain and exotic, fresh, marinated, dried and canned. If you're more stirred by the kind of fungus that gives old books their distinctive bouquet, don't miss **Baldwin's Book Barn** on Route 100 a mile outside West Chester (610-696-0816). On rough wood shelves and in old wooden fruit crates, it crams more than 300,000 used and rare books into 9,500 square feet. (A modern superstore like Barnes & Noble in Georgetown has 150,000 titles in a comparatively spacious 33,000 square feet.) Writes *Post* reporter Carolyn Spencer Brown: "Customers vary wildly—the 300-pound guy who pulled up in an 18-wheeler and bought two bags of books on Jungian psychology, the Bentley-driving dandy who buys his books by the yard. For the most part, though, the shoppers here are average folks who wander around in a state of reverence, voices hushed, murmuring polite excuse-me's when they pass one another."

GETTING THERE: The Brandywine Valley is about 110 miles north of the Beltway. Take I-95 to Wilmington, and then go north on Route 52 to U.S. 1 south. Expect a 2.5-hour ride for most destinations.

WHERE TO STAY: You'll find all of the brand-name hotel chains in and around Wilmington. The **Brandywine River Hotel** (610-388-1200; doubles start at $125 ♿) is a pleasant, 40-room hotel in Chadds Ford, a short drive from most attractions. The landmark **Hotel du Pont** (800-441-9019 ♿) is still the place to meet and eat in Wilmington; rooms range from $229 to $599, double. Ask about weekend packages. Better yet, ask about a package-deal room at the **Mendenhall Hotel** (610-388-2100 ♿). A recent special there for $155 included continental breakfast, tickets for Longwood Gardens, the Hagley Museum, Winterthur, the Brandywine River Museum and other spots, discount coupons for restaurants and tickets for dinner and a show at the **Three Little Bakers Dinner Theater**—plus clean, spacious accommodations for two. The second night was $69. The **Fairville Inn** (610-388-5900; doubles $150 and up ♿) offers 15 attractive rooms in the main house and the country-rustic annexes. **Abby's Agency** (610-692-4575) is a no-fee reservation service for scores of historic inns and B&Bs in the Brandywine Valley of Pennsylvania and Delaware.

A cozy, two-room West Chester B&B called the **Bankhouse** (610-344-7388; doubles from $70; no credit cards) is so named because the stucco-on-stone house was built into its embankment more than 200 years ago. The site was part of the original Pennsylvania land grant and was once owned by Quakers. Now it is on the outskirts of town, across from a horse pasture, and has a sitting room loaded with books, games and puzzles. In Glen Mills, **Sweetwater Farm** (800-793-3892 or 610-459-4711; doubles start at $175), a 50-acre working farm, was a stop on the underground railroad transporting escaped slaves in the Civil War. Most of the seven rooms in the 1815 Georgian wing and the original 1734 Quaker farmhouse have working fireplaces and four-poster beds, and five cottages also are available (pets allowed in cottages). There's a swimming pool, back porch with rockers, library and a sunset-facing parlor window seat. For a distinctive splurge: the 11 restored Du Pont millworkers' houses that make up the **Inn at Montchanin Village** (800-269-2473; doubles $150 to $325, including breakfast). A coat rack next to the door holds two huge umbrellas labeled with your room name, and a cunningly designed alcove holds a shiny new microwave, stocked coffee maker and half-fridge. The adjacent **Krazy Kat's** restaurant, in an old blacksmith shop, is superb.

WHERE TO EAT: For Old World elegance, the formal **Green Room** in the Hotel du Pont (302-594-3154 ♿) serves highly acclaimed (and priced) French cuisine. **Buckley's Tavern** (302-656-9776 ♿), a converted early 19th Century home in Centreville, Del., has been a popular eclectic restaurant for many years. The **Garden Restaurant and Tea Room** at Winterthur Museum (302-888-4855 ♿) and the **Terrace Restaurant** at Longwood Gardens (610-388-6771 ♿) are excellent places for luncheon stops during tours. The **Longwood Inn** (610-444-3515 ♿) in Kennett Square, near Longwood Gardens, serves American fare (with many dishes featuring the famed local mushrooms). The **Chadds Ford Cafe** (610-558-3960 ♿) has a creative menu and good food.

FOR MORE INFORMATION: Contact the **Brandywine Valley Tourist Information Center** (800-228-9933 or *www.brandywinevalley.com*) or the **Greater Wilmington Convention and Visitors Bureau** (302-652-4088).

BOILING SPRINGS, PA.

Golfers may dream of Pebble Beach, but serious trout anglers fantasize about the fabled limestone streams of the Cumberland Valley near Carlisle, Pa. *Post* contributor Bill Heavey, for example, is partial to Yellow Breeches Creek and the 250-year-old town of Boiling Springs, Pa. "The alkaline waters that percolate up here from the strongest springs north of Florida are magic," he says. "They support more pounds of trout per mile—and more big ones—than just about any place in the East. Rainbows here routinely reach 20 inches, a veritable torpedo of a trout. Some of the browns get bigger still, so large they turn cannibalistic, making hors d'oeuvres of their smaller kin."

Boiling Springs itself was placed on the National Register of Historic Places in 1984 and is charmingly spare and free of T-shirts. There is a neat self-guided walking tour of its restored Revolutionary-era blast furnace, a gristmill and many 19th Century houses and churches. The seven-acre lake in the middle of town is fed by 30 springs believed to lie 1,800 feet below ground. They supply 22 million gallons of crystal-clear water a day, all of it 53 degrees. Several roil the surface, hence the name of the town. The **Appalachian Trail** passes by the lake. Fishing licenses and the latest fly recommendations are available from Bill and Emily Zeiders at **Yellow Breeches Outfitters** (717-258-6752). They also provide guide services on a choice of Cumberland County limestone streams for $150 a day and $100 a half-day, including lunch; for two people, rates are $225 and $150. A three-day, non-resident license with trout stamp costs $20.50, and one-day fly-fishing schools and private instruction also are available. All fishing on the 1.2-mile section of the creek nearest town is catch-and-release, to promote conservation. You don't have to fly-fish, but no bait is allowed, and regardless of tackle, a "barbless hook" rule means you literally must put a crimp in your hardware. The **Kings Gap General Store** (717-486-5855 ♿), about 10 miles outside town on Pine Road, is worth a visit for its eccentric antiques and a bulletin board full of dead-deer snapshots taken by local hunters. Founded in 1893 and made unmistakable by its single, obsolete gas pump, the store is crammed with many of the useful things on earth, from fishing lures and spaghetti sauce to rubber boots and homemade cheese. The antiques are in the basement

GETTING THERE: Boiling Springs is about a two-hour drive from the Beltway. Take I-270 west to U.S. 15 north at Frederick. Continue about 55 miles to Dillsburg (about 20 minutes past Gettysburg) and turn left on Route 74 west. Go four miles and turn left again at the light onto Route 174. The first entrance to the stream is 10 minutes along, at the Allenberry Playhouse parking lot. Yellow Breeches Outfitters is ahead another mile on your left in the middle of Boiling Springs.

WHERE TO STAY: Choices are limited but elegant. **Garmanhaus** (717-258-3980), is a modest B&B with modest prices ($50-$95 doubles) overlooking Boiling Springs Lake. A five-minute walk from town, **Allenberry Resort Inn and Playhouse** (717-258-3211; doubles start at $125 ♿), set among 200-year-old trees on 57 acres, does triple duty. It is a theater (April through November), a restaurant and an inn with rooms in three lodges, including a limestone carriage house from 1812 and the Meadow Lodge overlooking the Yellow Breeches. In all cases, reserve well in advance for spring weekends, when anglers swarm the town.

WHERE TO EAT: Locals like the **Boiling Springs Tavern** (717-258-3614 &), which dates from the 18th Century and is conveniently located across the street from Yellow Breeches Outfitters. It serves reasonably priced seafood, pasta and steaks.

FOR MORE INFORMATION: Contact the **Greater Carlisle Area Chamber of Commerce** at 717-243-4515.

WESTMINSTER, MD.

If you head north on Georgia Avenue from the Beltway, the traffic starts to thin out after Olney. Eventually, so will those housing developments with names like Willow Crest Fox Brook Manor Meadows. Soon, you will find yourself motoring through hills where people actually make a living off the land, and that means you are in Carroll County. Your shoulders will relax, and that means you're in Westminster, Md., the red brick, 250-year-old county seat.

Post reporter Eric Brace suggests a first stop at the Carroll County Visitor Center. In an old brick building at 210 Main Street, it stocks racks of maps and pamphlets on things to do and see nearby, including area bike routes and a Civil War driving tour. You also can learn there about the town's legends and ghosts, many of which are related to Westminster's role as a Union supply depot during the Battle of Gettysburg. The **Westminster Fire Company** (410-848-1800; call in the early evening &) usually can find you the details on bingo, country dances and other events at its faded but still-gorgeous 1879 yellow-brick firehouse on Main Street. With its 1852 farmhouse museum and living-history demonstrations of blacksmithing, tinsmithing, weaving, wood carving and quilting, the 140-acre **Carroll County Farm Museum** (410-848-7775 &) offers a glimpse of farm life in the 19th Century. It is open daily, except Mondays, in July and August and on weekends only in May, June, September and October; it closes from November through April, except for special holiday tours. North of town, **Bear Branch Nature Center** (410-848-2517 &) has trails through forest and field, over creeks and ridges. At trail marker 12 on the 1.2-mile Vista Trail, Brace found a sturdy young tree with a large chunk of industrial steel embedded in its trunk. (The sapling must have been trying to grow from underneath this slab of metal, he says, and eventually decided that if you can't beat it, absorb it. The metal now hangs about five feet off the ground.) In Union Bridge, about five miles west of Westminster, is one of the prettiest railroad stations in the state, plus the small **Western Maryland Railroad Museum** (410-775-0150; open Sundays only, May-October, or by appointment) with its exhibits of equipment, pictures, charts and models. For antiques browsers, **Westminster Antique Mall** (410-857-4044; open daily &) houses 125 dealers in 20,000 square feet of space, with everything from Depression glass to old maps to rusted tractor parts. Antiques bidders can attend Monday morning and evening auctions at **T.R. O'Farrell's Auction Center** on Sullivan Rd. (410-848-5533 &). The real glory of Carroll County lies in its back roads and smaller towns. Even if you don't stop to read the roadside markers, you can't help absorbing history as you drive: the run-down tobacco barns, the single railroad lines cutting through hills and following creek beds, the almost ancient east-west roads like Baltimore Boulevard and Taneytown Pike. Driving such two-lane by-ways as Hoods Mill Road, Eden Mill Road, Klees Mill Road, Fridinger Mill Road, McKinstry Mill Road reminds you of the 31 mills that prospered here immediately after independence from Great Britain, when wheat replaced to-bacco as the area's primary crop. North of Westminster, a restored, 200-year-old example still stands at **Union Mills Homestead and Grist Mill** (410-848-2288), which in warmer weather schedules educational programs about the county's agricultural past.

GETTING THERE: Westminster is about a 90-minute drive from the Beltway. Head up Georgia Avenue (Route 97) to Old Westminster Pike (Route 140) north to Westminster. Signs lead you downtown.

WHERE TO STAY: A brochure available from the visitors center lists hotels and B&Bs. The **Westminster Inn** (410-876-2893; doubles $155 and up &) is in a converted brick schoolhouse. The swank **Antrim 1844** (800-858-1844; $160 and up &) is in nearby Taneytown; even if you don't stay at this restored former plantation, at least try to have a mulled cider in the bar. The **Wood's Gain Bed & Breakfast** (410-775-0308; $85-$140), also a few miles west of Westminster, is a lovely, old, out-of-the-way brick home with excellent break-fasts.

WHERE TO EAT: Cheesy pizza with a superb thin crust can be had at tiny **Adolpho's** (410-857-8055 &). For an upscale dinner, there's **Cockey's Tav-ern** (410-840-2134), but whatever you do, don't miss **Baugher's** (410-848-7413 &), the family-owned farmer's market and full-service, country-style restaurant. With great flapjacks and corn fritters, and a roast turkey plat-ter served up every Sunday, Baugher's is the kind of place where you want to order things like scrapple and eggs, fried pork chops and apple fritters—and our Mr. Brace did. "And after a small sundae, I asked them to box up one of their swell pies to go," he says. "It was still warm, and it filled my car with a delicious smell as I headed south, back to Washington."

FOR MORE INFORMATION: Call the **Carroll County Visitors Center** at 410-848-1388 or 800-272-1933. Web site: *www.carr.org/tourism.*

CAPE MAY, N.J.

Victoria's Seashore

By Daphne White

AT THE SOUTHERN TIP of New Jersey, a few miles south of Cape May, is a place called Sunset Beach. To get there, you just take—you guessed it—Sunset Boulevard. The road is flat and long and stretches straight ahead to the horizon, kind of like your life when you are about to turn 40. I had decided, in something of a panic over that prospect, that a cool-weather weekend in Cape May might help me get some perspective on life.

I remembered Cape May from a previous visit as a quaint town, a page torn out of time: Victorian houses dripping with gingerbread, wrap-around porches lined with rocking chairs, tidy perennial gardens. It seemed an ideal setting in which to think. So after a day that included breakfast in bed, a stroll on the boardwalk, a tour of Victorian inns and intensely pleasurable shopping, I found myself at Sunset Beach. About 20 people had already gathered for the nightly sunset-watching ritual, tourists combing the beach for shells, regulars bundled up in beach chairs sipping coffee. The beach was small and intimate. The remains of a sunken concrete ship loomed about a quarter mile offshore: A historical marker noted that 12 of these ships were produced during World War I before anyone realized that their weight made them "impractical."

Soon, the sound of bagpipes filled the air. A small group of people had just descended from horse-drawn carriages, and it appeared that two of them were about to be married. Right on the beach. Drawn in by the piper, we sunset viewers soon found ourselves in a loose, mesmerized circle around the wedding party. The sun, now a huge orb of shameless crimson, provided the ultimate processional.

As the bride's white cocktail dress fluttered in the wind, the couple's grown children from earlier marriages flanked them, and many of us in the outer circle found ourselves rummaging around for tissues even before the bagpiper began playing "Amazing Grace." Here was spontaneity, here was romance, here was drama. Maybe life in one's forties would be interesting after all.

The next day, I decided to check out the possibilities. Cape May is a former whaling port that still harbors many temptations. There are leisurely walking tours and heated trolley rides and restored Victorian mansions to prowl through. There are elaborate brunches and sit-down teas. Every fantasy you have ever had about Victorian life is here.

Ah, but it is a fantasy. The Victorians, tour guides will tell you, lived through a time of great change. Factory work was replacing farm work, urban slums and company towns were proliferating, child labor was a fact of life, while indoor plumbing was not.

The country that Oscar Wilde described in his 1883 "Impressions of America" does not sound very different from the America of the 1990s: ". . . everybody seems in a hurry to catch a train. This is a state of things which is not favourable to poetry or romance. Had Romeo or Juliet been in a constant state of anxiety about trains, or had their minds been agitated by the question of return-tickets, Shakespeare could not have given us those lovely balcony scenes which are so full of poetry and pathos."

The term "conspicuous consumption" was coined during this time, when factories made possible unprecedented material abundance. And middle-class Victorians, buffeted by change, tried to make sense of their world by accumulating objects for every conceivable purpose. Take spoons. There were different kinds for clear soup, cream soup, breakfast coffee, dinner coffee, tea, pastry and fruit.

After spending Sunday morning immersed in this historic clutter, I decided to head out of town. I was drawn to Cape May Point State Park, along the Atlantic Flyway on one of New Jersey's barrier islands.

As soon as I set foot on the nature trail, which cut through a freshwater marsh, I knew I had come to the right place. The narrow boardwalk plunged me straight into the heart of a surreal landscape. Tall reed grasses called phragmites, native to Asia and Europe, towered and crowded over me. The dense vegetation looked as if it could swallow the path up at any moment.

I had never walked through a tableau quite like this before. It is a borderline, a place between land and sea, where freshwater mixes with salt, where Southern trees and Northern trees merge at the very edges of their tolerance. In the autumn, huge flocks of hawks, songbirds, waterfowl and shorebirds pass through here on their way to other places.

Suddenly, the inner and outer landscapes seemed to merge—the vast expanse of marshland, the animals hiding in the reeds, the twisted path cutting through. Turning 40, I was thinking, may not be like Sunset Boulevard at all. It might be more like this marsh—wild and vibrant and full of hidden possibilities.

GETTING THERE: Cape May is about 4¼ hours from the Beltway. Take U.S. 50 east past the Bay Bridge to Route 404 east. Follow that to Route 18, pick up Rt. 9 into Lewes, Del., and follow the signs to the Lewes-Cape May Ferry (800-643-3779).

BEING THERE: Some people adore Cape May's celebration of all things Victorian. Others, finding themselves surrounded by so much refurbished fussiness and colorfully painted gingerbread houses, would just as soon hop on the next horseless carriage to the big city. In Cape May, these two kinds of people often arrive together in the same car, but they manage. This is because while Cape May indeed has more than 600 fine, late-Victorian homes (the entire town has been designated a National Historic Landmark), it also offers much for the avowedly non-nostalgic. It has one of the widest ocean beaches on the Jersey shore (not yet overrun by T-shirt shops or arcades). It has an abundance of relatively unspoiled natural areas (southeasternmost New Jersey is still much less densely populated than the rest of the state). It has some eclectic and excellent restaurants and historic sites, and it provides easy access to the 20th Century amusements of the Wildwoods and Atlantic City.

In town, the **Mid-Atlantic Center for the Arts** (609-884-5404 or 800-275-4278 &) keeps the torch burning for Victoria on a daily basis. It offers trolley tours through the gas-lit streets, musical and cultural festivals, a spring Tulip Festival, fall Victorian Week and Christmas candlelight programs, plus daily walking tours of many of the authentically restored Victorian homes. Not least of these is the **Emlen Physick Estate**, whose restoration in the late 1970s helped get the town back on its economic feet. The Physick house was built in the Stick style, so its gables and eaves lack the lacy details common to other Victorian structures. Inside, however, its Victorian bones show. Much of the original furniture remained in the house when the restoration began, and a good deal more has migrated back one way or another since. The furniture is low and heavy, and its carved contours dissolve in the dark murk of the rooms. The porch roofs were meant to keep out the high summer sun, and they do exactly that.

If there's not enough within the highly walkable streets of New Jersey's oldest and most often repainted beach resort, north of town is **Historic Cold Spring Village** (609-898-2300 &), where stone walkways take you back to a reenacted life at a typical South Jersey farm village of the 18th Century. More than 20 buildings have been moved from Cape May and Cumberland counties and restored on this 22-acre site. And **Wheaton Village** in Millville houses a "Down Jersey" folklife center and the **Museum of American Glass** (609-825-6800 &), a collection of more than 7,000 objects from hand-blown paperweights to Tiffany masterworks. Glassblowers, potters and woodworkers demonstrate their crafts. For eco-tourists and nature lovers, the **Cape May Whale Watch and Research Center** (888-531-0055 &) offers a popular three-hour offshore tour for $26 ($12 for children 7-14); reservations and cameras are recommended, though sightings aren't guaranteed. **Wildlife Unlimited** (609-884-3100) will take you into the coastal salt marshes to explore their ecology, wildlife and history. **Cape May Point State Park** (609-884-2159 &), better known as the site of the 1859 **Cape May Lighthouse** (it has 199 steps, but the view is worth it), also offers a popular hawk-watching platform and three excellent nature trails amid its 150 acres. The shortest trail is that half-mile boardwalk trek through an otherworldly freshwater marsh. Nearby is the **Cape May Bird Observatory** (609-884-2736; see box on next page) and, about two miles west of the park, the favorite local gathering spot, **Sunset Beach**, where a flag-lowering ceremony highlights the sunset

BIRD-WATCHING OPTIONAL

I T MAY BE the quintessential bed-and-breakfast getaway, but to those in the know, Cape May is also famous for two things unrelated to its Victorian gingerbread structures. Both involve **Higbee Beach**, a humble strip of shoreline along Cape May's west bank.

Among bird-watchers, Higbee is celebrated as a migratory ground for several species, guarded by the state's environmental protection agency and manned by the Audubon Society. Now, thanks to the Internet, it's also known for its nude sunbathing—or, as the signs say, "Clothing optional." Once in the Higbee parking lot, whether you turn left or continue almost straight on a little dirt path determines whether the white-rumped creatures you run into will be sandpipers or something a bit taller.

Searching for the beach, I found myself surrounded by bird-watchers and quickly lost sight of my goal, caught up in the crowd's excitement at spotting two female harriers. Identifying mark? "White rumps," a white-haired man whispered. (Everyone whispered.) "That reminds me," I whispered. "Does anyone know where the nude beach is?" I was pointed in the other direction.

A half-mile away, the path opened onto a narrow beach. Sailboats drifted serenely past. No nudes in sight. But wait—the man walking ahead of me, clothed moments before, was now wearing nothing but his sunglasses. Following him, I found two more nude men tossing horseshoes. One sporting a white safari hat greeted me, and I soon found myself making small talk in the midday sun with an elderly naked stranger. He attempted to persuade me that I should get naked. "People judge you

over the sunken World War I concrete ship "Atlantis," which has sat on the beach for more than 50 years after breaking loose from its moorings during a 1926 storm. If you or the kids crave more excitement, it's an easy drive up the parkway to **Wildwood** on New Jersey's southernmost barrier island, home to a fabulous boardwalk and the best amusement piers in the state—five of them, the best with a large water park and more than 30 rides, including a couple of memorable roller coasters.

WHERE TO STAY: There are more than 80 B&Bs in Cape May proper, and most are genuinely Victorian, with in-season rates mainly from $85 to nearly $300, double. Motel rooms start at $95 a night. For advance bookings (always recommended), **Cape May Reservation Service** (800-729-7778) handles 70 percent of Cape May's hotels, motels and B&Bs, and **Historic Accommodations of Cape May** (609-884-0080), staffed by innkeepers themselves, is a great resource for last-minute vacancies. Six-room, two-suite by your clothes," he insisted. "Take them off and everyone is equal."

Women alone on this beach do get hassled by "outsiders," he admitted. The key, he said, was to stick close to "the regulars." A few yards beyond, another "regular," this one tanned and burly, approached me— eek! —proffering a yellow business card. The card bore an illustration of an unclothed man and woman and listed several rules: no littering, no walking on the dunes, no photos or videos without consent, no overt sexual activity, no lewd or lascivious behavior. "Alternative lifestyles prefer the center portion of the beach," it read. "Harassment of ANY female is not welcome or tolerated."

I've been on nude beaches in the South of France, the Greek islands and Martha's Vineyard, but I've never come across such friendly or such aggressive nudists. Maybe it's the proximity to Atlantic City. Or maybe it's the preponderance of males. Men of all shapes and various states of sunburn roamed the shore. I finally spotted a few women sunning beside male companions. As I left the beach, the safari-hatted man waved. "Come back and try it sometime," he said. "I'm here all summer. I always have a big blanket and plenty of ice water and bananas." I pondered this invitation from the safe remove of the hawk observatory. Nice to know our right to public exposure is protected in the state of New Jersey, but I think I'll take up bird-watching instead.

DIRECTIONS AND MORE INFORMATION: From Cape May, take Lafayette, which becomes Sunset Blvd. (Route 606 west), and turn right on Bayshore Rd. (607 north). Then turn left on New England Road to the parking lot. Nude beach info can be found at *www. beachesbeaches.com/ higbee.html* or *http://cheef.com*. For birding information contact the Audubon Society's **Cape May Bird Observatory** at 609-884-2736.

—Cathleen McCarthy

Wilbraham Mansion (609-884-2046; doubles $135 and up) maintains a heated, indoor pool open year round and surrounded by stained glass rescued from an Atlantic City bar almost a century ago. **Angel of the Sea** (800-848-3369; doubles $155-$285), probably the highest priced (but still busiest) B&B in town, has 27 rooms with private baths in twin Victorians painstakingly renovated a decade ago for $3.5 million. The 24-room **Virginia Hotel** (800-732-4236) is similarly pricey, with doubles from $130 to $345, but a 1997 fire allowed for modernization of many rooms (cable TVs, VCRs and phones were added), making the Virginia a uniquely intimate full-service hotel. Its **Ebbit Room** restaurant (609-884-5700) is highly rated (and, yes, highly priced). On a smaller scale, Jack and Katha Davis at the **Inn on Ocean** (800-304-4477; doubles $129-$279) capitalized on their familiarity with business travel when they opted out of the rat race and opened their inn a decade ago. Deciding that guests are entitled to big-hotel comforts, they provided distinctly non-Victorian king-sized beds, air conditioning and cable TV in all rooms. A less expensive B&B a half block from the ocean is the modern **Carroll Villa** (609-884-9619; doubles $110-$180). It is distinguished by its "secret garden" and by breakfasts at the **Mad Batter,** a first-rate restaurant owned by innkeeper Mark Kulkowitz. Across the street, the immaculate, no-frills **Holly House** (609-884-7365; doubles start at $75, closed November-March), one of the Seven Sisters—seven identical houses built in 1891 as posh summer homes. Chain and small independent hotels can be found inland, closer to the Garden State Parkway. Wildwood, meanwhile, is chiefly a motel town—with a dominant decor straight out of the 1950s and rates that start, 1990s-like, at about $100 a night.

WHERE TO EAT: The best places include the casual and eclectic (though not entirely inexpensive) **Mad Batter** (609-884-9619) and the Virginia Hotel's more formal, seafood-bound **Ebbit Room**. You'll find more new-American fare at **Peaches at Sunset** (609-898-0100 ♿) and the **Water's Edge** (609-884-1717 ♿), and there's good fresh seafood at the **Lobster House** (609-884-8296 ♿) and—in a somewhat odd, taxidermy-prone setting—at the **Menz** in Rio Grande (609-886-9500 ♿).

FOR MORE INFORMATION: Contact the **Chamber of Commerce of Greater Cape May** at 609-884-5508 or the **Cape May County Chamber of Commerce** at 609-465-7181 or *www.cmccofc.com.*

ATLANTIC CITY

Of all Jersey Shore resorts, Atlantic City has the fewest problems with rainy days. Rain or shine, the beaches of America's most visited tourist destination are the least crowded places in town. Rooms—the great indoors, if you will—are what Atlantic City is all about. It has more than 16,000 hotel rooms covered in countless square miles of high-quality carpet. It has vast gambling rooms, filled with slot machines and blackjack tables and the distinctive clinking of legalized avarice, in each of the city's 14, fortress-like casinos. It has big dining rooms wired for light and sound and nonstop appearances by Jay Leno, Celine Dion or Bill Cosby. The beach, which lies beside them all, is beside the point.

Oh, you can complain if you want that the casinos have (ever since New Jersey voters legalized gambling on Absecon Island in 1977) dishonored their corporate citizenship by absconding with most of the money far beyond the many still-seedy streets of Atlantic City. Or you can mutter that gambling is a distasteful habit that begets other distasteful habits (smoking, prostitution, hard drinking and, these days, caffeine for the aging slot jockeys struggling to stay awake at their machines). Or you can do what a lot of Washingtonians do, at least once in a while--visit the home of the Miss America Pageant for a day or few days of pure, unadulterated fun, the kind of fun that appeals to a vacationer's basest emotions—greed, sloth, gluttony, envy—and for which Atlantic City is perhaps the most perfect place on the Eastern Seaboard. Then you can go back home and resume complaining, especially if the odds worked against you again (which, of course, they are scientifically designed to do).

Post contributor Adam Seessel's advice for Atlantic City visitors is to do the natural by day and the synthetic by night. "The casinos feel strange and alien in the morning," he writes. "There is something dispiriting about having breakfast and then walking around a casino floor full of senior citizens carrying quarters in huge plastic Slurpee cups. Save the casinos for the night: Somehow they feel better then, when the omnipresent haze of cigarette smoke and the constant jangling of the slot machines seem right." Each casino, Seessel says, has its unique appeal. The **Showboat** (609-343-4000 &) is light and breezy, sans souci and full of jazz—actually a very good replica of the New Orleans its name evokes. The decor is high bordello, and the centerpiece of the place is an atrium whose four walls are painted with a Vieux Carre scene complete with faux balconies and a Blanche DuBois look-alike dressed in a velvet dress with a bustle. In the mural, she looks down not on Stanley Kowalski but on a real live ragtime band playing in the lobby; the piano player wears a rhinestone waistcoat like Liberace used to wear. Upstairs there's also a bowling alley, which Stanley would have appreciated. At the other end of the boardwalk, **Tropicana** (609-340-4000 &) is brassy and sassy and full of a circus-like atmosphere, as befits the only casino in Atlantic City to contain a real indoor amusement park, complete with roller coaster. Other casinos are more formal and aspire to provide patrons with the illusion of grandeur. The **Trump Taj Mahal** (609-449-1000 &) has certain regal ambitions with its fuchsia carpet and huge chandeliers (which alone cost The Donald $14 million, he wants you to know). The **Claridge** (609-340-3400 &), built on top of the grand old hotel of the same name, naturally reflects the dimming glow of old-world luxury. But in Atlantic City, Caesar is king. Classic and somber, **Caesars Palace** (609-644-7777 &) is done in all white, giving one the impression that the entire place is draped in a toga. Upstairs, Seessel says, the hotel rooms themselves are much more inviting than Caesar's imperial-feeling, claustrophobic casino areas. "My wife was taken with the hand cream and conditioner in plastic bottles shaped like tiny Doric columns. I liked the hotel's slavolike willingness to serve (the customer-response card in the room said on the front, 'I, Caesar, care about your opinion') and the in-house television, which was showing half a dozen porno movies and a special casino-only channel designed to teach the novice the games of the house. But for actual gambling, I decided to avoid the pomp of Caesars and play the **Sands** (609-441-4444 &) instead. The Sands has an inviting feel to it, not to mention the biggest no-smoking section and an abundance of $5 blackjack tables."

Like any drug, the casinos after a time become numbing, and it's better to simply walk along the boardwalk, where there are the odd palm readers and greasy spoons and novelty stores selling cheesy T-shirts—plus the salt breezes and faded blue of, you know, the Atlantic Ocean. And there is more to do outdooors nearby: Across the bridge in Brigantine is the **Marine Mammal Stranding Center** (609-266-0538 &), where you can see distressed dolphins that have been fished from the sea. Farther north is some of the most pristine coastland on the Atlantic, thanks in large part to the **Forsythe National Wildlife Refuge** (609-652-1665 &), more than 40,000 acres of salt meadows, bays and marshes full of ibises and hundreds of Eastern migratory birds, and where thousands of Canada geese breed and teach goslings to swim. A series of levees allow you to drive through much of of it.

GETTING THERE: Atlantic City is 177 miles from the Beltway, about a 3¾-hour drive. Take I-95 north and follow the signs after crossing the Delaware Memorial Bridge to U.S. 40 east. NJ Transit operates daily commuter trains to Atlantic City from the same terminal Amtrak passes through in Philadelphia, and both US Airways Express and Continental fly to Atlantic City International Airport. Among the local operators with daily trips to Atlantic City is **Gray Line** (202-289-1995, roundtrip $29.95).

WHERE TO STAY/EAT: Access Atlantic City (888-777-2711) offers a free reservation service for such hotels as the Tropicana, the Sands, Atlantic City Hilton and Harrahs (rates range from $140 to $225 a night, in season), but any casino hotel on the boardwalk is decent. For grandiosity, try **Caesars** (800-524-2867); for pomposity, try the **Trump Plaza** (800-677-7378 ♿) or the **Trump Taj Mahal** (800-825-8786 ♿). You can save as much as 50 percent or more by going midweek or, especially, by visiting November to May. For meals, always avoid the casino restaurants: Amid the residue of secondhand smoke they serve mediocre food at inflated prices. Instead, go to the few good local joints still extant. Best and legendary is the **Knife and Fork** (609-344-1133), which has fabulous seafood, especially when it's steamed, stuffed or smoked. Also good are **Dock's Oyster House** (609-345-0092 ♿), owned and operated by the same family since 1897, when Atlantic City was still a small but popular Victorian summertime escape for railroad-bound Philadelphians; and the more downscale **White House Sub Shop** (609-345-1564) for New Jersey hoagies (more than 20 million sold).

FOR MORE INFORMATION: Contact the **Atlantic City Convention and Visitors Authority** at 800-262-7395 or *www.atlanticcitynj.com.*

THE NEW JERSEY PINE BARRENS

Protected by federal and state laws to varying and controversial degrees (since 60 percent of it is privately owned), the roughly 1.5 million acres of New Jersey's Pine Barrens constitute the largest contiguous wilderness area between here and Boston. The laws—including its designation 20 years ago as the country's first National Reserve—are especially meant to protect the buried treasure at the bottom of these shady savannahs and vast fields of chest-high pigmy pines known as the Plains. The treasure is a huge potable aquifer, an estimated 17 trillion-gallon underground lake fed over the eons by rainwater that has seeped, and is filtered by, the porous, nutrient-poor sand. It was this sand that prompted early Dutch and English settlers to first use the word "barrens."

The area is not, of course, barren; it's merely unique. Seen from a bus or car, the Pine Barrens' dry roadside face is more charred than inviting. The charring often has been done deliberately by state foresters hoping to preempt the destructive wildfires that visit every 10 to 20 years. The best way to see these sandy, scruffy pitch pine and oak forests and cedar swamps—which cover nearly a fourth of the otherwise most densely populated state in the country—is on foot or by canoeing or kayaking one of the Barrens' many rivers. (All of the waterways originate within the Pine Barrens). You can start with a tour of **Batsto**, the restored 18th Century village that was a major supplier of iron for cannons and shot for Revolutionary troops. It is in the southern end of the 300,000-

acre **Wharton State Forest** (609-561-3262), where you'll also find information about camping permits, hiking and the park's history and nature programs at Batso and along the Mullica River. Among the many trails that start in or pass through Wharton is the 50-mile **Batona Trail**, which takes you from here to **Bass River State Forest** (609-296-1114). You can rent canoes from **Mick's Canoe Rental** (609-726-1380) on Route 563 below Chatsworth. **Bel Haven** (609-965-2205), which is closer to the coast in Egg Harbor, rents canoes, kayaks, tubes and rafts and can get you almost anyplace in the Pine Barrens for trips of two hours or two days. (You can also get an extensive list of canoe and campground operators from the New Jersey tourism folks; see FOR MORE INFORMATION, below.) The best times to paddle or walk the pinelands are in early spring, weekdays in summer, or in the fall, when deer flies and ticks (but not mosquitoes, alas) are gone. The **Pinelands Preservation Alliance** (609-894-8000), a private nonprofit watchdog organization, offers occasional nature and conservation-related outdoor programs, as does the **New Jersey Audubon Society** (609-261-2495). For details on the annual **Cranberry Festival** (usually mid-October in Chatsworth, the epicenter of South Jersey's big cranberry and blueberry industry), as well as monthly weekend "ghost town" tours, check with the state tourism division at 800-537-7397. And for an entirely captivating sample of traditional pinelands music (it shares many roots with bluegrass, Ozark and country-western), check out **Albert Music Hall's** nifty year-round concerts, held on Saturday nights in Waretown (609-971-1593 ♿).

GETTING THERE: The Pine Barrens are a three- to four-hour drive from the Beltway (and a 30- to 60-minute drive from Atlantic City and most South Jersey beach destinations). Most parts are reachable via east-west Route 72, which intersects the New Jersey Turnpike on the western edge of the Pine Barrens and U.S. 9 and the Garden State Parkway at its eastern edge.

WHERE TO STAY/EAT: One thing this region is still a bit barren of: anything much beyond the kind of lodging that provides bed, bathroom and bar of soap. For helpful listings of motels and campgrounds in the middle of the Pine Barrens or not far away, contact the **Greater Hammonton Chamber of Commerce** (609-561-9080). The pines of **Wharton State Forest** (609-268-0444) also harbor nine cabins that can be rented from April to October for $28 (for a four-person cabin) or $56 (eight people) a night. Each comes with a kitchen, bath, shower and electric heater; you provide the utensils, bedding and linen. (Reservations should be made six months to a year in advance). In Pemberton, on the northern edge of the barrens, are the three-room, 1750 **Isaac Hilliard House** (800-371-0756; doubles $85-$155) and the **Main Stay B&B** in Medford (609-654-7528; doubles $80 to $125), with nine rooms. A lot of Pine Barrens visitors who aren't camping skip the motels along the state highways and stay at the beach.

FOR MORE INFORMATION: Contact the **New Jersey Tourism and Travel Division** at 800-537-7397 or *www.state.nj.us*. There's also an informative and helpful Burlington County web site at *www.burlco.lib.nj.us/pinelands*.

THE JERSEY SHORE

On the Road to Red Bank

By Roger Piantadosi

THANKSGIVING WEEKEND, on the road from Washington to not-quite-New York, seems a good a time as any to put your foot down—not on the gas pedal—and declare once and for all that getting there can indeed be half the fun.

We were going to stop at my parents' house for dinner and then head for nearby Red Bank, a nifty little riverside city near the top of the Jersey shore, to which we'll get in a moment. But first, on the very subject of getting somewhere in a moment: My wife and I decided that we were not in a hurry, so we would head through the flats of Maryland and Delaware to the Cape May-Lewes Ferry and then travel the truck-free Garden State Parkway, all the while avoiding I-95 and the New Jersey Turnpike. Besides, we'd heard that so many drivers had been seen muttering to themselves on the holiday-packed turnpike that the authorities were considering augmenting each toll plaza with a drive-through psychotherapy booth.

We had planned well for the good nine hours we'd be car-bound this weekend and packed a picnic in a cooler, music, a guidebook or two. The lovely ferry ride provided a chance to stretch. And my wife and I *talked* for nearly three consecutive hours.

Red Bank proved as transporting as the trip itself. I assume that nasty things sometimes happen in Red Bank, a reborn former seaport on the Navesink River's south bank. But on that Friday at 7 p.m., we were too busy running through an alley to notice any of it. We were dashing from our parking space about a block from the town's Christmas tree lighting ceremony on Broad Street. (Part of downtown Red Bank's plan for its own renaissance is the addition of some 4,000 cheap parking spaces within walking distance of most of its hundreds of shops and restaurants.)

Over the top of Broad Street's two-story, 19th Century brick buildings, we could hear the amplified voice of an emcee as he began leading a countdown chant: "10 . . . nine . . ." Exactly at "one," we skidded around the corner into a crowd of a couple of thousand cheering people, about half of them small and sitting on the shoulders of the other half. At that instant, the three-story evergreen and all of Red Bank's over-the-street Christmas decorations lit up.

The band, an ad hoc gathering of local rockers that spends the holiday season performing for disabled, sick and other under-cheered people, was superb. There is precedent for this: Red Bank is the birthplace of Count Basie, for whom its restored, 1,400-seat arts theater is named, as well as a known stomping ground of such former E Streeters as Bruce Springsteen and Clarence Clemons. It's also the home of locally grown filmmaker Kevin Smith, who shot his low-budget hits "Clerks" and "Mallrats" and the bigger-budget "Chasing Amy" within a few miles of his offices above the Bowknot restaurant on Broad.

Though Red Bank's year-round population is only about 11,000, there are three music stores in town—plus a half-dozen coffee shops for musicians and other artistic types and about 50 restaurants and a growing collection of galleries, theater and dance companies and yoga classes.

After the band, the Christmas festival featured a few gospel numbers by the Pilgrim Baptist Choir, which swayed up on the stage as kids in the street (and even grown-ups) danced. Eventually we found my Mom and my two brothers in the middle of the crowd (they had driven up to meet us), and we all squirmed our way through the maze of people toward dinner, me with a dopey smile on my face and Charmaine, my wife, doing a sort of path-widening rumba. It turned out that Basil T's, Monmouth County's first brew pub, also served excellent Italian food and huge, creative tossed salads.

We spent most of two days in Red Bank. We browsed among aisles without end of antiques in three converted warehouses and several shops in Red Bank's west end, near the train station. (New York is an hour's ride north.) Across the street we gorged on a $7 lunch buffet of pickled and roasted vegetable dishes, pastas and pesto-garlic bread at Mario's in the Galleria, a mini-mall of shops, restaurants and offices carved out of a factory on what 20 years ago was the wrong side of the tracks.

We admired, and then walked straight into, a two-story *trompe l'oeil* mural facing yet another midtown parking lot and noted the many restored storefronts on Front and Broad and Monmouth streets. Many of these were redone with the help of Red Bank's RiverCenter, a nonprofit downtown management agency that also organizes special events like the holiday concert and promotes Red Bank, which New Jersey Monthly magazine called "the hippest town in the state."

Shopkeepers and waiters all seemed to share a kind of casual friendliness here. This, combined with the seasonal presence of Santa and shops with such unusual specialties as garden Victoriana, rubber-stamp art and Asian clothing designs, conspired to make us feel very much at home. Back home and stressed out, I'd been having some trouble feeling that way.

Saturday, as we were checking out of the Molly Pitcher Inn, a fetchingly restored 150-room inn overlooking the Navesink at the north end of town, the Cheerful

Front Desk Person saw me begin to write a personal check and said, "Oh, we don't accept personal checks anymore." I looked up, suddenly noticing that she — and everyone else at the Molly Pitcher—was wearing a uniform.

"The teller machine I tried nearby didn't work with my card," I explained to the hotel woman, trying to keep in mind how nice everyone had been to us this weekend.

"Well," she said, and then she actually looked me in the eye, and made a decision. "Okay, sure."

My wife and I talked the whole way back to Washington, and when we got home, we felt very much . . . *at* home. Sometimes you just have to go somewhere for that to happen.

GETTING THERE: Take I-95 north to the New Jersey Turnpike to I-195 east (Exit 7A) to the Garden State Parkway north. Get off at Exit 109, and just follow the signs. The drive takes about four hours. (If you take the Cape May-Lewes Ferry to the Parkway north, the drive will take you between five and six hours.)

BEING THERE: In winter, Red Bank is an excellent cure for those whose hearts, minds and sinuses react badly to Shopping Mall Season. Every corner leads to a nice surprise, whether of the mom-and-pop or Starbucks variety, including a vegetarian restaurant and natural foods market, cool clothing and gift stores, old-time barber shops and a 24-hour chrome diner. In warmer weather, there are weekly jazz concerts on the river, and it's a short drive east to the beach, the most popular being Sandy Hook. This is an aptly named barrier peninsula that's part of **Gateway National Recreation Area** (732-872-0115), a place to which you'll want to arrive early in July and August or risk being turned away. And Red Bank's Independence Day fireworks display over the Navesink River, handled by Long Island's famous Grucci family, has become the largest Fourth celebration on the Jersey Shore.

WHERE TO STAY: In fall and winter, the renovated 1928 Greek Revival **Molly Pitcher Inn** (732-747-2500 ♿), on the north edge of downtown, has 158 rooms from $125 to $173 a night, the costliest a suite with a view of the hotel's marina and the river beyond. Just up the street is the **Oyster Point Hotel** (732-530-8200; weekend doubles $163-$173 ♿), a newer luxury-corporate hotel with 58 rooms. The **Courtyard by Marriott** (732-530-5552 ♿), closer to the Garden State Parkway than downtown, has weekend rates from $99 to $179. **Seascape Manor** (732-291-8467; doubles start at $95) is a four-room B&B in nearby Highlands, overlooking Sandy Hook (and, on a clear day, the skyline of Manhattan, which is a ferry ride away).

WHERE TO EAT: For lunch or a snack, sample the smart deli fare at **Mario's** in the Galleria (732-747-8181), or the curries, tempura and other vegetarian specialties of the cozy **Garden Restaurant** on Front Street (732-530-8681). For dinner, **Basil T's** (732-842-5990 ♿) is a popular—and noisy—spot. Quieter and more continental is **Little Kraut** (732-842-4830 ♿), and quieter still, for a special dinner, are the restaurant at the **Molly Pitcher Inn**, with its panoramic Navesink River views, and the **Shadowbrook** (732-747-0200), serving continental fare in a Georgian mansion in nearby Shrewsbury.

FOR MORE INFORMATION: RiverCenter offers toll-free event info at 1-888-HIPTOWN (1-888-447-8696) and an excellent web site at *www.redbank.com.* Or try the **Monmouth County Department of Public Information & Tourism** at 800-523-2587.

SPRING LAKE

Spring Lake's development as an exclusive beach resort for well-to-do city dwellers goes back to Victorian times. It stops there, too.

If you've always liked ocean-side boardwalks but have had your fill of junk-food emporiums, rock-and-roll bistros, amusement arcades and T-shirt shops, Spring Lake is your kind of beach town. With the exception of a pavilion at either end with food and restrooms, the **Spring Lake boardwalk** is just a boardwalk, bounded on one side by the beach, the other by dunes. In the blocks leading away from the sea, many of the town's original summer houses still stand— Italianate villas, rambling English Tudors, dignified Colonial revivals and, most popular, the Queen Anne-style manse, with its Gothic shingles, stained-glass windows and wraparound porches. A good number of these are now inns, guest houses and B&Bs. The town's namesake lake winds through the center of the village for five blocks, with the willows on its banks weeping alluringly. The lake's Giverny-like pedestrian bridges and boat-sized swans are a pleasant counter to the tempestuous Atlantic. Quaint **Third Avenue**, the shopping district, is a 3½-block thoroughfare with boutique-like stores for groceries and kid's toys and religious artifacts, along with coffee bars and cafes and an Italian joint with arguably the best pizza this side of Sicily. The town, though, is known as "the Irish Riviera," because many early settlers and visitors were of Irish descent.

Unlike Cape May, a larger and more deliberately commercial Victorian resort further south, Spring Lake's unadorned beaches, quiet streets and manicured lawns allow the seaside surroundings to function as they were meant to back in 1898—as a restorative, a place to escape the pressures of the modern world. And this isn't just a summer pastime—many of the town's hotels and guest houses remain open year round.

Post writer Carolyn Spencer Brown says that the town doesn't actively dislike tourists but that it welcomes them with less than open arms. "On the beach, town regulations seem designed to scare day-trippers away," she says. "You can't picnic on the beach. Don't even think about changing into your bathing suit in one of Spring Lake's boardwalk bathrooms—it's illegal. It'll cost you $5 to access the beach each day." But people do come. "I've returned again and again over the past 10 years, because it's like visiting a museum and going to the beach at the same time."

GETTING THERE: Spring Lake is about four hours from the Beltway. Take I-95 to the New Jersey Turnpike to Exit 7A and follow I-195 east to Route 34 south. At first traffic circle, go three-quarters of the way around to pick up Route 524 east to Spring Lake.

WHERE TO STAY: There are numerous B&Bs; rates at the 16-room Italianate **Normandy Inn** (732-449-7172), listed on the National Register of Historic Places, start at about $153 in season. The more modern-amenity-prone **Chateau** (732-974-2000 ♿) has 30 rooms and six suites, starting at $199, three night minimum, not including breakfast. Up in the north end of town amid the oak trees, **Hollycroft** (732-681-2254; doubles $125 and up) is a cross between a beach house and an Adirondack lodge; trout fishers and birdwatchers like it here.

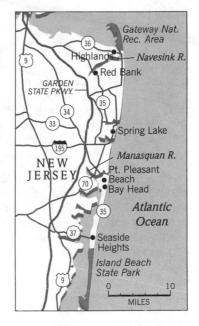

WHERE TO EAT: Several older Spring Lake hotels—including the **Breakers** (732-449-7700 ♿)—offer public dining, and other eateries are within walking distance of the beach. For special occasions, the **Old Mill Inn** (732-449-1800 ♿) overlooking a millpond in neighboring Spring Lake Heights, specializes in seafood and steak. In town, the **Sandpiper** (732-449-4700 ♿) is a popular Sunday brunch spot that also serves lunch and dinner in a cozy and candle-lit Victorian room.

FOR MORE INFORMATION: Contact the **Greater Spring Lake Chamber of Commerce** at 732-449-0577 (open daily; hours vary) or *www.springlake.org.*

POINT PLEASANT BEACH/BAY HEAD

The homey and seasonally overcrowded Barnegat Peninsula is connected to the New Jersey mainland about 30 miles due south of New York's fabled Coney Island. Here you'll find **Point Pleasant Beach**, an aptly named, semi-sleepy home to a small commercial fishing fleet, great seafood restaurants and the most well-rounded New Jersey beach experience available. The point about Point Pleasant is that it has something for everyone, starting at the **Manasquan Inlet** to the north. There, at one end of the three-quarter-mile boardwalk, are fishing boats, charters and pleasure craft that make their way between the open ocean and their Manasquan River or Barnegat Bay slips. There's also a miniature train right on the sand to take you to the arcade-and-restaurant cluster farther south. The stretch between here and the concessions, bars, pizza stands, arcades and amusements at the foot of Arnold Avenue is quintessential Jersey Shore: row upon row of medium, small and very small beach houses in the gravelly block between the boardwalk and Ocean Avenue. The houses are well-tended, with kids often playing paddleball out front while mom, dad, aunts and uncles huddle over a card game on the screened-in porch. On the boardwalk or Ocean Avenue you'll find food, restrooms and changing facilities; a small but satisfying (for kids under 12) amusement park; free concerts on Wednesday nights in summer; a wide, pretty and clean beach, and (for us kids well over 12) all the latest hiresolution video games, electronic air-ball batting cages, pinball wizardry and, for the beach dinosaurs among us, Skeeball.

Point Pleasant Beach has also become a modest antiques and collectibles center—try the three floors of the **Antique Emporium** (732-892-2222), which now has three coffee shops as well. At the inlet are riverboat-style dinner and specialty cruises on the **River Belle** (732-892-3377 ♿) and half-day sport-fishing trips on the **Norma K III** (732-892-9787 ♿). At both **Jenkinson's Beach** and the somewhat quieter **Risden's** (732-892-8412) in Point Pleasant Beach, beach access is about $5 weekdays, slightly more on weekends, and $1.75 for ages 5-11 (Jenkinson's) or $1 for 4-12 (Risden's).

All this is in sharp contrast to **Bay Head**, the next town south. There the meticulously maintained beach is free of any piers or fences, boardwalk or concessions, outdoor showers or even public restrooms. In other words, the oceanfront here lacks noisy crowds (you don't take kids to a beach that doesn't sell snowcones or offer plumbing). While Bay Head property owners have season beach badges, visitors need to stop in at the Bay Head Improvement Association office for a $5 daily badge required for access by anyone 12 or older. (If you rent a room at one of Bay Head's numerous guest houses, the badge will be included in your room rate.) For food or drink you have to walk the three or four blocks into Bay Head's similarly low-key business district. It can make for a satisfyingly long and restful day. (If you want to speed things up, you can rent in-line skates—as well as windsurfers and kayaks—at **Bay Head Windsurfing**, 732-899-9394).

GETTING THERE: Point Pleasant Beach and Bay Head are about four hours from the Beltway. Take I-95 to the New Jersey Turnpike. At Exit 7A, take I-195 east to the Garden State Parkway south, exiting immediately on Route 34 south. Just before the Manasquan River, pick up Route 35 south into Point Pleasant Beach. Route 35 continues south to Bay Head.

WHERE TO STAY: For basic needs (per-night prices will exceed $100 as you get close enough to the beach), motels abound along Route 35 from Point Pleasant through Seaside Heights (and Routes 88, 37, 70 and 9 on the mainland). On a quiet residential street—within walking distance of the beach and Point Pleasant Beach's eclectic, resurgent downtown—is the friendly B&B **Gull Point Cottage Inn** (732-899-2876), where rooms with a full bath start at $109 weekends (when there's also a two-night minimum). Bay Head has the most gracious B&B inns south of better-known Spring Lake. Try the **Bentley Inn** (732-892-9589; the 20 rooms with private baths start at $145 a night in season, including beach passes, breakfast and parking), as well as the beautifully restored Victorian **Grenville Hotel** (800-756-4667; $175-$295 a night weekends in season ♿), a block from the ocean and with its own formal and highly rated restaurant.

WHERE TO EAT: For fine dining, try the restaurant at the **Grenville Hotel** in Bay Head. On the Point Pleasant Beach boardwalk, there are the open-air, food-and-drink emporiums of **Martell's Sea Breeze** (732-892-0131 ♿) and **Jenkinson's** (732-899-0569 ♿). On the Manasquan Inlet in Point Pleasant Beach, check out **Jack Baker's Lobster Shanty** (732-899-6700 ♿) for the

Great Adventure

SAFARI TIME IN NEW JERSEY

CARVED OUT of the pine and oak forest some 30 miles inland from the shore resorts, **Six Flags' Great Adventure/Hurricane Harbor** theme park is a huge, day-long family destination, with more than 100 rides, shows and other attractions and an adjacent 350-acre, drive-through safari park with some 1,500 animals. On weekends, the lines start forming out at the Great Adventure exit lane off Interstate 195 and continue afoot at the log flume, the "Lethal Weapon" water show and just about every serious roller coaster and food counter. Both the theme park and safari park are open April through November, daily till late from Memorial Day to Labor Day and mostly weekends otherwise. Reach the park via I-195, which runs east-west between the New Jersey Turnpike on the west and the Garden State Parkway/Route 9 on the east. (For details, call 732-928-1821; admission starts at $38.50 for adults, $27.50 for those older than 3 and shorter than 54 inches. But late-day and other discounts are available).

best Jersey Shore seafood-lounge ambiance, and the no-frills **Shrimp Box** (732-899-1637 ♿) and **Red's Lobster Pot** (732-295-6622). Right on the border of Bay Head and Point Pleasant Beach, the **Ark** (732-295-1122 ♿) is worth a visit for its casual, classic pub atmosphere, its satellite sports channels and its often excellent but not expensive meals. And if you just came to Jersey for the pastries, both the Italian kind and the kind that is otherwise not part of your calorie-watching plan, stop in for an espresso drink and anything baked at **You Take the Cake** (732-714-7004 ♿)

FOR MORE INFORMATION: Contact the **Greater Ocean County Tourism Council** at 732-929-2138, the **Point Pleasant Beach Area Chamber of Commerce** at 732-899-2424 or the **Bay Head Business Association** at 800-422-9433. Online, consult the *Asbury Park Press'* extensive Jersey Shore web page, at *www.injersey.com* or the Ocean County information page at *www.vitinc.com/ocean.*

SEASIDE HEIGHTS/ISLAND BEACH STATE PARK

Head south from Bay Head on Route 35 and you'll come to **Seaside Heights**. High above the ocean, Seaside Heights a generation or two ago built two large piers. These make it a crummy place to sit on the beach all day but great for cloudy-day or after-dark amusement rides (including edge-of-the-pier roller coasters and water slides, fun houses and a few dozen stomach churners).

The town is known for its post-adolescent nightlife, which makes it a wilder place after dark than Wildwood, the other area amusement nexus to which it's most often compared. Seaside also is known for its well-lit array of boardwalk places with pizza, zeppoli and games of chance, staffed by the kind of mysterious-looking young men and women who normally arrive in town with the circus. Which is what Seaside Heights is, really—particularly on the boardwalk at night, when everything is lit up and loud. That includes many of the passersby, most of whom come here from North Jersey and New York, where the rules governing the public display of enthusiasm are different from those at, say, the Smithsonian's Air and Space Museum. If you don't get it—hey, fagettaboudit.

As Assateague Island sits just across the inlet from the bright lights of Maryland's Ocean City, so will you come to another world at the southern end of Seaside Heights, after you pass the gravel parking lot and one last steak-and-lobster joint. There, through a gate, you enter **Island Beach State Park** (732-793-0506). It's a largely wild, 9.5-mile-long, 3,000-acre barrier peninsula with a wildlife preserve and nature trails in its northern half, a guarded beach with concessions and restrooms about four miles from the gate, and another six miles or so of relatively untouched, sparsely populated ocean beach and bayside marsh. Some 10,000 to 15,000 people come to Island Beach State Park on a sunny Saturday or Sunday in midsummer. (Admission is $4 a car weekdays, $7 weekends and holidays. The gates close when the parking lots are full, usually by 10 a.m., though you can always bike in free.) A remarkable number of visitors fail to venture up or down the beach away from the public beach, which is their loss. The park is divided into three sections: the northern natural area (also known as the botanical preserve) limited to nature tours and surf fishing; the recreation area with guarded beaches (10 a.m. to 6 p.m. Memorial Day-Labor Day), and the southern natural area, a wildlife sanctuary, its ocean beaches open to surf fishers, strollers, picnickers, scuba divers and surfers. An 8½-mile bike lane runs from the gate to the southern area. The park provides a number of nature tours, including canoe and kayak tours through the Sedge Islands wildlife area in Barnegat Bay on Sundays, Tuesdays and Thursdays (pre-registration required). Not far from the park entrance, you can rent bikes (and, if parking lots are full, get in the park for free, minus calories burned) at **Tyres Bicycles** in Seaside Park (732-830-2050).

For details on getting here, and nearby places to stay and eat, see **Point Pleasant Beach/Bay Head** on page 87 and just follow Route 35 at Bay Head farther south to Seaside Heights.

Chapter 3

Hightailing It West By Northwest

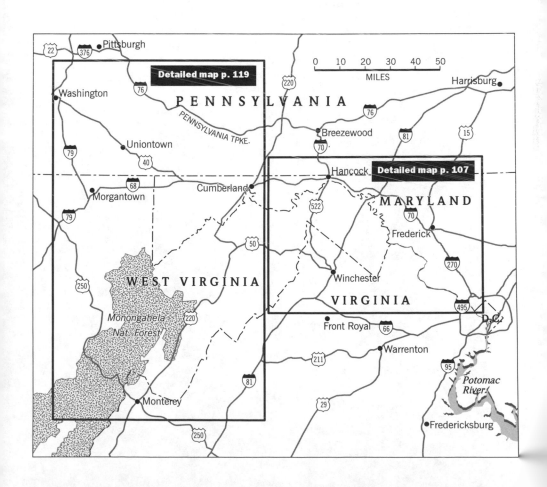

The Other Side
Of Camp David

By Craig Stoltz

HERE IT IS, a mere 53 minutes into our weekend away, and much to the delight of the under-6 squad in the back seat, we already are "there yet." Sure, the beach may be more popular, the Florida Keys more exotic. But at the moment on Friday afternoon when others are trapped on U.S. 50 behind some poor schnook whose radiator is smoking like a hibachi, or sweating in line at the airport as a foreign student with a metal plate in his skull negotiates the X-ray gate, our family already is startling a family of deer along a winding, two-lane road in Maryland's Catoctin Mountains.

A weekend taking in the subtle but considerable charms of these brushy, long-worn hillocks may not yield the most spectacular postcard photos, but let's put it this way: It is one of the most time-efficient escapes these parts have to offer.

Of course, we're not the first stressed-out, time-pressed Washington folks to figure this out. All U.S. presidents since Franklin Roosevelt have cruised out to the Catoctin getaway originally called Shangri-La—now known as Camp David—for rest, relaxation, relief from the summer heat and, every now and again, some diplomacy alfresco. Modern presidents and their entourages pretty much keep to themselves within the Catoctin Mountain National Park zone described only as "Camp Number 3" by some menacing signs and fence work lining Park Central Road. Too bad for them, I say, because the area has plenty else to offer: some excellent hiking on miles of mountain trails; a handsome freshwater lake for swimming, boating and fishing; a splendid 78-foot waterfall at the adjacent Cunningham Falls State Park; a scattering of quirky historical and natural sites; some memorable restaurants, and even a small and funky private zoo.

There's also Thurmont, where you should stay if you can get reservations, not always easy during summer and fall weekends. An alternative is a room in Frederick, 15 miles southwest on U.S. 15, but you'll miss the sense of isolation of spending all your time in and around the mountains. Both Catoctin Mountain Park, administered by the National Park Service, and Cunningham Falls State Park offer many fine campsites, if you're so inclined. Or you can rent a rustic cabin at Camp Misty Mount within Catoctin Mountain Park.

Thurmont derives much of its personality from a curious local institution known as the Cozy, a campus consisting of an inn, several cottages, a restaurant and a number of "shoppes." The restaurant is a sprawling, jerry-built affair, each of its many rooms decorated in a different theme. One room has faux Victorian storefronts and is hung with cut-glass lamps; elsewhere, a red caboose with accompanying rails juts from a hallway. Out on the terrace is a goldfish pond and a remarkable, tin-roofed dog house, the only one I've ever seen with a miniature replica TV antenna.

The Cozy's accommodations are named and decorated for the presidents who have visited Camp David. I coveted the thought of spending the weekend in the Nixon Room (no smoking, queen-size bed, $71.50 a night). I'd even have settled for the Reagan Cottage ("queen-size water bed and a corner-mirrored Jacuzzi," $105). And the Kennedy Room is equipped with a bidet! But, alas, a wedding had the entire Cozy booked the weekend we went, so we wound up at the Rambler, a clean, well-lighted place alongside U.S. 15. (A bit too well-lighted, as it turned out. The "24-hour deli" the brochure advertises turns out to be the convenience store of the gas station that shares the Rambler's driveway.)

My wife, Pam, the kids and I spent most of our time at the lake, the falls and along the many miles of hiking trails offered by both the state and federal parks. The strenuous hike to Wolf Rock nearly exhausted 4-year-old Jordan and 5½-year-old Caleb. But as is so rarely the case with family hikes, the destination turned out to be as memorable as the journey. Located around 500 vertical feet above—and about two miles down the trail from—the handsome park Visitors Center where the route begins, Wolf Rock is a dramatic upthrust of 500-million-year-old quartzite that provides a generous view of the surrounding countryside and a rare chance to do some full-contact geology.

The massive white rock face is riven with dozens of vertical chutes that look as if they could swallow a 4-year-old boy in a single gulp, and the further you wander from the trail head, the more the rock is splintered into islands and towers. Caleb sighted a lizard we later learned was a skink, and he managed to lay a hand on it before it disappeared into a narrow crevice. The hike back to the car was long, and Jordan had to finish on my shoulders. That night the boys slept like stones.

Still, I'd have to say the highlight of our trip came on Saturday afternoon, just after we'd finished touring Hunting Creek Lake on a pair of preposterous aquacycles (if you've never had the pleasure, imagine a cross between a Big Wheel, a monster truck and a Jet Ski). Suddenly the sky over Cunningham Falls turned the color of pig iron, and the rangers' jeeps began to circulate around the park, flashing their lights and warning people to get off the lake and run for cover. We hightailed it for the station wagon and, like everyone else, drove away. We were nearly in Thurmont when heavy sheets of rain began sweeping down the mountain.

For several minutes the wind was so strong and the rain so hard we had to pull off the road, and as we sat there, our wagon rocking heavily in the wind, we watched a slab of vinyl siding tumble across a lawn. The boys were quiet. They'd never witnessed such a powerful dose of nature at one time. The storm passed quickly, and afterward, everything felt clean and aroused.

Which may be as fitting an ending for a weekend in the Catoctins as you'd ever hope for.

GETTING THERE: Thurmont is about an hour from the Beltway. Take I-270 north and, at Frederick, get on U.S. 15 north. Thurmont is just south of the intersection of Maryland Route 550.

BEING THERE: If the beach-versus-mountains debate resounds repeatedly at your house, **Cunningham Falls State Park** (301-271-7574) is a place to enjoy a day of détente. It's both: a beach in the mountains. Actually, it's two beaches, nice, long, sandy ones facing each other across one end of 43-acre Hunting Creek Lake (for non-motorized boating and canoeing, aquacycles, swimming and fishing) within the park woods. Next to a bathhouse, ranger station and snack bar, beach people can sunbathe on the sandy beaches or on the wide, grassy clearings that flank them. Mountain folks can hike the trails, including the shaded and lovely (but rocky) one-mile hike through a moss-bottomed hardwood and conifer forest to the park's namesake falls. (The best part: At the falls you can climb the rocks alongside and wade in the pools below and within.) The falls are handicapped-accessible from a tiny parking area on Route 77. Next door, **Catoctin Mountain National Park** (301-663-9388) offers great trails, a charming and informative exhibit area in the Visitor Center, and tours of the Blue Blazes Whiskey Still and a 19th Century charcoal-making site. Within both the national and state park are 47 miles of trails for cross-country skiing and snowshoeing, trails designed to educate visitors on nature, three trails that are handicapped-accessible, and one trail for horseback riders. Fly-fishing fanatics also enjoy hunting the rainbow trout in catch-and-release **Big Hunting Creek,** which runs through both parks in a narrow gorge darkened by overhanging conifers and hardwoods. Also nearby is **Catoctin Wildlife Preserve and Zoo** (301-271-4922), a privately owned small zoo with nearly 300 species, some of them endangered. Kids usually are impressed by the Andean condor, which look as big as a Cessna when it spreads its wings.

Antique browsers can easily fill up a weekend in the Catoctins. To the south of Thurmont and east of Frederick is **New Market**, a town on the National Register as a historic district. Founded in 1793 as a stop along the Baltimore Turnpike, (which later became part of the National Pike, the first federal highway), New Market nowadays is a one-stop antique-shopper's theme park.

95

Antiquers not exhausted by canvassing New Market's 30 or so shops should hit the area's ever-widening metropolis of **Frederick**, which has more than 300 antiques dealers housed in warehouses and old commercial buildings. In addition, Frederick has much of historic interest. You can visit Francis Scott Key's grave in **Mount Olivet Cemetery** or the house of **Barbara Fritchie** (301-698-0630), who reputedly flew the Union flag in the face of Stonewall Jackson as Frederick was falling to his troops. Or check out the **Children's Museum of Rose Hill Manor Park** (301-694-1648 &) depicting 19th Century family life and the **Schifferstadt Architectural Museum** (301-663-3885), based on excavations of a 1756 house. The Community Bridge, with its *trompe l'oeil* murals, also is well worth a look. South of Frederick, Civil War buffs can visit **Monocacy National Battlefield** (301-662-3515), where Rebel Gen. Jubal Early's advance on Washington was stopped; self-guided tours and a diorama depict the battle. Adjacent to the battlefield, **Sugarloaf Mountain** (301-874-2024) isn't much of a mountain (it's about 1,300 feet), but it is the highest stack of ancient rock for miles around, and it offers picnicking and hiking in a postcard setting.

WHERE TO STAY: Thurmont's **Cozy Country Inn** (301-271-4301; doubles $52-$130 &), loaded with anachronistic charm and still family-run, is the place to stay. The **Rambler** (301-271-2424; doubles $52-$72) is clean and conveniently located. **Ole Mink Farm** (301-271-7012 &) is deep within the woods down a long gravel road. Offerings include high-class luxury cabins ($250 for two nights) and camping cabins (which feature electricity and running water but no toilet and go for $60 a night), a game room, restaurant and outdoor pool. In New Market, the **Strawberry Inn** (301-865-3318; doubles $95-$125, including full breakfast &) has five pleasant rooms in a restored 1837 farmhouse and a Victorian gazebo out back that looks like a perfect place to drowse away a summer afternoon. Cascade, a woodsy mountain village just shy of the Pennsylvania border, once was a summer getaway for the wealthy of Baltimore and Washington, who built substantial vacation cottages there. A few remain, including **Bluebird on the Mountain** (800-362-9526; doubles $105-$125), a 1900s-era home that is now a five-room B&B beneath towering trees on the edge of town. Bluebird's decor is distinctly frilly. Two of the rooms have wood-burning fireplaces, and massages by area practitioners are an inn specialty.

In the parks around Thurmont are six campgrounds or cabin-lodge areas, two in the state park and four on the federal land.

WHERE TO EAT: Thurmont features two all-you-can-eat family buffets. **Mountain Gate Family Restaurant** (301-271-4373 &) is a country-style, family-ready, carpet-stained operation offering steam trays of chicken, ham, potatoes, salads and desserts. It is excellent for tour groups and grumpy families on a budget. The **Cozy Restaurant** (301-271-4301 &) is a more upscale version of the same, adding fresh seafood and prime rib to a basic menu of pies, chicken, mashed potatoes, steamed vegetables and the like. In New Market, **Mealey's Restaurant** (301-865-5488; closed Mondays &) is the only real restaurant if you want more than light fare. It's popular with the locals, so reservations are recommended. The food is good, mainstream Ameri-

The W&OD and the C&O

RAIL TRACK AND CANAL TRAILS

BICYCLISTS, hikers and runners looking to get upriver of the Beltway without having to use the Beltway—or cross the Beltway or any other motorway, for that matter—have two well-looked-after but distinctly different choices in the **Washington & Old Dominion (W&OD) Railroad Regional Park** (703-729-0596) and the **C&O Canal National Historical Park** (301-739-4200). The W&OD is a 45-mile-long, 100-foot-wide park with an asphalt trail (and, for 30 miles, a parallel gravel bridle path) running from southern Arlington to Purcellville in western Loudoun County. The C&O's somewhat rougher trail covers 184 riverfront miles between Georgetown and Cumberland, Md. The C&O's towpath, once followed by barge-toting mules, is mostly gravel and (in spring) can be muddy and slow in spots. But it offers many access points to natural sites (Great Falls, Point of Rocks) and historic places (Antietam, Sharpsburg) and is quite amenable to being enjoyed one small bite at a time.

The W&OD takes its name from the railroad whose tracks ran along the right-of-way from 1859 to 1968, and the scenery along the trail progresses, railroad-like, from high-rise and interstate to backyard single-family suburbia to rolling farmland. The two trails don't intersect, but they come close not far from Leesburg; you can make the Potomac crossing at tiny **White's Ferry** (301-349-5200; 5 a.m. to 11 p.m. daily, surface permitting). For a helpful trail guide and list of lodgings that are near both paths, send $1 to the **Tri-State Bike Trail Group** (800-644-1806), or you can download the guide for free at *www.norrishouse.com.*

can, and a relish tray of coleslaw, apple butter, beets and cottage cheese before the meal adds an ingratiating country touch.

FOR MORE INFORMATION: Contact the **Tourism Council of Frederick County** at 800-999-3613 or *www.visitfrederick.org.*

LOUDOUN COUNTY, VA.

Many of the thoroughbred towns and tiny hamlets of Loudoun County remain among Washington's favorite weekend escape routes. Up on the Maryland border, Loudoun's commercial hub is Leesburg, whose old-town streets are filled with Colonial-era architecture (much of it looking like it was built yesterday), quite a few good restaurants and shops, and easy access to several restored plantations and historic homes open to the public nearby. These include **Oatlands Plantation** (703-777-3174, closed January-March), whose 1803 mansion and adjacent gardens attract some 70,000 visitors annually for house and garden tours as well as for such special events as its May Sheep Dog Trials and Farm Days, October's Middleburg Kennel Club All Breed Dog Show, April and September Antiques Fairs and November and December "Christmas at Oatlands" events. Six miles south of Leesburg on U.S. 15, Oatlands was built by George Carter, great-grandson of early Virginia settler Robert "King" Carter. The estate was purchased in 1903 by prominent Washingtonians Edith and William Corcoran Eustis, whose daughters donated the furnished house and land in 1964 to the National Trust, **Morven Park** (703-777-2414 ♿) is another, a miniature White House whose Greek Revival mansion was home to two governors and whose 1,500 acres are home to a serene array of flowering trees and gardens. In town, self-guided walking tours start at the small **Loudoun Museum** (703-777-7427), whose exhibits span the region's settlement by Native Americans to mayhem and confusion hereabouts during the Civil War. (The Union defeat and disastrous retreat at Balls Bluff is commemorated in a small national cemetery up on U.S. 15.) For curious kids and young teens, Leesburg's little-known **Naturalist Center** (800-729-7725, closed Sunday-Monday) has a vast cache of bones, rocks, shells, fossils, leaves, nests, preserved dead animals and other oddments collected by the Smithsonian's National Museum of Natural History and representing each of the museum's major scientific disciplines: mineral sciences, paleobiology, zoology, anthropology and botany. Kids 10 and older are welcome in the main research room, where much of the collection is accessible in drawers and shelves.

At the county's southern edge, amid the tree-lined highways and fenced estates of Virginia's hunt country, lies **Middleburg**, a tiny, well-heeled crossroads that attracts a more or less continuous stream of daytrippers looking for a bite and a bit of window shopping. Middleburg packs them in every May for the **Virginia Gold Cup** steeplechase (703-253-5001) and again for late summer's **Middleburg Wine Festival** (540-253-5000). **Waterford** is an 18th Century Quaker village whose annual population explosion occurs during October's **Waterford Homes Tour and Craft Exhibit** (540-882-3018). Most Sundays in the town of **Aldie** on U.S. 50, you'll find a popular flea market at which everything from antiques to junk is available. You can spend a lot of quality time browsing through old prints and magazine ads at the **Rare Print Wagon** (540-364-3671), which is here whenever it's not at a bigger convention.

For other things to do nearby—as well as places to stay and eat—see the section on **This Side of the Shenandoah** on Page 34.

GETTING THERE: Leesburg is about an hour from the Beltway. The fast toll route: Take the Dulles Toll Road (Route 267) and stay on it after it becomes the Dulles Greenway extension, and follow the signs into Leesburg on Business 15 (or U.S. 15 for points south). The scenic route: From Beltway Exit 13, take Georgetown Pike (Route 193), which slowly curves west to Route 7 west, and follow the signs.

WHERE TO STAY: Creek Crossing Farm (540-338-7550; doubles $135-$175, including breakfast and afternoon tea) is a gracious 18th Century farm-

LONG NOTED, LITTLE FORGOTTEN

FROM THE boulder-strewn crest of Little Round Top, the lush farming land of Pennsylvania is a beautiful scene, checkered with white farmhouses, fields of corn and pastures dotted with rolled mounds of hay. But scattered across those peaceful fields are stone, bronze and steel reminders of events of more than a century ago. The objects—400 cannons and more than a thousand monuments—tell us that something terrible happened here. For three days in the summer of 1863, Gettysburg was witness to the greatest battle fought in the United States. The epic struggle began almost by accident on July 1, when a small party from Gen. Robert E. Lee's 65,000-man Confederate army entered this community looking for, of all things, shoes. The Southern soldiers ran into forward elements of Gen. George C. Meade's 95,000-man army, and the battle was joined. The next few days were filled with the horror of war. On July 3rd, the climactic event of the battle came when Maj. Gen. George E. Pickett's 15,000-man division attacked the center of the Union line. The Virginians charged, reached the line of blue soldiers and died. And the battle was lost.

On July 4th, the battle ended, and Lee's defeated army began the long retreat to Virginia. Four months later, the nation turned its eyes to Gettysburg again, this time for a cemetery dedication at which President Lincoln spoke briefly but with words that still echo through history: "We cannot dedicate—we cannot consecrate—we cannot hallow—this ground. The brave men, living and dead, who struggled here, have consecrated it, far above our poor power to add or detract. The world will little note nor long remember what we say here, but it can never forget what they did here."

Nowadays, those events are remembered daily in Gettysburg, where the aura of war sometimes is so real that a hint of gun smoke seems to linger in the air. The Civil War is served up almost every imaginable

house in Lincoln. The innkeeper allows children and pets and will fix a light dinner at the farm. The **Norris House Inn** (703-777-1806; doubles $100-$150, two night minimum) is well run and comfortable and particularly helpful to bikers and hikers along the C&O and W&OD trails (see box above). Other options include the simply furnished **Laurel Brigade Inn** (703-777-1010; doubles $60-$90), with gardens and a highly praised restaurant in the center of town, and the **Fleetwood Farm B&B** (800-808-5988; doubles $110 and up) on Route 621 not far from Oatlands. In Middleburg, the 33-room **Red Fox** way—from wax figures to Abe Lincoln impersonators—but those looking for the truest and unadorned glimpse should focus on **Gettysburg National Military Park** (717-334-1124), which covers more than 5,900 acres of the battlefield. Stop by the visitor center for maps to the battlefield's 36 miles of roads, 1,300 monuments and 400 Civil War cannons, then head to the adjacent Cyclorama Center for a film and more exhibits on the battle. Admission to the park is free (but there is a fee for some programs at the Cyclorama Center). If you want more than a simple map-led, drive-it-yourself tour, hire one of the battlefield guides licensed by the National Park Service. (The fee for a two-hour tour is $30; you can hire the guides at the center, on a first-come, no-reservations basis.

Adjoining the battlefield is the **Eisenhower National Historic Site**, the farm where President Eisenhower lived in retirement. The site is open to visitors, but you need tickets. Buy them at the National Park Service's Visitor Center, where free shuttle buses will take you to the farm.

The Civil War is big business in Gettysburg, with battle-related attractions competing with more touristy showplaces like **The Land of Little Horses** (717-334-7259 ♿) and the **Hall of Presidents and First Ladies** (717-334-5717). Then there are the artifacts at **General Lee's Headquarters** (717-334-3141), where the Confederate leader planned his strategy for the battle. If you are interested in toy soldiers, stop by the **Gettysburg Battle Theatre** (717-334-6100), a war room with a miniature battlefield and more than 25,000 toy soldiers poised to fight. The **Lincoln Train Museum** (717-334-5678) will thrill any railroading buff with its displays of more than 100 model trains and railroad memorabilia. And if the sight of trains sends you into a reverie, drop by the **Gettysburg Railroad** (717-334-6932 ♿) and take a 16-mile ride on a sightseeing train. Check the schedule before you go; it does not run every day. For guided group tours, check with **Gettysburg Battlefield Bus Tours** (717-334-6296) or the **Ghosts of Gettysburg Candlelight Walking Tours** (717-337-0445 ♿).

Inn (800-223-1728; doubles $135-$245 ♿) has been taking in weary travelers along the old traders' route (now followed by U.S. 50) since 1728. Though it looks like a corporate conference center—which it is—**Lansdowne Conference Resort** (800-541-4801; doubles $209-$309, golf and "getaway" packages available ♿) has developed a terrific business as Washington's closest, full-service golf resort; its 18-hole Robert Trent Jones Jr.-designed course, amid the hills between Route 7 and the Potomac just southeast of Leesburg, is one of the area's best. The back nine is the real showpiece, laid out in a

GETTING THERE: Gettysburg is about two hours from the Beltway: 65 miles away via I-270 north to U.S. 15 and the U.S. 15 Business Bypass.

WHERE TO STAY: Most major hotel chains and associations have locations in and around town. For period accommodations, consider the **James Gettys Hotel** (717-337-1334; doubles start at $115 &), built in 1804 but offering modern kitchenettes and cable TV in each of its 11 rooms; the **Battlefield Bed & Breakfast Inn**, an eight-room inn on a 46-acre farm on the south side of the battlefield (717-334-8804, doubles $147-$193); and the 10-room **Brafferton Inn** (717-337-3423; doubles $92-$115), a 211-year-old home that was the first private house built in Gettysburg. The **Farnsworth House Inn** (717-334-8838; doubles from $95) was used as Union head-quarters, and the 187-year-old, five-room inn has been restored to its 1863 appearance, furnished with 19th Century antiques. (The south wall of the inn is pockmarked with about 100 bullet holes.) And the **Brickhouse Inn** (800 864-3464), a turn-of-the-century Victorian home, offers families a two-room suite and a swing set (used by the resident 7-year-old) for $140 a night for adults, $15 for each child under 16 and more for older children. The visitor center of Gettysburg National Military Park is a 10-minute walk.

WHERE TO EAT: The **Blue Parrot Bistro** (717-337-3739) is a lively continental-cuisine restaurant that also displays paintings by local art-ists. Continental fare is also featured at the **Dobbin House** (717-334-2100 &), in the five-room **Gettystown Inn** and at the **Herr Tavern & Publick House** (717-334-4332). Colonial-style dishes—peanut soup, game pie and the like—can be enjoyed at the **Farnsworth House Inn** (see **where to stay**, above). The local land-mark is **Ernie's Texas Cafe** (717-334-1970), which features, as its sign says: "hot wieners." The locals say they can tell who ate at Ernie's the moment they walk in the door.

FOR MORE INFORMATION: Contact the **Gettysburg Convention & Visitors Bureau** at 717-334-6274 or *www.gettysburg.com*

—*Larry Fox*

large oval that runs away from the main building out into woods thick enough to make you feel like you're a million miles away from civilization. The hotel-conference center itself has all the modern conveniences and more—including a fitness center and spa where you can get a massage, pedicure or manicure.

WHERE TO EAT: In Leesburg, the buffalo burgers and wines are worth check-ing at **Tuscarora Mill** (703-771-9300), set in a restored 19th Century grain mill at the Market Station complex downtown. In Ashburn, the **Old Dominion Brewpub** (703-724-9103 &) is worth the trek. In addition to food and drink, it offers brewery tours Saturdays at noon and 2 and 4 p.m. and Sundays at 2 p.m. In Purcellville, there's **Mario's Italian Food** (540-338-3555 ♿), **Fran's Place** (540-338-3200 ♿) and **Candeloria's** (540-338-2075). **Planet Wayside** in nearby Hamilton (540-338-4315, closed Monday-Wednesday) has a good reputation among families and young professionals, despite (or more likely because of) its funky, friendly quarters in what once was a chicken coop and later a biker bar.

FOR MORE INFORMATION: Contact the **Loudoun Tourist Council** at 800-752-6118 or *www.visitloudoun.org*, or call the **Middleburg Visitor Information Center** at 540-687-8888.

ALONG THE UPPER POTOMAC

Soaking It Up
In Berkeley Springs, W. Va.

By Roger Piantadosi

FIVE HUNDRED YEARS ago, they say, Native Americans came from as far away as Canada to soak in the "medicine waters" that still flow from the ground in Berkeley Springs State Park. I journeyed only two hours to this spot, with its 2,000 gallons a minute of 74.3-degree water bubbling out of the native sandstone, but it seemed like light years from Washington.

In one of the 13 private baths in this hospitable park, among the antique shops, holistic emporiums, amiable restaurants, sand mines and tire factories of not-quite-beautiful downtown Berkeley Springs, I soaked quietly in 750 gallons of heated, 102-degree mineral water. My $60 check to the state of West Virginia bought me not only 15 minutes in the baths but a subsequent hour of full-body massage.

It's no accident that so many city folk come to this corner of West Virginia to soak away—or ski, swim, hunt, fish or hike away—their hard-won urban crusts. If there's one thing West Virginians know a lot about, it's recovery. The state itself has spent the last half century recovering—from timber companies that carted off most of its towering oaks, hickories and chestnuts and from mining firms that extracted so much coal that some West Virginians grew up thinking that the natural color of creek water was black.

West Virginia's modern recovery began when the state began buying park lands in the 1930s—bleak, clear-cut mountain moonscapes went for less than a dollar an acre back then—and developing them with the aid of some public officials its voters helped send to Washington. Through World War II, thousands of workers from President Roosevelt's Civilian Conservation Corps built the dams, cabins, lodges, roads, bridges and trails that remain the foundation of the state's extensive state park system.

From the worn-smooth oak porch of one of the CCC-built log cabins in Cacapon Resort State Park, about nine miles south of town, you can see all this for yourself. At the bottom of this eastern slope of 2,300-foot Cacapon Mountain is the CCC's stone-core dam and the lake it spawned, circled by a beach. Beyond that, shady picnic areas sprawl where once the men and boys of the CCC bunked in simple barracks.

In the distance, the dark bulk of Sleepy Creek Mountain lurks between the relatively slim trunks of this second-growth forest—the naturalist's term for the young hardwoods (and, on this slope, dogwood, redbud and mountain laurel) that have replaced their slashed and burned predecessors. On a three- to four-hour hike through Cacapon's long sliver of 6,115-acres, stretching from the West Virginia line to a high point overlooking the Potomac and Maryland beyond to the north, you may encounter the occasional blackened trunk of a primeval oak.

Cacapon is favored by golfers and families—the former for the public course that's below the 49-room main lodge, the latter for the park's modestly priced cabins. But any visitor who pays attention will find clues throughout Cacapon to a distinctively dogged West Virginia spirit. On the practice green near the lodge, for instance, 47-year-old assistant superintendent Tom Ambrose, who grew up at Cacapon (his father worked here, too), points to the unlikely stone chimney rising from one end of the putting oval. "We maintain that as a reminder," he says with a smile, describing the farmhouse it once adjoined, "of what came before."

From the gazebo at Berkeley Springs State Park, you might want to turn your back on the 18-wheelers on Route 522 and look west. You have to crane your neck as your eyes follow the sharp rise of Warm Springs Ridge. When Sam Ashelman stayed in town around Easter 1961, he couldn't see past the ridge either—but he did see an ad for a 1,200-acre estate tucked in a small valley on the other side. On a whim, he drove up to see it.

"I thought it was just great, and I made a ridiculously low offer for it, half what they were asking," says Ashelman. "They accepted it."

Former economist Ashelman, now in his mid-80s, is still running what he made of that estate, Coolfont Resort, with his wife Martha, 70, who joined both him and his homey, family-oriented spa in 1977. Together, Martha and Sam have made the best of Berkeley Springs' urban proximity by offering workaholic city folk two decent choices. You can come out to stop working and be pampered (or to be fed healthy food and organized exercise) in the fully equipped, 14,000-square-foot Spectrum Spa. Or you can come out and *keep* working: Coolfont's large conference center has all the standard equipment, plus glass doors and windows that open onto a serene mountain lakefront.

Coolfont guests have a choice of the main lodge, log cabins, modern chalets (many with hot tubs, few televisions) that dot the surrounding slopes or one of the private vacation homes built by the Ashelmans on Coolfont land. Reflecting the Ashelmans' own interests in the global economy and environment (their solar-heated and -cooled spa has won two national energy awards), guests and conference attendees tend toward a similar axis. Martha's been quoted as saying Democrats stay at Coolfont while Republicans head for the more polished Greenbrier; one of the resort's best known guests in recent years, in fact, was Vice President Al Gore.

"We've always wanted to make this more of an international thinking, discussing center," says Martha, sitting with Sam in the Treetop Restaurant. "The first AIDS report was written here," Sam adds. "And the United Nations' first report on the ozone and global warming . . ." And, well, a glance around the room, with its treetop-level view of the lake, reveals a surprising number of discussions—earnest, alarmingly Washington-like—taking place all around.

GETTING THERE: From the Beltway, take I-270 north to I-70 west to Exit 1B (Hancock, Md.) and follow Route 522 south across the Potomac into town. For Coolfont, turn right on Route 9 west and take it over the ridge to a left on Cold Run Valley Road. The resort is four miles down.

BEING THERE: Berkeley Springs State Park (304-258-2711 or 800-225-5982) is the center of town, geographically and historically. It sits on four acres amid the town's restaurants and fine Victorian homes (a few of which are small B&Bs) and several antique and crafts emporiums, including the **Curiosity Shop** (304-258-8019), **Mountain Laurel Crafts** (304-258-1919) and **Berkeley Springs Antique Mall** (304-258-5676 ♿). The park has an outdoor pool plus (quieter, more expensive and worth every penny) mineral baths, Roman baths, steam cabinets and massages in the adjacent Depression-era bathhouses, which are clean, politely staffed and just begging to be the setting for a John Grisham mystery. A 15-minute bath and one-hour massage is $60 on weekends (bath with half-hour massage, $35); reservations are taken up to a month in advance. There's also an open-air market here Saturday mornings, April through November. The privately owned **Bath House Massage and Health Center** offers indoor and outdoor hot tubs and several types of massages nearby at 110-114 Fairfax St. (304-258-9071 or 800-431-4698), and the Country Inn's **Renaissance Spa** has similar services (see WHERE TO STAY/EAT below). **Cacapon Resort State Park**—on U.S. 522 about nine miles south of town (800-225-5982)—has an 18-hole golf course, a lake with swimming, fishing and rowboat and paddleboat rentals, hiking trails, horseback riding and year-round nature programs, plus cabins and a lodge (see WHERE TO STAY/EAT below). The **Homeopathy Works** (304-258-2541) makes and sells homeopathic medications and features antique pill-making equipment and homeopathic displays. Overlooking the state park is **Berkeley Castle** (800-896-4001), a stone castle built in 1885 by Col. Samuel Taylor as a wedding present for his bride, Rosa Pelham. You can giggle at this unlikely scale model of an English castle, but you'll settle down when you realize that you can see four states from atop the three-story turret. In town, you'll also find a great old 1940s movie palace in the **STAR Theatre** (304-258-1404), whose first-run films are $3 (with a reservation and 50 cents extra, you can watch the movie from an overstuffed sofa). The **Morgan Arts Council** also sponsors events worth noting at the **Ice House** community center (304-258-2300). West of town on one of the sharp curves of Route 9 (about 20 minutes from downtown), there's a peerless scenic overlook—especially around sunset or during a thunderstorm—of the Potomac and Great Cacapon valleys at **Prospect Peak**, which looks out onto West Virginia, Maryland and Pennsylvania.

WHERE TO STAY/EAT: Coolfont Resort and Conference Center (800-888-8768 or *www.coolfont.com)* has spa packages starting at $315 for two nights (per person, double occupancy, midweek). The resort shares a border with Cacapon State Park, where guests can eat, play golf, hike and ride horses, and most rates include buffet breakfast and dinner. Non-package room rates range from the rustic Woodland House Lodge (doubles $210 on the weekend) to log cabins and small chalets ($240) to Alpine Village Chalets, with double Jacuzzis for each bedroom ($260). The resort's **Treetop Restaurant** has a rotating and health-conscious buffet available nightly. Two centrally located and nicely restored B&Bs hereabouts are the four-room **Manor Inn** (304-258-1552; doubles $85-$130) and the 10-room **Highlawn Inn** (304-258-5700; doubles $85-$195, including breakfast), two of which are honeymoon suites with double whirlpool tubs. At **Cacapon State Park** (see BEING THERE on previous page), the 49-room main lodge (doubles about $60 and up Memorial Day through Labor Day) is easier to book than the 30 rustic-to-modern cabins (single nights available only in off-season, from $65 to $108 &); in season, one- and two-week cabin rentals need to be reserved as much as a year in advance. Next door to the downtown baths, the 70-room **Country Inn** (800-822-6630 &) offers a Spa Get-Away Weekend at $420 a couple, including meals, massages and mineral baths, and standard double rates that start at $96. Nearby, **Tari's Cafe** (304-258-1196 &) is always worth a stop for its friendly atmosphere and innovative menu (it also has four upstairs guest rooms to rent, doubles from $53), and distinctive Italian sandwiches and take-out are to be found at **La Fonte** (304-258-1357). If you forgot to bring a picnic lunch up to Prospect Peak, the **Panorama Steak House** (304-258-9370, closed Mondays) is right there and can usually find you a filet-laden table with the same view.

FOR MORE INFORMATION: Contact **West Virginia Tourism** at 800-CALL-WVA (that's 800-225-5982). You also can call up *www.state.wv.us/tourism*, or **Travel Berkeley Springs** at 800-447-8797 or *www.berkeleysprings.com*.

MARTINSBURG, W.VA.

Martinsburg is one of those towns that's "near" a better-known place but rarely near enough for travelers to make the short side trip. But the town—with its streets of 18th and 19th Century homes and buildings complemented by a huge outlet mall and a growing number of antique shops—is a destination worth seeing. Its history is one of textile mills and rail lines—the latter a mixed blessing. The railroad brought a century of prosperity but also war and labor strife. Stonewall Jackson's troops burned most of the B&O buildings here in 1861, and a local work stoppage by railway workers exploded into the Great Railroad Strike of 1877, the first nationwide labor walkout. While the strike

eventually was crushed by federal troops, it sowed the seeds of America's national labor movement. Homes here reflect almost every architectural style, from late Colonial stone houses to Greek Revival, from Queen Anne to High Victorian Gothic. Start a visit at the 165-year-old **Boarman House** (208 S. Queen St.), home to the **Martinsburg-Berkeley County Convention & Visitors Bureau** (304-264-8801 ⟂), which has free brochures and maps of the region. The Boarman House also is home to the **Boarman Arts Center** (304-263-0224), which exhibits works by area artists. It's a short walk from here to the golden-domed, antebellum **Berkeley County Courthouse** (304-267-3000 ⟂) and the **Gen. Adam Stephen House** (304-267-4434; closed weekdays), a stately, native-limestone home built by the Revolutionary War general and city founder sometime between 1774 and 1789. Facing the Stephen House is the **Triple Brick Museum** (304-267-4434), in a three-story red brick home built in 1784; the museum displays early surveying equipment and railroad artifacts. The **B&O Railroad Depot**, built to replace the building burned by Stonewall Jackson, has been restored, and though the town's many textile mills are now closed, some of the turn-of-the-century brick buildings have acquired new lives as antique or outlet centers. The **Blue Ridge Outlet Center** (800-445-3993 ⟂) houses more than 50 name-brand stores (Polo/Ralph Lauren, Tommy Hilfiger, Nautica, Levi's, Dress Barn, Britches Great Outdoors and such). Nearby is **Olde Kilbourn Mill**, a seven-acre complex with scores of antique vendors, a crafters gallery and other diversions (304-263-2900). Martinsburg's 85-year-old **Apollo Civic Theater** (304-263-6766), which offers musicals and plays, was the work of the same architect who designed Washington's legendary Knickerbocker Theater, which collapsed after a blizzard in 1922.

GETTING THERE: Martinsburg is just over 90 minutes from the Beltway. Take I-270 to I-70 west to I-81 south or, from Virginia, follow Route 7 west to Route 9 west to the town.

WHERE TO STAY/EAT: Boydville (304-263-1448; doubles $100-$125 with breakfast) is a six-room B&B on 10 heavily shaded acres, and features wallpa-

Antietam

MANY LIVES, LITTLE GAIN

THE EPIC BATTLE near Antietam Creek at Sharpsburg, Md., marked the high point of Robert E. Lee's first attempt to carry the war into the North. After his great victory at the second battle of Manassas in August 1862, Lee had marched his army into Maryland. Union Gen. George B. McClellan and the Army of the Potomac followed. When two Union soldiers happened upon a copy of Lee's battle plan that had been used to wrap three cigars, which had been left behind when the Rebels broke camp, McClellan wrote President Lincoln: "I have the plans of the rebels, and will catch them in their own trap. Will send you trophies."

But McClellan, perhaps the most cautious Civil War general, never sprang the trap. Instead of attacking—historians say he could have destroyed Lee's army and all but ended the war—he hesitated, over-estimating the size of Lee's force. By September 17, the two great armies faced each other in the gently rolling woods and farmland east of Sharpsburg.

The conflict unfolded in three stages throughout the day over the 12-square-mile battlefield. Strategic ground was taken, lost, retaken and lost again by both sides. In a now-famous dispatch, Union Gen. Joseph Hooker reported: "In the time I am writing, every stalk of corn in the northern and greater part of the field was cut as closely as could have been done with a knife, and the slain lay in rows precisely as they had stood in their ranks a few moments before." When the sun set, more than 23,000 men were dead, wounded or missing in action, and the two armies were positioned almost exactly as they had been before the battle. The Civil War would drag on for another three years.

Unlike Gettysburg (which has a McDonald's on the battlefield) or Manassas (which is hemmed in by housing developments), Antietam

per that was hand-painted in England in 1812, French chandeliers and two-foot-thick stone walls. A short walk from the Blue Ridge Outlet Center is the two-room Victorian **The Pulpit & Palette B&B** (304-263-7012; doubles start at $80), whose odd name is descriptive of owners Bill and Janet Starr—he's a retired minister and she's an artist. Several national motel chains also are in Martinsburg, near one or the other of the I-81 interchanges. As for

still looks pretty much as it did at the time of the conflict. Some of the families that farmed the area then—the Mummas, Roulettes and Poffenbergers—are still here, still farming. At the somber stone Visitors Center, the only food you can buy is a sample of hardtack biscuit that carries a warning that broken teeth are not the baker's responsibility.

Post contributor Bill Heavey and his wife, Jane, rented a cassette tape to guide them along an 11-stop driving tour of the battlefield, but they quickly found themselves overwhelmed by the many attacks and counterattacks in places like the Cornfield, the Sunken Road, Burnside Bridge and the North Woods. Everywhere there were iron tablets, cannons buried muzzle-first where generals had fallen, marble soldiers on pedestals, sabers aloft as if to battle the clouds. Contrasting with this was the earth itself, some of it seeded with corn or soybeans, some just wet and brown, bordered here and there by split rail fences. They found it hard to make the two match up, hard to grasp the scope of what happened here. But if you stand long enough, you're likely to see something like they did.

A man drove up in a little white car with Ohio plates as they were parked at the Sunken Road, known after the battle as Bloody Lane for the 5,000 men killed or wounded there in less than four hours. He got out and stretched. He was about 50, a strong-looking guy with white hair and clear blue eyes and the ruddy color of someone who works outdoors for a living. He walked to the edge of the fence, moving from plaque to plaque until he found the one he was looking for. He stopped and stared out across the land for a few minutes. Finally, he tucked his chin into his chest and bowed his head for a few moments. They met the man as he was walking back to his car. He bobbed his head and smiled, blinking hard. "Beautiful day," he said.

GETTING/BEING THERE: Antietam National Battlefield (301-432-5124) is less than two hours from the Beltway. Take I-270 north to I-70 west to Exit 29 (Route 65). Follow that south 10 miles. The Visitors Center is open 8:30 a.m. to 6 p.m. daily; admission is $2 per person, $4 per family, and includes a battlefield map. Besides the half-hour Visitors Center movie and tour tapes for rent, rangers conduct walks, talks and demonstrations daily, Memorial Day through Labor Day. For places to stay and eat, see Sʜᴇᴘʜᴇʀᴅsᴛᴏᴡɴ on next page.

cateries, the **Peppermill Gourmet Grille** (304-263-3986 ♿) offers American cuisine, and the **Historic Market Street Grill** (304-263-7615 ♿) features Cajun dishes. For more options, see BERKELEY SPRINGS, page 106, and SHEPHERDSTOWN, below.

FOR MORE INFORMATION: Contact the **Martinsburg-Berkeley County Convention & Visitors Bureau** at 800-498-2386 or 304-264-8801. Web site: *www.travelwv.com.*

SHEPHERDSTOWN, W.VA.

"Endearing" is a good word for Shepherdstown, a place of considerable but low-key charm. It's not a "destination" sort of place. There are no outlets, no sites of major historical events, no Civil War battlefield. But there are some excellent places to sleep and eat before and after visiting such other nearby places. Shepherdstown's streets are lined with 18th and 19th Century buildings, a 1909 movie theater called the Opera House, a library that was once the Order of Odd Fellows' hall, an 18th Century gristmill with a 40-foot wheel that operated until 1939 (sorry, it's now a private home), and a monument to James Rumsey, the man who really invented the steamboat before that Fulton guy stole all the credit. Shepherdstown is determined to right the historical wrong done Rumsey, possibly because he made his successful trial run (in 1787) a few hundred feet upriver. A museum contains a scale model of his boat—a little thing, about the size of a modern motorboat. There's also an impressive-looking monument erected in 1915 on a cliff overlooking the Potomac: a globe atop an Ionic column in a pleasant, park-like setting less than a half-mile walk from the center of town. On the way into town on Route 230, you can rent a bike ($7 for three hours) at **O'Hurley's General Store** (304-876-6907), which also carries handmade wooden toys, pottery and cast-iron goods. Downtown are a number of small galleries, between which you can catch an espresso at the **Uptown Cafe** (304/876-2111) or the **Lost Dog** (304-876-0871 ♿). The **Historic Shepherdstown Museum** (304-876-0910) displays exhibits and artifacts relating to Thomas Shepherd's founding of the town and offers guided walking tours of the historic sites, which include, on the edge of town, the **Christ Reformed Church** and its yard full of 18th Century graves. The original settlers in the area came from German immigrant communities up north, and their simple headstones are inscribed in an angular and condensed German script that fills the tablets, looking more like ancient monuments than Revolutionary War relics.

GETTING THERE: Shepherdstown is 1.5 to 2 hours from the Beltway. Take I-270 west to U.S. 340 south. After crossing the Potomac, turn north on Route 230, a winding, hilly, sparsely populated road that goes directly into downtown. If you prefer Civil War scenery, small towns and roadside antique shops, take I-270 instead to I-70 west to U.S. Alternate 40 west (at Braddock Heights, exit 49). In Boonsboro, turn left on Route 34 south, which will pass through Antietam National Battlefield and Sharpsburg before crossing the Potomac (where it becomes Route 480).

WHERE TO STAY: The **Thomas Shepherd Inn** (304-876-3715; doubles $85-$135), built in 1868 and once a Lutheran parsonage, is a stately, Federal-style row house that offers seven rooms with private baths and a superb breakfast (locally made sage sausage, chilled spiced pears and chestnut soup have been among the offerings). The four-diamond AAA and four-star Mobil **Bavarian Inn** (304-876-2551; doubles $85-$250 ♿) has 73 rooms (some with Potomac views) and the full-service **Bavarian Inn Restaurant**. The **Little Inn** (304-876-2208; doubles $75-$85) actually is just two rooms, with private baths and 11-foot ceilings, above the restaurant in the Yellow Brick Bank (see WHERE TO EAT). And the **Mecklenburg Inn** (304-876-2126; doubles $55) has two rooms that share a bath in an updated Revolutionary War-era building with a bar downstairs featuring live music Tuesdays and Saturdays. Nearby are also some interesting B&Bs, including **Piper House** (301-797-1862; doubles $85-$95, including breakfast), which is smack in the middle of the Antietam National Battlefield. Regina and Lou Clark, who run the frame-and-log farmhouse, think it's the only B&B in America where you can sleep on a Civil War battlefield in a structure that not only was standing during the conflict but also briefly played a role in the fighting. Confederate Gen. James Longstreet commandeered it for his headquarters, and both sides used it as a hospital. (This distinction helped earn the place a Travel Holiday magazine's Insider's Award for 1997, and during Civil War high season, April through October, the three-bedroom inn is a favorite with visiting historians, Civil War buffs and re-enactors.)

WHERE TO EAT: The **Bavarian Inn** (see WHERE TO STAY) serves German cuisine. The **Old Pharmacy Cafe and Soda Fountain** (304-876-2085) serves up entrees like pecan catfish and pie made from local peaches. One of its walls is still lined with old darkwood pharmacy cabinets, and the soda fountain bar is a slab of white marble. The ceiling, like many of the ceilings in town, is pressed tin, this one painted a dark green. For sandwiches, there's the **Town Run Deli,** which stands over the Town Run, the stream that courses through Shepherdstown; the deli advertises itself with the slogan "A Run Runs Under It." The high-end restaurant in town is the **Yellow Brick Bank** (304-876-2208 ♿), housed in an ornate building of ordinary, sandy-colored brick. (Yellow brick turned out to be either unaffordable or unavailable when the bank went up in the 19th Century, but the builder's ambition lives on in the name.) Inside are high-ceilinged dining rooms where you can eat corn chowder and inventively prepared meat, poultry, fish and pasta. Also check out the Cuban coffee creme brulee, a concoction that by itself should be enough to put Shepherdstown on the Must Eat Here map. It should be noted, however, that others have been less enamored of this restaurant, complaining particularly of poor service.

FOR MORE INFORMATION: Contact the **Shepherdstown Visitors Center** at 304-876-2786 or *www.intrepid.net/traveler,* or call up the **Martinsburg-Berkeley County Convention & Visitors Bureau** at 800-498-2386 or *www.travelwv.com.*

HARPERS FERRY, W.VA.

On a moonless night in October of 1859, the Provisional Army of the United States—14 whites and five blacks led by abolitionist John Brown—made its way down a winding Maryland road and crossed the covered wagon bridge adjacent to the B&O railroad. The men concealed their weapons under heavy gray shawls. The objective in their silent advance: to capture the United States Armory and Arsenal and incite a rebellion to free the slaves of Virginia (whose subsequent division into two states would be the only permanent change to the U.S. map caused by the Civil War). Initially, all went as planned, but as day dawned and the townspeople became aware of the armory's capture, confusion led to chaos and bloodshed. Shots were fired. Local militia began to arrive and, woefully outnumbered, John Brown retreated into the town fire station with hostages. The mayor, mistaken for a sharpshooter, was killed, as was a local businessman and two raiders sent out to negotiate an escape. By the time a trainload of U.S. Marines arrived—under the command of Lt. Col. Robert E. Lee—the crowd was vengeful, and many were drunk. Battering the fire station door with sledgehammers and a large ladder, the Marines brought the invasion to a conclusion in a matter of minutes. John Brown was beaten into unconsciousness and later was hanged at Charles Town for treason, murder and inciting slaves to rebellion.

Congress set aside 1,500 acres in 1944 for a monument to Brown's abortive raid and to the repeated skirmishes between Confederate and Union forces that followed for control of Harper's Ferry. The Confederacy considered the town—where both the rushing Shenandoah and powerful Potomac rivers meet the Blue Ridge Mountains—a crucial gateway to Washington. In 1963 the monument became **Harpers Ferry National Historical Park** (304-535-6298), and today's popular 2,200-acre park is surely one of the most evocative and stirring sites administered by National Park Service rangers and guides. In the restored 19th Century Lower Town, reached via shuttle bus from the park's Visitors Center on U.S. 340, are more than a dozen restored houses and buildings. In town, hikers can walk to **Jefferson's Rock**, from which Thomas Jefferson once pronounced the view "one of the most stupendous scenes in nature," or they can venture across the Potomac River bridge to the **C&O Canal towpath** or the **Appalachian Trail. Ghost Tours** (304-725-8019) is a popular company in a town truly haunted by historical events, and gift-shopping in Harpers Ferry is always a treat. The **Herb Lady** (304-535-6570) offers handmade potpourri and wonderful soap. Check out **Molly the Rebel** (304-535-2217) for flowers, garden items, antiques and West Virginia folk crafts, plus **Westwind Potters** (304-535-2511).

The abundant moving waters of Harpers Ferry also are known to support many underwater creatures and, more obviously, the gear-laden bipeds who follow them around. For a good shot at spring's trout and summer's and fall's elusive smallmouth bass, check with guide **Mark Kovach** (301-588-8742), a former K Street professional based in Silver Spring, Md., who has developed a boat for the demands of the shallow but fast-moving waters here. It's a 14-foot inflatable raft with 10-foot oars, aluminum decks and two swivel seats that let you cover the water like an artillery officer laying down fields of fire. Kovach is a burly fellow with a walrus-like mustache and a collapsing cowboy hat that competes with his raft in its array of dangling attachments. He also is arguably the Potomac's most famous fishing guide, a man expert in delivering customers through hurtling Class III rapids while narrating the history of the area and pointing out spots where smallmouth bass congregate. Kovach's trips on the Potomac near Harpers Ferry—which usually aren't whitewater runs—go on April through November and cost $350 for two people. If you don't have your own fishing gear, Kovach will supply it for $10 a person. You also may need a Maryland fishing license, which usually is available at **River and Trail Outfitters** just down river in Knoxville, Md., (301-695-5177 or *www.rivertrail.com*), a well-regarded supplier of gear and guides for hikes or trips on whitewater rafts, canoes, inner tubes and cross-country skis on and around the upper Potomac and lower Shenandoah.

GETTING THERE: Harpers Ferry is a 55-mile, 75-minute drive from the Beltway. Take I-270 to Frederick, then I-70 west for less than a mile to the first exit (Exit 52). There, follow Route 340 south for 16 miles. MARC trains (800-325-7245) run out to Harpers Ferry each evening.

WHERE TO STAY: Lots of visitors to the historic park stay in nearby Shepherdstown or somewhere between here and Frederick, Md., but Harpers Ferry itself has a few interesting choices. Worn but homey **Hilltop House** (800-338-8319 &) has traditional rooms for two for $70 a night on weekends. **Between the Rivers B&B** (304-535-2768; doubles $85-$95) was built in the 1890s, and its front porch and Balcony Room offer peerless views across the Potomac and the mountains. Breakfasts here include homemade breads and muffins, fresh fruit and quiche, and it's just two blocks to the magnificent Shenandoah overlook. The **Cliffside Inn** (304-535-6302; doubles $60-$76 &) has a dining room and woodland views near the Park Service parking area, with shuttles into the Lower Town. The **Harpers Ferry American Youth Hostel** (301-834-7652; $13 members, $16 non-members) is just down river near Knoxville, Md., where the C&O Canal meets the 2,100-mile Appalachian Trail, the longest continually marked footpath in the world. (This is one of several American Youth Hostels that have been turned into "sustainable living centers" through the installation of water-saving devices, insulation, energy-efficient fluorescent lighting, recycling and composting programs and use of environmentally friendly cleaning products.) There's also a 50-room **Comfort Inn** (304-535-6391; doubles start at $65 &) on U.S. 340 at Union Street.

WHERE TO EAT: The food at historic **Hilltop House** (see WHERE TO STAY) ranges from ho-hum to nearly as excellent as the view. The **Mountain House Cafe** (304-535-2339) on High Street has a lovely outdoor patio. Across the street, the **Garden of Food** (304-535-2202 &) features live folk music on warm-weather weekends, a back bar that sells only microbrews and a spirited menu of local specialties and wines.

FOR MORE INFORMATION: Contact the **Harpers Ferry Visitor Center** at 304-535-6298 or *www.nps.gov/hafe,* or the **Jefferson County Chamber of Commerce** at 304-725-2055.

WILDER WEST VIRGINIA

Higher Learning Atop North Fork Mountain

By Bill Heavey

TELL YOUR FRIENDS you're headed to West Virginia for the weekend and you'll notice a verbal-facial disconnect. While they may remark, "Oh, that's nice," their look says: You *really* think that's a good idea? Actually, it's a heckuva good idea. West Virginia is the anti-Washington: a place where people have four-wheel-drive because they need it to get to work, where you haven't had breakfast if it didn't include bacon, and where folks pat you on the arm, as if to say nobody's perfect, when you tell them you're from the nation's capital.

Hiking up a mossy, rocky path to the trail that runs the length of North Fork Mountain, my wife, Jane, and I experience another disconnect. We're puffing uphill through a forest of maple, oak and laurel, but what's ahead sounds like the West Virginia National Seashore, something gathering itself and then surging like surf. Suddenly, we're on a spectacular sandstone outcropping looking far across a deep valley at a succession of ridges and peaks stretching into infinity. The wind blows so hard it makes my eyes tear up and my trousers flap. Even the vultures riding the updrafts above the cliffs look a bit unsure of themselves, as if they remember how they got up here but aren't so sure about getting down. Drop a stone here and it might roll until it plunked into the North Fork of the South Branch of the Potomac, 2,000 vertical feet below.

I check my "Monongahela National Forest Hiking Guide" for the North Fork Mountain Trail. Its difficulty is rated as moderate, its trail condition good, its scenery exceptional. And there's not a soul in sight.

We got here by dumb luck, after booking a night in one of the 49 log cabins that Jerry Hedrick built near Smoke Hole Caverns. (We splurged on a honeymoon cabin: heart-shaped Jacuzzi, fireplace, front and back porches, full kitchen for $110 a night.) Our original destination was Dolly Sods, the famous upland bogs nearby that are like a piece of Canada that migrated south. It's late March, meaning snow is still likely there, so the gate to the road through the sods is still closed. It was Jerry, a hillbilly with a master's degree in business administration, who directed us to North Fork Mountain, 24 miles of some of the best walking in this part of the country. He suggested that we do a seven-mile loop: Park at Landis Trail, hike up to the ridge trail, then descend back to the road on Redman Trail and hitchhike back to the car.

"Hitchhike?" I asked. "Is that, you know, okay?"

"Sure," he said. "Anybody'll pick you up, long as you don't look like a convict or something."

It's an overcast day, but every so often an arrow of sun illuminates a patch of mountain against the purple ridges. Two hours into the hike, I'm able to determine—after a lengthy computation involving compass, topographic map and watch—that I'm really hungry. Jane and I snuggle into a grassy spot behind a rock and break out cheese, apples and pita bread. For dessert, we have a chocolate bar that turns out to contain equal amounts of dark chocolate and ground espresso beans. It's gritty, sweet and has the effect of attaching jumper cables to your legs. "C'mon, babe," I tell Jane as we shoulder our daypacks. "If we miss the cutoff we'll just walk the whole dang trail."

The path runs mostly just below the ridgeline through wild azaleas and rhododendron, with spurs to the better overlooks. One spur leads to a honeycombed sandstone wall about 40 feet high. Another ends at a little hunk of rock that looks like a sacrificial altar. These are old places, known to the Seneca and Shawneee for centuries before settlers showed up in the 1700s. About 4 o'clock we hit the turnoff for Redman's Run and turn left, back to the road. On the way down, we hear crashing sounds in the brush and can just make out the flags of two whitetail deer as they bound out of sight.

Sure enough, the first vehicle to pass stops to let us in. Its occupants are three guys in chest waders who've been fishing for trout and are now firing up cigars to celebrate. One is getting a degree in geology and tells us of the 1989 "debris flow" that happened near here. A debris flow is when the mountain simply sloughs off the top layer of rock, dirt and trees and sends it down the mountain at 60 mph, leveling everything in its path. "These mountains here," he says, shaking his head, "make a man feel like a little bitty speck."

GETTING THERE: Plan on three hours driving time to cover the 170 miles to the trail. Take I-66 west to I-81 south to Exit 74, and pick up Route 55 west. After passing through Petersburg and the tiny town of Cabins, turn left at the sign for Big Bend and Smoke Hole and take the bridge across the river. The first trail head (three-quarters of a mile up the road) is **North Fork Mountain Trail. Landis Trail** is another two miles or so. (For North Fork Mountain, you should have the U.S. Geological Survey "quad" maps for Hopeville and Petersburg West. To include the **Dolly Sods Area** as well, get the adjoining maps, Blackbird Knob and Blackwater Falls. All are available at REI and most Hudson Trail Outfitters in the area. Or call the USGS at 703-648-6892. "Monongahela National Forest Hiking Guide" is the area hiking bible, usually also in stock at REI and Hudson Trail Outfitters.

BEING THERE: Once a paradise for spruce- and hardwood-hungry timber companies, most of West Virginia's 901,000 acre **Monongahela National Forest** (304-636-1800) is—in its second-growth prime—enjoying a second life. Mostly now it is an outdoor recreation nirvana for skiers, hikers, mountain bikers, fishermen, hunters and fresh-air fans from Ohio to the Chesapeake and New York to North Carolina. The forest's northern **Potomac Ranger District** (304-257-4488), its most easily reached section from Washington, includes all of Canaan Valley and the Dolly Sods Wilderness (see the AROUND THE CANAAN VALLEY section, below.) as well as **Spruce Knob** (at 4,862 feet the highest point in West Virginia) and the better-known sheer sandstone face of 1,000-foot **Seneca Rocks**, a must stop on every serious rock-climber's East Coast itinerary. (If it's on yours, contact the **Seneca Rocks Climbing School** at 800-548-0108, **Seneca Rocks Mountain Guides** at 800-451-5108 or the **Blackwater Outdoor Center** in Davis at 800-328-4798. The last outfit also can equip or shuttle paddlers, rafters and fishermen on the Cheat and North Fork rivers.) If climbing sheer Tuscarora sandstone is not your bag, you can use the telescopes at the **Seneca Rocks Visitor Center** to watch, or bring your own binoculars and have a pizza across the highway on the front porch of the **Front Porch** restaurant (304-567-2555). Ninety-minute trail rides to Seneca Rocks are available three times a day, from about Easter through Thanksgiving, at **Yokum's** (304-567-2351), which also has two campgrounds and a motel scattered about its significant acreage here. **Smoke Hole Caverns** (800-828-8478) offers year-round guided tours of its 225-million-year-old caverns, which were used by the Senecas as shelter and to smoke and store game, and by both Union and Confederate troops as an ammunition depot and later as a safe place to make moonshine.

WHERE TO STAY/EAT: Besides the cave tours and gift shop, Hedrick's **Smoke Hole Caverns** (800-828-8478) offers a range of accommodations (40 motel rooms; 23 "family" cottages with two bedrooms and a loft; 32 "honeymoon" cabins with Jacuzzi and fireplace) that are quite reasonable, ranging from $45 to $130 a night on weekends. The **North Fork Mountain Inn** (304-257-1108; doubles start at $90, including a full breakfast) in nearby Cabins has six guest rooms and a larger guest house, all rooms with private baths (and a two-night minimum), some with whirlpools. In Seneca Rocks is the **4-U Restaurant** (304-567-2111), features homemade pies, breads and mashed potatoes. For more nearby options, see the following section, AROUND THE CANAAN VALLEY.

FOR MORE INFORMATION: Contact the **Potomac Highland Travel Council** at 304-636-8400 or **West Virginia Tourism** at 800-225-5982.

AROUND THE CANAAN VALLEY

The big attraction of West Virginia's Canaan Valley and the northeastern reaches of **Monongahela National Forest** (304-636-1800) is outdoor sports. In warm months that means climbing, hiking, canoeing, fishing, swimming, rafting, caving, mountain biking, golfing and trail riding. In fall it's most of the above plus hunting, and in winter downhill and cross-country skiing. There are few other places in the mid-Atlantic where you can conveniently take part in so many vigorous recreational activities—and in such an inviting, laid-back setting. About 15 miles long and three miles wide, **Canaan Valley** itself is a geographic anomaly. In a state that seems to consist of nothing but up and down, it's some of the flattest territory around, almost a plateau encased by mountain ridges, a topography that naturally enhances the sense of isolation. At 3,200 feet it's the highest "valley" this side of the Mississippi, and that altitude also makes Canaan (pronounced kuh-NANE by the locals) a natural snow bowl, averaging about 180 inches a year, twice what some parts of Vermont receive. Centrally located **Canaan Valley Resort State Park** (800-622-4121 ♿) sits on a hilltop surrounded by 6,000 acres of forest and fields. Its 250 modest but comfortable rooms, some with excellent views, are in a series of two-story, motel-like wings. Family-friendly facilities include an indoor pool, a heated outdoor pool, an 18-hole golf course, miniature golf and eight tennis courts. Miles of country roads around Canaan make it an appealing place to bicycle, and mountain bikers will find many challenging routes on former logging roads. Park cabins are rented only on a weekly basis in summer, but rooms that sleep up to four in the lodge cost about $85 a night on weekends. Just 15 miles away, a network of hiking trails and narrow but driveable gravel roads climb into the open, rugged landscape of the **Dolly Sods Wilderness Area**, a strange, windswept land of unusual rock formations, gnarled spruce trees and tundra-like plant life—the largest inland wetlands area in the United States. (In June and July, blueberries flourish in Dolly Sods' natural sphagnum bogs and chilly, Canada-like climate.)

The interconnected network of trails here also makes one of the best spots for wintertime Washingtonians to indulge their growing cross-country ski habit. Both Canaan Valley Resort and nearby **Timberline Four Seasons Resort** (800-766-9464; $375-$500 for two-bedroom condos midweek, three night minimum); have trails set aside for cross-country skiers (ski packages and mountain biking rentals available). **White Grass Ski Touring Center** (304-866-4114) has 36 miles of cross-country trails and daily lessons and rentals (lessons $10, rentals $15), as well as a homey lodge, a full ski shop and a natural-foods cafe. Cross-country skiing competes with sledding in wintertime at 1,700-acre **Blackwater Falls State Park** (304-259-5216; doubles $70 ♿), which has a 54-room lodge and 25 cabins (the cabins are by the week only from June through Labor Day), and is known in summer for its namesake falls cascading through a 60-foot gorge, its hiking, horseback and mountain-bike trails and swimming and boating in the lake.

GETTING THERE: The Canaan Valley is roughly four hours from the Beltway. Follow I-66 west to I-81 south and take the second exit to Route 55 west. Turn right on Route 32 north at Harman and follow the signs to Canaan or one of the other parks or resorts.

OTHER PLACES TO STAY/EAT: In Davis, the **Bright Morning Inn** (304-259-5119) has eight rooms with private baths that start at $60 double, and **Meyer House Bed and Breakfast** (304-259-5451; doubles $75, some rates including breakfast) has five rooms in a restored 1860 Victorian home. The

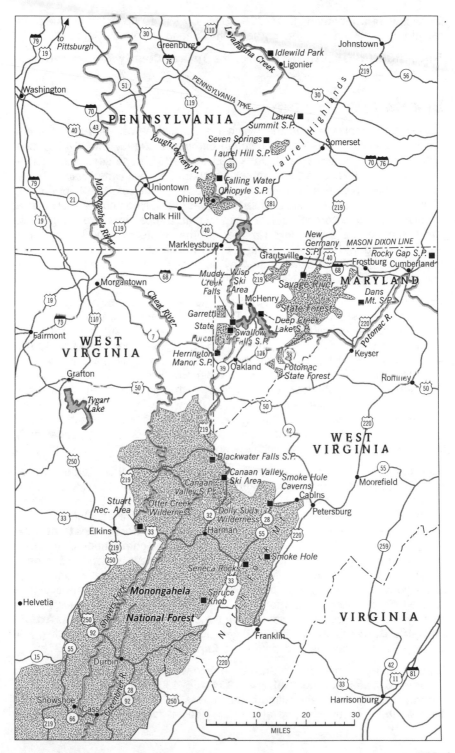

79 to Pittsburgh
19
30 Greenburg
110
Loyalhanna Creek
Idlewild Park
Ligonier
Johnstown
219
56
76
Washington
51
PENNSYLVANIA TPKE.
30
Laurel Highlands
219
70
43
119 PENNSYLVANIA
Laurel Summit S.P.
Seven Springs
Somerset
70 76
40
381
Laurel Hill S.P.
Youghiogheny R.
79
21
Uniontown
Falling Water
Ohiopyle S.P.
281
219
Monongahela River
19
119
Chalk Hill
Ohiopyle
40
New Germany S.P.
MASON DIXON LINE
Markleysburg
Grantsville
Rocky Gap S.P.
68
40 Frostburg Cumberland
68
19
Morgantown
Muddy Creek Falls
Wisp Ski Area
219
Savage River State Forest
MARYLAND
Dans Mt. S.P.
110
Cheat River
McHenry
79
7
Fairmont
Garrett State Forest
Deep Creek Lake S.P.
220
Potomac R.
WEST VIRGINIA
Swallow Falls S.P.
Herrington Manor S.P.
135
Keyser
Grafton
39
Oakland
28
Potomac State Forest
Romney
50
50
Tygart Lake
50
220
WEST VIRGINIA
219
42
250
Blackwater Falls S.P.
55
219
Canaan Valley Ski Area
Smoke Hole Caverns
Monrefield
Canaan Valley S.P.
Cabins
Stuart Rec. Area
Otter Creek Wilderness
32
Dolly Sods Wilderness
28
Petersburg
33
Elkins
33
55
220
219
250
Smoke Hole
259
Helvetia
Seneca Rocks
Monongahela
33
VIRGINIA
Shavers Fork
National Forest
Spruce Knob
North Fork Mt.
250
92
Franklin
15
55
220
42
Durbin
81
11
Snowshoe
28
92
33
Harrisonburg
219
66
Cass
Greenbrier R.
250

0   10   20   30
MILES

119

Oriskany Inn restaurant (304-866-4514 ♿) serves up a thoughtful continental cuisine by candlelight, not far from Canaan Resort on Route 32.

FOR MORE INFORMATION: Contact the **Tucker County Tourist Information Center** at 800-782-2775.

ELKINS AND BEYOND

Like a lot of small towns in the Alleghenies, Elkins, W.Va., is a cool place—close to schools (the beautiful Victorian campus of **Davis and Elkins College**), shopping (antiques and crafts lead the list), historic sites and sublime trout streams. To a devoted weather watcher like *Post* writer Nancy Lewis, however, Elkins also has become an icon of actual coolness. She kept noticing that the temperature in Elkins consistently was 20 degrees cooler than that at Reagan National, a compelling fact when you are trapped in a sweltering Washington summer. So it was only a matter of time before she and her husband, Gene, checked into a small inn and spent a weekend taking in not just Elkins' temperatures—which are moderated by its nearly 2,000-foot altitude and its proximity to Monongahela National Forest—but also its small-town charms.

Elkins is dominated for six weeks in summer (and sustained the rest of the year) by activities of Davis and Elkins College. In the summer, the college hosts week-long classes in traditional crafts—from Zydeco rubboard to twig furniture construction to intensive clogging. These annual **Augusta Heritage Arts Workshops** (304-637-1209 or *www.augustaheritage.com*) culminate in the craft fairs, folk music, dance and storytelling performances of August's **Augusta Festival**. The metaphysical center of town is the large landscaped city park, with a Victorian-style bandstand and old-fashioned swings for the kids. During the five weeks leading up to the August festival, concerts are given here at least twice a week, with unscheduled jam sessions occurring almost daily. During the festival there are nightly performances.

Cool, entertaining summers, however, are not Elkins' only draw. As soon as the snow flies, cross-country skiers flock to town and nearby resorts in Monongahela National Forest (see WHERE TO STAY). Rounding out the seasons are festivals celebrating fiddling and trees and hikers and mountain bikers, the largest of which is probably September's annual **Mountain State Forest Festival** (304-636-1824), which has wood-chopping and sawing competitions, a parade and the crowning of a queen. Downtown Elkins has several good shops offering great bargains on crafts, at least compared with Washington price tags. Lewis bought a two-foot long birdhouse with a slate roof and a meticulously detailed checkerboard design for $65—a third, she says, of what such a creation would have cost in the city. Among the shops worth checking out: **Artists at Work Gallery** (304-637-6309), an aptly named local cooperative, and the handcrafted baskets and pottery of **Expressions** (304-636-5087).

South of Elkins on the road to Snowshoe (see WHERE TO STAY), the town of Cass is home to **Cass Scenic Railroad** (304-456-4300 ♿). This is an old-time, steam-powered, mountain railroad that makes daily runs to 4,842-foot Bald Knob during the summer and also offers special fall and spring trips, along with occasional dinner excursions. Reservations are required. Tickets include admission to the park's museums on logging and area wildlife. Also down this way is **Elk River Touring Center** (304-572-2771), one of the East Coast's most highly developed mountain-biking and cross-country skiing outfitter/guide centers. (Tour prices range from $240 for three days/two nights to $600 a person for week-long trips, including everything but equipment). The center's amenities also include a dozen lodging units and small communal restaurant (see WHERE TO STAY).

GETTING THERE: Elkins is about 200 miles from the Beltway (driving time: about five hours). Take I-66 west to I-81 south about four miles to the Strasburg exit. There, take Route 55 west into West Virginia for about 90 miles to U.S. 33 west into town.

WHERE TO STAY: In a hillside farmhouse built as a private home in 1939, **Tunnel Mountain Bed and Breakfast** (304-636-168; doubles $70) offers three comfortable rooms at the edge of the national forest, along with inn-keepers Anne and Paul Beardslee's useful advice and many publications on area activities. More upscale and pricier (but a definite possibility) is the **Graceland Inn and Conference Center,** (800-637-1600; doubles $118-$180 ♿), located in what was the Victorian mansion of coal and railroad baron Henry Gassaway Davis. The place is operated by future hoteliers—specifically, students from the college's Robert C. Byrd Center for Hospitality and Tourism. The inn's trappings are fitting, from a massive fireplace in the entrance to claw-foot bathtubs in some rooms. The adjacent motel-type conference center is less expensive (doubles $70). The **Cheat River Lodge** (304-636-2301; doubles $58-$63, cabins $146-$166) is a fine place to rent comfortable and spacious two- to four-bedroom deluxe cabins. Each includes a full kitchen and a hot tub and private deck, and some are right on the trout-stocked Cheat River, across from which are the national forest's Stuart Recreation Area and the birds, bears and deer of Otter Creek Wilderness. South of Elkins on 188 wooded acres outside Durbin is the **Cheat Mountain Club** (304-456-4627; doubles $160 to $330, including breakfast, lunch and dinner). Built a century ago on a fetching knoll some 3,700 feet up the side of Cheat Mountain as a private hunting club, the property remained testosterone- and cigar-friendly until the late 1980s. That's when the logging company that had used it as a private executive retreat sold it to a group of Charleston investors, who opened its 10 simple, clean rooms and cross-country trails (for walking, skiing and biking) to the rest of us. There's only one private bath in the stately, two-story, red-spruce lodge, but the communal bathrooms are vast and well-kept, and unless you're fogged in or snowed under (there are two fireplaces and a large library for such days), what are you doing indoors, anyway? Nearby activities include hiking (one trail leads the entire 18 miles south to Bald Knob), and trout fishing at the Shavers Fork River, which winds through two miles of club property. The river is stocked with rainbow, brown and brook trout. The Greenbrier River, also nearby, has trout as well as smallmouth bass. The inn provides fishing gear to guests for no charge, as well as bikes and cross-country skiing equipment. A bit farther south is the **Snowshoe/Silver Creek Mountain Resort** (304-572-4000 ♿), the largest ski resort in the

THE WEST VIRGINIA ALPS

IN 1869, a small party of Swiss immigrants arrived in a valley at the headwaters of the Buchanan River in central West Virginia. The newcomers—farmers, teachers, musicians, innkeepers, beekeepers, cheesemakers—thought they were coming to a town, not a wilderness. After overcoming their disappointment, they decided to found their own town, Helvetia, which still has so much of its original Swiss character that a spokesman for the Embassy of Switzerland once described it as the "purest example of Swiss culture" in the United States.

About 30 miles south and west of Elkins, Helvetia (population: about 20) is where you will find the **Beekeeper Inn** (304-924-6435; doubles $85, including breakfast; 30 percent less mid-November to mid-April). It is owned by Eleanor Mailloux, who grew up in the village, went away and returned about 30 years ago. "Almost everyone here is a Swiss descendant," she says, adding quickly, "not everyone, of course, but we try to make them one." Mailloux also owns the **Swiss Huette** (same phone), a restaurant with a Swiss-German cuisine—sauerbrauten, bratwurst and "our own sausage." The inn is in one of the oldest buildings in the village. "It belonged to the original beekeeper," Mailloux says. It has three bedrooms with private baths. The decor is country antique "with a bit of sophistication."

Traditions live on here. "My ancestors were innkeepers 400 years ago in Zurich," Mailloux says. "There still are beekeepers in town—the Burky family . . . We have a teaching family, the Zumbachs. We have musicians. And cheesemakers—almost every family knows how to make cheese."

As small as it is, Helvetia isn't backward, Mailloux says. "We have an inn. We have a public library, which is very well attended and supplied. We have a church, a store, a post office, a museum, a community hall, a youth center. And we have goats and ducks." The town retained its character because of its location, Mailloux believes. "We are at the end of the pavement. It's the isolation, and we have worked on it, too."

GETTING THERE/BEING THERE: Take I-66 west to I-81 south to U.S. 250 west to Huttonsville, W. Va. Bear right on U.S. 250/92, drive north a mile, go left on state Route 46 and drive two miles to Helvetia.

— *Larry Fox*

mid-Atlantic (it can accommodate 7,000 guests a night). Its winter ski season and holiday rates go from $116 a night for a hotel room all the way to $615 a night for a 4-bedroom condo. Corresponding summer prices range from $65 to $146, with many others in between in both cases for efficiencies, smaller condos, town houses and homes. Ski, golf and family packages also are available. Snowshoe has 53 trails and new terrain parks for snowboarders and skiers, plus snowtubing, sledding and lights on the slopes to permit nighttime skiing. A single lift ticket gets you into both ski areas, and for warm-weather visitors there's fishing, swimming and mountain biking in addition to golf. Speaking of mountain biking, **The Inn at Elk River** (304-572-3771; doubles $50-$85, including breakfast ♿) now offers a dozen rooms, about half in a converted 100-year-old farmhouse, to the cross-country skiers and mountain bikers outfitted by Gil and Mary Willis' adjacent Elk River Touring Center (see BEING THERE). Even if you don't stay here, the inn's fresh, plentiful and vegetarian-friendly meals, served at tables around the fire, are worth a stop (a recent sample: fresh West Virginia rainbow trout, feta-stuffed mushrooms, herb roasted potatoes and just-made apple-cranberry crumb pie).

WHERE TO EAT: Everyone Nancy Lewis asked in Elkins suggested the **Red Fox Restaurant** (304-572-1111 ♿) at Snowshoe as the area's best. "It may be the best around," she says, "but we didn't feel that the $100-plus price tag was justified by the meal (and it only included a couple of glasses of wine). The food was good, however, and in the winter the view would be spectacular." In town, the fanciest place is the **Mingo Room** (304-637-1402) in the Graceland Inn, offering surprisingly good but limited fare for dinner year round and for lunch as well in spring and summer. **C.J. Maggie's American Grill** (304-636-1730) is a roadhouse and bar plopped in the middle of town and cleaned up sufficiently to have families queued up outside by 6 p.m., waiting for tables; burgers, pasta and a few Tex-Mex specialties are what you'll find on yours. There's a separate bar that offers snacks (salted and spicy still-in-the-shell peanuts) out of grain feeders, and a motto: "Get in Here." Next door to the unrelated Cheat River Lodge, the **Cheat River Inn** (304-636-6265) is perched like a lake cabin on the bank of the southern branch of the Cheat River and seems to fancy itself as a Key West fish house. The trout isn't local and the crabs obviously don't come from here, but it's a local favorite.

FOR MORE INFORMATION: Contact the **Randolph County Convention and Visitors Bureau** at 800-422-3304 or *www.randolphcountywv.com*, or the **Potomac Highlands Travel Council** at 304-257-9315 or *www.potomachighlands.org*.

Our Cabin in the Woods
At Herrington Manor State Park

By Jay Mallin

FROM A CANOE in the middle of our 50-acre lake, my wife, my toddler son and I could survey the whole scene—our sandy beach with its roped-off swimming area, the beach house with picnic tables and bathrooms, our lake itself, surrounded by deep woods and low hills.

Of course, since this was a state park, it wasn't really all ours. But it felt like it was. For while other visitors occasionally would wander by and sit on the beach or even trek through the woods, they had to leave by sunset. We, on the other hand, lived here—at least for a while.

Among its many state forests, preserves and wildlife management areas, Maryland has five state parks where visitors can rent cabins and stay overnight. These range from New Germany State Park, also in Western Maryland, with 11 cabins, to Martinak, with a single cabin near the Delaware line at the other end of the state. It was at the oldest of these, the 365-acre Herrington Manor State Park near Deep Creek Lake in far western Maryland, that we decided to spend some time.

Because we were coping with a one-year-old newly discovering the joys of bipedal locomotion, my wife had been a bit skeptical of the whole notion. To her, a cabin is a place for roughing it, with none of the amenities inside and the only facilities in an outhouse. And we were still too sleep-deprived from regular nighttime wake-ups for rough-and-ready cots or additional strange noises in the night.

Arriving at Herrington Manor, though, we found that we need not have worried. The cabins were well furnished, with bathrooms, fully equipped kitchens and reasonably comfortable beds. Outside, they had porches with lounging furniture and picnic tables with grills.

It's no wonder they're so cozy. Half of the 20 cabins at Herrington Manor (named for a Revolutionary War sergeant and a mansion that no longer exists) were built by Franklin Roosevelt's Civilian Conservation Corps in the 1930s and early 1940. Back then people knew what a cabin should be—not skylights or picture windows but hardwood floors, wood paneling and rough-cut interior beams. The three of us went for a four-person cabin, which

125

turned out to be a roomy affair with two single beds downstairs and two more upstairs in the loft. We didn't use the loft much. Instead, we blocked the base of the stairs from our miniature mountaineer and quickly had a more childproof place than our own home—nothing really fragile or breakable, few electrical outlets and only battered pans under the sink.

As for the rest of the park, it was simply beautiful. The trout-stocked lake was not outside the cabins and thus not a drowning hazard, as my wife had feared. Rather, it was a short hike or drive away. The pleasant little sandy beach had roped-off shallow and deep swimming areas, and the acres of forest had marked trails.

Even better, from my viewpoint at least, was the flotilla of canoes, rowboats and paddleboats on the lake. During the summer season, according to the guide that comes with each cabin, overnight visitors often can have free use of a boat if they are not all rented out through the concession stand. During our non-summer-season stay the deal was even better. The park office opened the concession stand long enough for us to take out a couple of paddles and three life preservers (one sized for a small child). We propped this equipment behind a drink machine, available to pull out whenever we wanted to go for a cruise.

The area had other attractions as well. Our favorite was just up the road at Swallow Falls State Park, where Maryland's largest waterfall is just a five-minute hike from the parking lot. Further on is the Deep Creek Lake resort area, which you actually pass through on Maryland Route 219 to get to Herrington Manor.

Herrington Manor, though, is quite a ways off from the main road running through Deep Creek Lake. It's far enough that anyone staying in the cabin would want to take advantage of the cabin kitchen or grill to do most of their own cooking, rather than running out for meals.

The kitchen did indeed come with almost everything needed for ordinary cooking except dish soap and a towel. Ours had both an electric can opener and a microwave—the two keys to many successful vacation meals. As for food, there were perfectly good grocery stores on Route 219 and in Oakland, the nearest town. But a cook who plans to take vacation time to prepare something special would be advised to bring the essential ingredients from home. I couldn't find a red bell pepper anywhere, and if there's anyone in Oakland who eats tofu, they must get it by mail order.

I'm sure it's a great place to visit in summer, too, but another advantage of staying at this park during the off-season was that the week-long rental required of summer guests is eliminated. Instead, if you spend two nights Sunday through Thursday, you get the third free. And the cabins are open through winter, with trails for cross-country skiers. We don't know yet what these old cabins are like in winter, with snow on the ground and a biting chill in the air, but with both heating and wood-burning stoves or fireplaces, they look as though they'd be pretty cozy. Some day soon we may just find out.

GETTING THERE: Herrington Manor State Park is close to four hours from the Beltway. Take I-270 north and then I-70 west to get to I-68 west through Cumberland, Md. At Exit 14A, take Route 219 south. Continue two miles past the Deep Creek Lake Bridge, turn right onto Mayhew Inn Road, and follow the signs to Herrington Manor.

BEING THERE: There are 20 two-, four- and six-person cabins available at prices ranging from $75 to $95 a night in the off-season (before Memorial Day, after Labor Day). Reservations (888-432-2267 May-Sept, 301-334-9180 otherwise ♿) can be made up to a year in advance. Indeed, they *should* be made a year in advance for fall foliage and peak snow season stays. Leashed pets are permitted in the off-season in the state park, which is inside 6,800-acre Garrett State Forest. Depending on the weather, be prepared to take advantage of the hiking trails, the beach, the lake for fishing and boating, the tennis courts or the 10 miles of well-groomed and frequently cleared cross-country ski trails. The kitchens are well equipped, and bed linens and pillows are provided, but bring your own towels for bath and kitchen as well as soap and food. For more on the other attractions in the neighborhood, including **Deep Creek Lake State Park** and resort area, **Swallow Falls State Park** (which has five similar rental cabins), **Wisp ski area, Backbone Mountain** and **New Germany State Park** (which rents 11 cabins), see the following section on **GARRETT COUNTY, MD.**

GARRETT COUNTY, MD.

Garrett County, on the Allegheny Plateau in its very own panhandle surrounded mostly by West Virginia and Pennsylvania, is to the rest of Maryland what Alaska is to the Lower 48: remote, distant, different—and known for its longer, colder, snowier winters. In summer, there's swimming and boating on Deep Creek Lake, a serpentine reservoir created by a Pennsylvania utility in the 1920s. In winter, there's skiing, downhill at the locally owned Wisp resort and cross-country at three state parks. (A recent winter snowfall in Garrett County: 12 feet.) Year round, the county's rural roads reveal stunning mountain vistas but only a few houses and fewer vehicles. This is a vast county: 662 square miles, but only 30,000 or so people who are sufficiently cut off from their fellow Marylanders that when state judges can't find an unbiased jury elsewhere, they'll often send their most notorious cases to Garrett for trial.

Deep Creek Lake has long been the vacation center of Western Maryland. The state's biggest lake, created by a dam in 1925, is 12 miles long and has 65 miles of shoreline; most houses are built behind a line of trees, which occasionally creates the illusion that the lake is undeveloped. It is not. For many years, it was a quiet, middle-class, family-oriented getaway. You came and rented a cottage for a week or two, did some fishing (the lake is noted for its bass, walleye and trout), let the kids splash in the lake and tried to forget what your boss's face looked like. The secluded spot has been discovered by upscale folks from here and Pittsburgh and Baltimore, so nowadays a visitor can find stinky fish bait and even stinkier French cheese within a mile of each other. As the past decade's construction boom continues (mostly vacation homes, rental properties and condos), the quiet lake now has more anglers, pleasure boaters and members of the Hell's Angels Personal Water Craft Club per square mile than any place on the Chesapeake Bay. The first million-dollar lakefront home went up not too long ago, and the locals still can't quite believe it. Indeed, in an attempt to avoid overdevelopment, the state announced plans in 1998 to buy the lake. At **Deep Creek Lake State Park** (301-387-5563) on the east side of the lake (two miles east of Thayerville off Route 219), there are 108 reservable campsites, horseback riding, trailer hookups and flat-water canoeing. For rafting on the upper and lower Youghiogheny, contact **White Water Adventures** (800-992-7238), **Precision Rafting** (800-477-3723) or **Laurel Highlands River Tours** (800-472-3846). For boat rentals, check with **Bill's Marine Service** (301-387-5536), **Crystal Waters Boat Rentals** (301-387-5515) or **Deep Creek Outfitters** (301-387-6977). For personal watercraft rentals, call the **Aquatic Center** (301-387-8233).

In winter, **Wisp Ski Resort** (301-387-4911), overlooking the village of McHenry, is the area's biggest attraction, drawing skiers and snow-boarders to its 23 trails day and night. Cross-country skiing is at nearby New Germany State Park (see below), where the trails are cleared and marked. (Good cross-country skiing also is possible at Herrington Manor, Deep Creek Lake and Swallow Falls state parks, which ring the lake.) Snowmobiles are allowed in **Savage River State Forest** (301-895-5759) and other state forest lands, where 35 miles of trails are marked. In recent years, ice fishing has been drawing fans when thick ice forms in January. The feature almost everyone mentions about **Swallow Falls State Park** (301-334-9180), nine miles northwest of Oakland on county Route 20, is the 53-foot **Muddy Creek Falls**. The park also has hiking trails, campsites, five rental cabins and a pet loop (both Swallow Falls and Herrington Manor parks permit dogs on a leash—except between Memorial Day and Labor Day). A bona fide cross-country trail also leads during the snowy season to **Herrington Manor** (see previous section). But the big attraction is the falls, a short hike from the parking lot. Even in winter, it's worth the (careful) trek on the snow-covered wooden stairway down the side of the gorge, following the length of what is, in January, virtually one large icicle down to the creek below. Cross-country skiing is free at Swallow Falls (and $1 a person at Herrington Manor). **New Germany State Park** (301-895-5453) often is so crowded with urbanites on winter weekends that *Post* writer Eugene Meyer once likened the intersection of two trails there to Connecticut and K. St. But he says that the relatively level trail by the parking lot, which actually is a snow-covered road that parallels a creek, "is like Beach Drive in Rock Creek Park when it's closed to traffic on weekends, except instead of in-line skating, biking and jogging, these city folks are on cross-country skis." For $2 a head on weekends and holidays (free other times) cross-country skiers have the run of trails at New Germany State Park. Cars with anyone 62 or up always get in free. The park also has a 13-acre lake, 39 campsites and 11 cabins.

Not far from New Germany park on the old stagecoach route west is Grantsville, where the humpbacked **Casselman River Bridge** was built 50 feet over the water just east of town to allow for an extension of the C&O Canal that never materialized. At the time of its unveiling in 1813, it was to be the longest single span bridge in the country—80 feet—and more than a few folks were skeptical that it would stand at all. The night before the official opening, the contractor secretly had the supports removed to test it. The next morning, he was standing confidently beneath the keystone when the wooden beams were taken away. Today, it's a great spot for a picnic lunch. A few hundred yards away is the nonprofit **Spruce Forest Artisan Village** (301-895-3332; closed Sundays), founded by a Mennonite woman 40 years ago. Local potters, blacksmiths, spinners, weavers and woodcarvers demonstrate and sell their crafts in 12 restored log houses and buildings, two of which date to the Revolutionary War. It's a nice setting and refreshingly non-commercial. Next door is the Penn Alps restaurant (see WHERE TO EAT).

GETTING THERE: The westernmost county in Maryland, Garrett is closer to Steubenville, Ohio, than to Washington—which is three to four hours away via I-270, I-70 and I-68, all of them west. For Deep Creek Lake, McHenry and Oakland (and Wisp, Swallow Falls and Herrington Manor), take U.S. 219 south from I-68's Exit 14.

WHERE TO STAY: Around Deep Creek Lake, the **Carmel Cove Inn** (301-387-0067; doubles $120-$180) has 10 rooms in a former monastery 200 yards from the lake (with a tennis court, hot tub, billiard room, canoes, bicycles and private fireplaces). **Haley Farm** (888-231-3276; doubles start at $130 ♿) is a 65-acre farm B&B with orchards, horses and a trout pond. Minutes from the lake, it also has bikes, canoes and hot tubs. The **Lake Pointe Inn** (800-523-5253; doubles from $138 weekends, $123 weekdays, with full breakfast) has nine rooms right on the lake. **Red Run Lodge** (800-898-7786; doubles $89-$135), is a six-room B&B on one of Deep Creek's western fingers, not far from Oakland.

One of the best deals in the Grantsville area is the single private room in the main building of the **Casselman Motor Inn** (301-895-5055 ♿). Forget the 40 motel rooms in the back building. The other three guest rooms in the 1824 inn, built to serve travelers along the old National Road (for a thumbnail history of this first U.S. interstate highway, see PENNSYLVANIA'S LAUREL HIGHLANDS, Page 136), are smallish and share a single bath. But the large, $75-a-night main room has a four-poster bed and a big bathtub. If its taken, the **Grantsville Holiday Inn** (301-895-5993; doubles $69-$89) has an indoor pool and a large fireplace in the lobby, and it's right off I-68 at Exit 22, a few minutes from New Germany State Park.

There are cabins and camping at Herrington Manor (see previous section), Swallow Falls, New Germany and Deep Creek Lake state parks (see preceding page), and primitive camping within the vast **Savage River State Forest** south of Grantsville (301-895-5759) and in **Potomac and Garrett state forests** (301-334-2038) farther south and east.

WHERE TO EAT: In Oakland, **Towne Restaurant** (301-334-3300 ♿), near the domed courthouse, has down-home food that sticks to your ribs but hardly touches your wallet. At the **French Cafe Bakery**—within the **Cornish Manor** (301-334-6499 ♿), a fancy Victorian eatery—try the cheeses or the pastries, such as the Key lime mousse, baked by Fred Bergheim. He and wife Christine own both establishments. The **Deer Park Inn** (301-334-2308 ♿), three miles from the southern end of the lake off Route 135, is elegant, a restored Victorian mansion with a five-star chef imported from Washington. Whatever the season, a favorite eating place on Deep Creek Lake is **McClive's** restaurant in McHenry (301-387-6172 ♿), known for its prime ribs and its two-for-one meal for $20, Sunday through Tuesday night. There's also a **Pizzeria Uno** in McHenry, next to the locally popular **Honi-Honi bar** (301-387-4866) and the **Arrowhead Market** (301-387-4020 ♿), which carries portabello mushrooms in its well-stocked deli, three flavors of cappuccino (including the ill-advised Banana Nut) and a full-service business center. Up in Grantsville, the Mennonites who run the **Casselman Inn** (301-895-5055 ♿), formerly a drover's stop on the old National Road, also rent rooms and sell antiques. Just east of Grantsville is **Penn Alps** (301-895-5985 ♿), also Mennonite-run, serving Pennsylvania Dutch cooking in a restored stagecoach stop dating to 1818.

FOR MORE INFORMATION: Contact the **Deep Creek Lake-Garrett County Promotion Council** at 301-334-1948 between 8 a.m. and 8 p.m., or try *www.garrettchamber.com.*

AROUND CUMBERLAND, MD.

Allegheny County and particularly Cumberland are hoping to regain a bit of their old glory days—when everyone, starting with young George Washington on his way to the French and Indian War front, made extended stops here on their way west. There is a new $54 million golf resort and conference center. An $87 million project is under way to re-water the terminus of the C&O Canal and create a park in downtown Cumberland. And there's a plan to continue propping up the area's historic rail tour (which runs from Cumberland to Frostburg and feeds patrons to a little "olde" restaurant that the state coincidentally just bought).

Part of the reason so few modern-day Washingtonians ever really see this part of Maryland is, paradoxically, that the road out here is too good, says *Post* contributor Bill Heavey. "Interstate 68 starts at Hancock—the spot where a long cannon shot fired north from West Virginia might easily fly two miles over the skinny 'wrist' of Maryland and cross the Mason-Dixon line into Pennsylvania—and heads west with astonishing purpose. When the hills go up, it cuts through them. When the valleys go down, the road rides above them on pylons. It's a masterpiece of engineering and, as you whiz along at the posted 65, people pass you so fast they'll suck the daisy right out of your radio antenna. So you speed up to join the herd, and the next thing you know they've led you straight to the gourmet cheeses and flavored cappucinos of Deep Creek Lake's Arrowhead Market [see GARRETT COUNTY, WHERE TO EAT, above]. At which point you might as well have taken two orbits around the Beltway and returned to downtown Bethesda. If you want to see what you're traveling through, you must force your car into an exit lane and get on the small roads."

You won't want to miss the town of **Cumberland**. With a population of 24,000, it's the biggest town in western Maryland and marks the terminus of the 184.5-mile C&O Canal that starts in Georgetown. The last stone mile marker stands in a field of grass. Construction has begun on a program to re-water the canal to its end, though the project is not scheduled to be completed until 2005. In the meantime, there's a full day's worth of sightseeing in Cumberland, which has an array of interesting restaurants, pubs and places to stay. You can take a 28-stop walking tour through the **Victorian Historical District** along Washington Street in Cumberland's polished West End. There you'll see houses built for railroad and coal barons as well as the soaring spire of the **Allegheny County Court House**. You also can peer through the window of **George Washington's Headquarters** (301-777-8214), the one-room cabin that was his first command post and is the last remaining building of Fort Cumberland. (Inside is a mannequin of the Father of Our Country, with his sword, bugle and chamber pot). Don't miss **History House** (301-777-8678; closed Mondays), an opulent, 1867 mansion built for the C&O Canal's president that's been restored and filled with paintings, costumes and Civil War artifacts. The scenic train to Frostburg (see next page) leaves from the **Western Maryland Station Center** (800-508-4748 🔕), a 1913 Victorian structure restored to its original splendor and a must stop even if you're not railroad-bound. It houses the local visitors center and the **C&O Canal Visitors Center** (301-722-8226). It also contains the **Transportation and Industrial Museum** (open May-October, closed Mondays), which traces the city's development as a transportation hub in the 18th and 19th Centuries and the boom and bust years that followed the rise and fall of bituminous coal. Cumberland also is surrounded by hiking, mountain biking, rafting, caving, kayaking and cross-country skiing opportunities; besides the C&O's National Park Service, for guidance—or guides—check with **Allegeny Adventures** (301-729-9708) or **Allegheny Expeditions** (800-819-5170.)

As you head out of town on 40-Alt, you pass through the thousand-foot wall of the "narrows" between Will's and Haystack mountains. Before long you'll arrive in the funky little country village/college town of **Frostburg**, home of **Frostburg State University** (and summer home to the **Washington Redskins**). In the basement museum of the turn-of-the-century **Hotel Gunter** (see WHERE TO STAY/EAT)—which has its own jail, a gamecock fighting arena (now a bar) and a mock-up of the inside of a coal mine—you get a sense of how the discovery of coal in the surrounding mountains in 1810 changed this part of the world. For the next century, coal was king, and this valley was a jewel in its crown. Miners from England, Ireland and Wales came and asked the way to George's Creek to work the 12-foot-wide seam of coal under Big Savage Mountain and Dan's Mountain surrounding the town. Cumberland coal was of such quality that ships of the Cunard line would burn no other. In 1840, the railroad arrived, making the area an important commercial center. It all collapsed when oil replaced coal. The devastation is hard to imagine today. In the Gunter museum, the writings of F. DeSales Meyers, a boy who had grown up during the boom and returned many years later, gives you a glimmer of what it must have been like—how the creeks no longer ran yellow with sulphur from the crushed rock, how the forest, greener now, crept back down the hills to the edge of town. "The old folks talk of how the forest may take over the town and it will all look the way it did 200 years ago."

There's also a gem of a carriage museum near the Old Depot Restaurant, where the train from Cumberland stops. The **Thrasher Carriage Museum** (301-689-3380; closed Mondays ♿) houses more than 50 beautifully restored 19th and 20th Century carriages, terrific examples of what you drove to impress the neighbors before Henry Ford. All were collected by a local, James Thrasher, who restored closed carriages, open sleighs, funeral wagons, even dog and golf carts to road condition. There is a five-windowed carriage that belonged to Theodore Roosevelt and a sleigh used by the Vanderbilt family. Perhaps the most interesting carriage is the oldest, a modest little family coach called a Germantown Rockaway that dates from 1850. There's a luggage rack on the back, panes of glass that slide down into the doors and—most significant—an extended roof to shield the driver (usually the father) from rain. This was a new feature in the history of carriage making. In Europe, no one had ever given any thought to the comfort of the servants driving the vehicle.

Don't overlook the **Western Maryland Scenic Railroad** (800-872-4650 ♿). It's a bargain at $18 for a three-hour, 32-mile round-trip down a mile-long gorge, over an iron truss bridge and through the 914-foot Brush Tunnel. (PBS found it worthy of inclusion in its "Great Scenic Railway Journeys" TV show.) The railway runs May through October, with trains leaving Cumberland at 11:30 a.m. Tuesday through Sunday, returning at 2:30 p.m. (Weekend-only service continues into December.) Reservations are recommended. There are also several theme trips, including Halloween, Santa and Murder Mystery trains and an early October trip to Brunswick, Md., to coincide with its "Brunswick Railroad Days," a celebration of railroading with displays, family activities, antiques, tours and entertainment at the rail station there. Should old railroad cars be of interest to you, just 30 miles south on Route 28 near Romney, W.Va., the **Potomac Eagle** (800-223-2453 or 304/822-7464 ♿) runs weekends May through October. Among other things, its diesel engine pulls restored rail cars from the 1920s along the South Branch of the Potomac on a tour of the mountainous West Virginia panhandle. Reservations are a good idea.

Just east of Cumberland, **Rocky Gap State Park** (301-777-2139) sits on Lake Habeeb between Evitts and Martin mountains. It has three swimming beaches and a bathhouse, 278 campsites, boat rentals, a visitors center and a huge resort/conference center (see WHERE TO STAY/EAT). Farther east, the mountainous, 38,800 acres of **Green Ridge State Forest** (301-478-3124) are worthy of exploration—experienced exploration, that is, with primitive camping in roughly 90 designated areas. The forest (a good place to wear blaze orange in fall and winter, to ensure that you won't be mistaken for a deer, black bear or large turkey) is adjacent to the C&O Canal. Thus, trail hikes can be combined with towpath bicycle trips along the Potomac, including those through or around the canal's 3,120-foot-long **Paw Paw Tunnel**. (The tunnel has no lights, so make sure to bring that flashlight.)

GETTING THERE: Cumberland is about three hours from the Beltway. Take I-270 to I-70 to I-68 (or the more interesting U.S. 40 and 40-Alt), all of them west. Amtrak has limited service to Cumberland (800-872-7245).

WHERE TO STAY/EAT: In Cumberland, the **Inn at Walnut Bottom** (800-286-9718; rooms start at $87, including full breakfast) offers elegant accommodations in two adjoining 19th Century houses. The inn's **Oxford House Restaurant**, moreover, is one of the better watering holes in town. The **Cumberland Holiday Inn** (301-724-8800; doubles $89 and up &) is a good bet if the best surprise is no surprise and you want to be near Exit 43-C of Route 68. The **Rocky Gap Lodge & Golf Resort** (800-724-0828; doubles start at $135; packages available) has 220 rooms on Rocky Gap State Park's 243-acre lake. It also has a lakefront restaurant, private beach, indoor-outdoor pool, fitness center and one of the country's few Jack Nicklaus-designed golf courses open to the public. The 7,100-yard beauty, with enough underground water pipes to supply a small city, was due to open in the spring of 1999. North of Cumberland is the one-of-a-kind **Castle at Mt. Savage** (301-264-4645; doubles $95-$125, including breakfast), a brooding Gothic stone castle surrounded by a 12-foot-high stone wall. The 24-room mountaintop inn is a copy of the Craig Castle near Inverness in the Scottish Highlands. It was built in 1840 by an Englishman who was the doctor for the mining company that built and once owned the town of Mt. Castle itself. Since then the castle has served variously as a bar, a brothel, a casino, an apartment building and a private home. William and Andrea Myer bought it in 1986 and turned it into an inn, furnishing its six guest rooms with exquisite antiques from the 17th and 19th Centuries. The baths have seven- and eight-foot-long claw-foot tubs. The grounds have formal English gardens and a croquet court, and of course there's afternoon tea. In Frostburg, the 1896 Failinger's **Hotel Gunter** (301-689-6511; doubles start at $65, including breakfast) has 18 apartments and 17 hotel rooms, each furnished in Victorian style with cable TV and air conditioning. In its turn-of-the-century heyday, the hotel featured tame fawns on the lawn. The lobby still has its original oak staircase, a splendid "Gone With the Wind" affair that required 179 gallons of stripper to restore. Restaurants in Cumberland include the **Bourbon Street Cafe** (301-722-1116 &), a New Orleans-style spot downtown serving Cajun specialties, and, beneath its distinctive neon flying-pig logo, **When Pigs Fly** (301-722-7447 &), a popular place among locals, serving ribs, chicken, seafood and lots of microbrews. For a filling and inexpensive lunch on the way out to Western Maryland, the **Park-n-Dine** in Hancock (301-678-5242 &) is open 6 a.m. to 9 p.m. daily to meet all your needs for homestyle pork-chop, mashed-potato and pie.

FOR MORE INFORMATION: Contact the **Maryland Office of Tourism** at 800-394-5725 or *www.mdisfun.org*, or the **Allegheny County Visitors Center** (301-777-5905). A helpful web site is the privately run *www.mdmountainside.com*.

SIX FLAGS OVER . . . EASY

EACH YEAR as summer wanes, if you haven't made the annual trek to Six Flags Over Asphalt, younger family members may start lobbying hard. They think that standing in line, paying $4 for souvenir cups of soda and perspiring profusely is their birthright. So you will cast about for an excuse, like a week-long East Coast power failure, to stay away. But there's an alternative. Think cool. Think green. Think—dare we say it?—cheap.

Idlewild Park, a family-owned amusement park in Pennsylvania's Laurel Valley, four hours from Washington (see next section), is all those things, and, in a way, less: natural, unhurried and charming. Indeed, Idlewild might be described as Idlemild. It's a park for low-tech expectations: not the highest rides or the newest but the twirled-and-true. Its biggest roller coaster isn't The Mauler but the Wild Mouse. Kids' attractions even include a trolley ride through Mister Rogers' Neighborhood, inspired by the PBS kids' show that never raises its voice.

Its physical layout, moreover, is a pleasure. No attraction, from the Tarzan lines to the nine-acre lake and water park, is more than a 10-minute stroll under towering trees. Even ride lines—if you encounter any—are guarded by shade trees. And the view from atop the old Ferris wheel is of blue-green hills, rather than a sea of parked cars.

When Idlewild was founded in 1878, the property owner specified that "no timber or other trees be cut or injured" on the 350-acre tract. Honored ever since, that clause has kept the park a cool jewel. Its elevation in the Laurel Highlands, close to Seven Springs and other ski resorts, keeps down both the humidity and the crowds. The Loyalhanna Creek, source of Rolling Rock beer, threads through Idlewild and is another factor in keeping you cool. Its footbridges, linking different park neighborhoods, are a pleasant place to loiter. Canada geese patrol the banks below. And as we chugged across the railroad bridge from Hootin' Holler to Raccoon Lagoon on the miniature Lakeview Railway, we watched a snake below race us across the creek.

Neighboring **Ligonier**, an old-money enclave with small-scale charm, is a good place to spend the night and a morning. The town offers two motels and a cluster of bed-and-breakfasts. Brick-front shops fan out from "The Diamond," the town-square gazebo that hosts Sunday evening concerts each summer. Sextets of young performers stage the usual song-and-dance shows throughout the park. For the past few seasons, the Royal Hanneford Circus has performed under a big top. The five-act show, with elephants, riding acts and aerialists, runs just under an hour. It's free on weekdays and an extra $2 on weekends. Coaster cognoscenti will approve of the Rollo Coaster and Wild Mouse, both clackety fun. Anyone who's thrilled to beat the four-foot height requirement will leap on the centrifugally powered Round-Up and the equally stomach-churning Spider. Our kids rode them twice in a row, a monument to youthful equilibrium. All told, Idlewild offers 45 attractions, including the impressive water slides of the H2Ohhh Zone. Bumper cars, a restored pastel merry-go-round, games for a quarter a chance—no classic park element is missing, except the lines.

There is, for example, a lake where you can rent a paddleboat or small outboard and share a placid pond ringed in yellow-flowered spatterdocks with the swans, bass and bluegill lurking in the shallows. There is Storybook Forest, one of the park's oldest sections, where characters kids encounter aren't Mickey and Minnie but the Old Woman Who Lived in a Shoe, the Three Billy Goats Gruff (played by real billies) and other fairy tale figures. Even the shyest toddler will be thrilled.

Despite souvenir stands and Idelwild's modest midway, there just aren't many opportunities to blow big bucks. We won a plush Flipper on the first try, so the cost-per-dolphin was delightfully low. Our weekend admission for a family of four was under $60. Even with a pasta dinner, cotton candy and other trinkets, we got away for less than $100. We "did" Idlewild in about five hours. Although we could have stayed till dark, we headed to the car, walking slowly, as the sun set over the Laurel Ridge. From the stage echoed the final chorus of "God Bless America." No one was crying. No one was muttering. In fact, no one was talking at all. We were just charmed.

GETTING THERE/BEING THERE/STAYING THERE: Idlewild Park (724-238-3666; open May through August), is about four hours northwest of the Beltway on U.S. 30, three miles west of Ligonier, Pa. Take I-270 to I-70 west to the Pennsylvania Turnpike. Head west to Exit 9 (Donegal), and follow Route 711 north to 30 west to Ligonier. Admission to Idlewild and the adjacent Soak Zone (14 water rides) is $18.95 for anyone aged 3 to 54 (55 and older, $14). Park opens at 10 a.m., most rides at 11 a.m., and closing time, which depends on crowds and weather, usually is about 9 p.m. Closed Mondays. The **Ramada Inn** in downtown Ligonier (724-238-9545; weekend doubles start at $84 ♿) is within walking distance of shopping and dining and features a pool and restaurant. The **Fort Ligonier Motor Lodge** (724-238-6677; weekend doubles start at $60 ♿) is two miles from the park on U.S. 30 and has standard motel rooms (and no restaurant). It offers discount tickets to the park, good for any day.

FOR MORE INFORMATION: Contact the **Ligonier Valley Chamber of Commerce** at 724-238-4200 or the **Laurel Highlands Visitors Bureau** at 800-333-5661.

—Christine H. O'Toole

Pennsylvania's Laurel Highlands

Due north of Maryland's western edge, in the woods and hills south of Pittsburgh, you'll find two popular ski resorts, one bombastic but excellent full-service spa and resort, some of the best and most serious whitewater rafting around, and an old, scenic and not-quite-forgotten byway through the Alleghenies. You'll also encounter—characteristically melded into the scenery—Frank Lloyd Wright's **Fallingwater** (724-329-8501; closed Mondays and open weekends only, weather permitting, in mid-November and March; closed January and February). This icon of American architecture has stunning rectangular forms cantilevered over a waterfall a few miles north of Ohiopyle, Pa. It has been joined now by a second Wright-designed home seven miles south in Chalk Hill: **Kentuck Knob** (724-329-1901; also closed Mondays and open by appointment only, November-March). This is a relatively undiscovered, privately owned treasure that opened to the public only in recent years.

Near both houses, the tiny town of Ohiopyle is a big whitewater rafting center for the Youghiogheny River (that's YOCK-a-GAY-nee, or "Yock" to its friends), which runs through the 30 square miles of **Ohiopyle State Park** (724-329-8591). The park also has 27 miles of riverside biking trails and 41 miles of hiking trails, both of which convert easily to cross-country ski territory in winter. If it's whitewater rafting that calls to you, **Laurel Highlands River Tours** (800-472-3846) can get you in a raft (as well as a canoe) pretty swiftly. Cross-country skiers are welcome on the 20-plus miles of trails through **Bear Run Nature Reserve** (also 724-329-8501), and downhill skiers on the slopes of either **Seven Springs Mountain Resort** (800-452-2223 for reservations, 800-523-7777 for snow reports) in Champion or nearby **Hidden Valley** (800-443-7544 for reservations, 800-443-7544 for snow reports). If it's mid-summer and you'd prefer a place where it's always 52 degrees, the spot for you is the **Laurel Caverns** (724-438-3003; closed December-February and all but weekends in March, April and November). This is Pennsylvania's largest cave, with more than two miles of passageways that reach a depth of 450 feet.

And if you're fascinated by more recent history than the million-year-old stories told by underground rock formations, follow the example of *Post* writer Eugene Meyer, an experienced wanderer who headed out one of his favorite highways, U.S. 40, into "the uncharted wilderness" beyond Uniontown. "Well, actually, it's well charted," Meyer says:

"That's because U.S. 40 is also the **National Road,** the first federally funded interstate highway, built between Cumberland, Md., and Wheeling, W.Va., early in the 19th Century. And before that, during the French and Indian Wars, it was Braddock's Road. And before that, [Delaware Indian chief] Nemacolin's Path. The road once much traveled is now not very, which makes it a kind of interesting time warp. A Uniontown bypass is up to interstate standards, but then the road narrows to two lanes as it winds over hill and dale, past the Coal Baron Restaurant, Searight's Tollhouse, the Brownsville Drive-in (really big screen, two movies), a Madonna of the Trail statue, an abandoned farmhouse next to an occupied trailer, and the wide and muddy Monongahela River. The scenery is arresting, if not spectacular, and then there is Scenery Hill. This is not much of a hill, but it is a town that is enjoying a small renaissance as a pit stop for tourists. Located along its Main Street (U.S. 40) are 16 antique and gift shops and places to eat. 'I'm here to make a living, not to entertain you,' says a sign outside one shop specializing in 'early American' furniture and bric-a-brac, but the owner doesn't mean it. He can't stop talking, though we don't buy a thing. At another shop, we exchange life histories with the proprietor, who really ought to write a book, but find nothing to buy."

GETTING THERE: Most Laurel Highlands destinations are within four hours of the Beltway. Take I-70 to I-68, exit at Keyser's Ridge onto U.S. 40 west and 381 north into Pennsylvania. (For such locations farther north as Seven Springs, keep going on 381 north.)

WHERE TO STAY: The eccentric personal stamp of Joe Hardy, founder of the timber enterprise called 84 Lumber Co., is all over the 1,260-acre **Nemacolin Woodland Resort** (800-422-2736 ♿). The lobby has a portrait of Hardy slouching in a chair with his belly overhanging his trousers and a big stogie in his left hand. The resort displays his eclectic and often astonishing art collection. Lake P.J. is named after his grandson, and Hardy Boulevard traverses this personal Disneyland. The kingdom, still growing, has more than 200 rooms (including those in the new luxe-redux **Chateau Lafayette**, audaciously modeled after the Ritz in Paris). The rooms come in many sizes, the largest with whirlpools and balconies. You'll also find a toy store and other pricey "shoppes," two golf courses, hiking trails, stables, a ski area, a rose garden, seven (yes, seven) restaurants, surrey rides, tuxedoed butlers and bellmen and a large, well-equipped spa with enough masseurs to set every major muscle group atingle. Staying here is not cheap, but the dazzling array of packages makes it seem just a bit more affordable. A mid-week package for two includes unlimited access to the spa and a choice of 18 holes of golf and a massage or a facial for $322. Two *Post* writers have thus far come back alive from the lush wilds of Nemacolin, and when asked if they *liked* it, both more or less rolled their eyes, shook their heads disparagingly—and then said, "Yes."

Arrival at the 94-room **Summit Inn** (724-438-8594 ♿), just east of Uniontown at the crest of Chestnut Ridge, puts you about 2,418 feet above sea level and roughly 35 years back in time. A venue for summertime torpor since it opened in 1907, it was touted as the best hotel between, well, Baltimore and Wheeling. The low-key, 1,200-acre, family-owned resort (with its own golf course) is open from April to early November and offers a variety of modestly priced packages (doubles $79-$195 a night; some rates include breakfast and dinner). Staying in rooms that are not posh but are comfortable and clean, many with four-county mountain views, generations of guests (including two presidents, neither of whom a 65-year-old could have voted for) have languished at the Summit. Many still do, sipping afternoon tea on the veranda, taking meals in the main ballroom, playing shuffleboard and eight ball and reading poolside. The large lobby, where a fire burns even on some chilly midsummer nights, is the Summit's heart. It seems straight out of a 1930s movie, with its Mission furniture, dim lighting and a century-old wall telephone with a detachable ear piece and a side hand crank (not an artifact but a working house phone). Hotel lore has it that George Gershwin once played the parlor grand piano, which at last report was missing a couple of keys. Somewhat closer to sea level, the **Lodge at Chalk Hill** (800-833-4283; doubles $79-$111) has simple, comfortable rooms overlooking a small lake. **Benner's Meadow Run Camping and Cabins** (724-329-4097; $10 per person, or $15 for a rustic cabin) is close by and has a pool, playground, store and room for 250 campers.

WHERE TO EAT: Aside from the pricey restaurants at the Summit Inn and Nemacolin Woodlands (the latter's best are highly rated; jackets and reservations are required; see WHERE TO STAY), there's the **Stone House** (724-329-8876 ♿), another longtime Route 40 landmark. This is a place of contrasts: On one side is an upscale, very good Italian restaurant, on the other an unabashed blue-collar bar. And **Glissen's** (724-329-4636 ♿), in Markleysberg, not far from Nemacolin, is a real find: It's cheap, it's good (the home fries are outstanding), and you can buy a complete dinner special (meat, potato, vegetable, soup, bread) for $4—or wonderful home-baked pies for $5.75. And there are jukeboxes at the tables.

FOR MORE INFORMATION: Contact the **Laurel Highlands Visitors Bureau** (800-333-5661).

Chapter 4

Hotfooting it
East
By Southeast

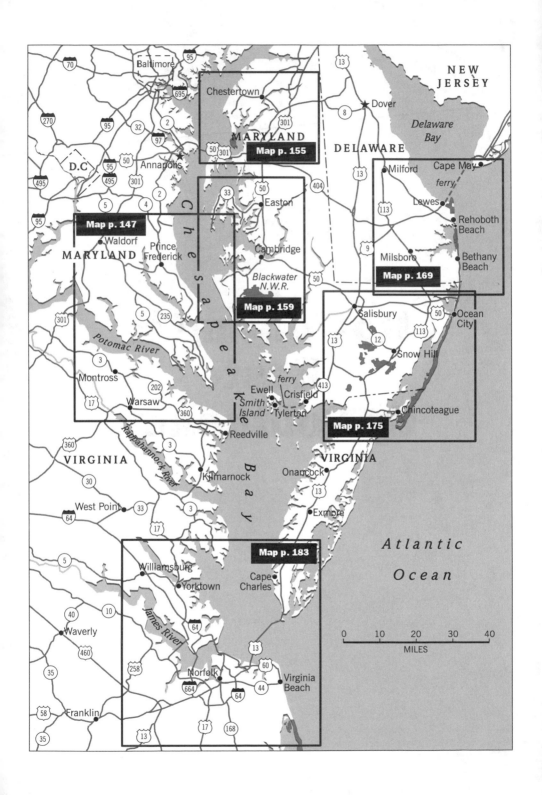

Calvert Cliffs Notes

By Susan Glick

ONE OF THE best things about day trips is that no one has to know about them. You can just hit the road and, as long as you're back by dinner, the whole trip can be your little secret. My latest such outing was to Matoaka Beach Cabins along the Chesapeake Bay's Calvert Cliffs. Usually I go there with my kids, but now that they're teenagers, day trips don't fit easily into their schedules. Besides, I needed a day away, a day just for me.

I packed some stuff and stashed it in my car when no one was looking: an old journal from a trip I'd taken to Europe the summer after high school, a fresh notebook, some jeans and duck boots.

Matoaka Beach Cabins, 12 miles north of Solomons Island in Calvert County, is owned by Connie and Larry Smith, who rent out cabins and daytime beach access. Calvert Cliffs, stretching about 30 miles from North Beach to Solomons Island, is a fascinating place where the sandy cliffs erode a little bit each day, exposing shells and bones and anything else that was on the floor of the shallow ocean that covered southern Maryland in the Miocene Epoch. A couple of feet of the Smiths' cliffs crumble each year, tossing fossils onto the beach and into the surf.

After you've been collecting ancient fossils for a while, you home in on your favorites, which is a good thing, because it's not possible to pick up everything. I like barnacles and coral and Maryland's state fossil, a snail referred to in books as the "ecphora quadricostata." And I always look for teeth—shark, of course, and crocodile and horse teeth.

Fossil hunting is a Zen-like activity, kind of like weeding or highway driving or channel surfing. But on this late spring day, I'm having a hard time finding that "zone." I've taught an 8 o'clock writing class on my way here and I can't seem to relax.

It's nonetheless a perfect morning for the beach. The sun is out, the breeze is warm, the air is damp and salty. The waves block out all other sounds. The best part is that the beach and water are empty. It's never crowded, but today I'm completely alone. (Secret Outing Tip: Ignore weather reports. The forecast today was for chilly wind and rain.)

The winter storms have left logs all along the beach and small ledges in the sand that drop off near the water, making perfect seats. I move up the beach, sitting on one ledge and then another, lazily sifting through the sand on the shore. After a while, I find a shark's tooth. It's tiny, so tiny that it would be lost in my pocket, but I'm pleased. I slip it into a plastic bag and pull out my old journal, a record of my thoughts as I wandered through Europe, young and free and ready for adventure.

The first couple of pages are full of names and addresses of people all over the world, but I remember none of them. I turn to my first day: "Today Gail and I saw Eiffel Tower, Napoleon's Tomb, Champs-Elysees, La Seine, *et* Notre Dame . . . My feet hurt but I feel great." Where's all the good stuff? Why didn't I describe the smell of raisin bread at dawn in a bakery on the Greek island of Ios, or those pencil sketches in the Picasso museum in Barcelona that changed the way I think about abstract art?

I pull myself to my feet and keep on walking, hoping to find some quick treasure in the sand. The sun is getting hot. The beach is still empty. And fossils, suddenly, are everywhere. More coral than I've ever seen. Perfectly preserved scallop shells. Barnacles! I walk, I spot something, I pick it up, I walk, I spot something, I pick it up. I walk some more. I think of nothing else. I'm in the zone.

I do this for a long time, until I'm tired, and then I sit down and pull out the other notebook, the empty one, the one I'm going to put poems in. It's taken me a long time to come to poetry. "I feel like I'm about to be a poet," I said to a friend last year, like I was about to come down with the flu or something. Then I gave it a try and loved how it felt, compressing and condensing complex images and feelings into a few careful words.

Here on the beach I write freely and privately, trying to capture things that are hard to describe—longings for times past, the feel of salty air at a beach miles from home. Finally it's time to go. When I get to the car, I find it's hours later than I thought. For some people, losing track of time may be an ordinary occurrence, but for me it's rare. It feels strange as I drive away from prehistory and poetry back to daily life.

GETTING THERE: The Calvert Cliffs are about 40 miles from the Beltway, or about an hour's drive. To get to Matoaka Beach Cabins, from the Beltway (Exit 11) take Route 4 south six miles to a left on Calvert Beach Rd. Then go about 1.5 miles to the bright yellow signs on the left marking the dirt road to the cabins. To reach Calvert Cliffs State Park, stay on Route 4 south and follow the signs.

BEING THERE: About eight miles south of Matoaka Cabins, **Calvert Cliffs State Park** is a 1,313-acre wooded park, open sunrise to sunset, with picnic areas, fishing, swimming and an unpaved, two-mile trail leading to beach access for fossil hunting. To hunt for fossils, wear boots and (in any season but summer) dress in layers. Take along a small trowel and sieve. Zippered plastic

142

bags, buckets and film canisters work well for holding finds. A $3 donation per vehicle is requested. For more information call 301-872-5688 or check www.dnr.state.md.us/publiclands/southern/calvertcliffs.html. (A word of caution: Do not, under any circumstances, climb in the cliffs. Their unpredictable shifts and slides have produced more than one casualty.)

WHERE TO STAY: Matoaka Beach Cabins, St. Leonard, Md. (410-586-0269) was a girls' camp from 1924 to 1956. The Smiths, who raised four kids there, bought it in 1960 and have been renting out cabins ever since. The 50-acre property includes a vineyard, hiking trails and a half-mile beachfront for fossil hunting, swimming, crabbing and boating. No dogs are allowed. Rustic, six-person, all-in-one-room cabins rent from April 1 through October for $160 for two nights (the minimum stay). Cabins with two bedrooms go for $195 for two nights. Camping also is available. The beach is open all year. Beach access is $3 for adults, $2 for children under 12. Unlike some other fossil-hunting spots in the area, the beach here is an easy hike from the car.

Also, ever more small B&Bs are springing up in nearby hamlets, including the two-room **Cliff House** overlooking the bay in Prince Frederick (410-535-4839; doubles $95-$129, including breakfast) and the four-room **Serenity Acres Bed & Breakfast** in Huntingtown (410-535-3744; doubles $99-$114). Each has a pool and hot tub. For others, see CHESAPEAKE BEACH, Page 146, and SOLOMONS ISLAND, Page 147.

WHERE TO EAT: You can't beat the view from the picnic tables overlooking the bay atop the cliffs where the Smiths' home and cabins are located. For fancier dining, Connie Smith recommends **Adam's the Place for Ribs** in Prince Frederick (410 586-0001 &) for a relaxed family setting and **Stoney's Seafood House** in Broomes Island (410-586-1888 &) for seafood and scenery.

FOR MORE INFORMATION: Contact the **Calvert County Department of Economic Development** (410-535-4583 or 800-331-9771, or www.co.cal.md.us/cced/guide/guide.htm).

ANNAPOLIS

Annapolis has, among other things: (1) the oldest U.S. legislative building continuously in use (the 219-year-old Maryland State House); (2) scores of historic houses, some now distinctive inns and restaurants; (3) the country's third-oldest college (**St. John's**, of the Great Books curriculum); (4) an antique row, and, of course, (5) boats. Lots of boats.

Maryland's state capital has embraced its image as America's "sailing capital," with 17 miles of waterfront, a home port to more than 2,500 boats, picturesque creeks, the **U.S. Naval Academy** and 200 maritime businesses. Head down Main Street toward the harbor and you'll bump into **Market House**, a sort of small-scale version of Baltimore's Lexington Market, and **City Dock**, where tour boats, pleasure craft and an occasional work boat tie up. Before it was spruced up in the early 1970s, the dock area was known as Hell's Point. Now many know it as Ego Alley, where to-die-for boats glide to a halt to impress the crowds.

With a permanent population of just 35,000, Annapolis is at heart a small-town state capital and county seat that's also a maritime theme park—one that includes the 4,000 midshipmen (and women) of the Naval Academy, whose spotless grounds beckon visitors.

Annapolis parking is tight. Try one of three garages in or near downtown. Better yet, take advantage of the $3 all-day parking ($4 on weekends) at the **Navy-Marine Corps Stadium** (turn right from Rowe Blvd. onto Taylor Ave.) and take the shuttle bus (10 a.m.-6 p.m. weekends, when it's free, 6:30 a.m.-8 p.m. weekdays, when it's 75 cents). In town, forget all mechanized forms of land travel. Annapolis, conveniently compact, is for walking.

Consider starting at the **Annapolis Visitors Center** at 26 West St.; walking tours leave daily at 10:30 and 1:30 ($8, $3 for students). At the **Historic Annapolis Foundation's** store at City Dock (410-268-5576), you can rent ($5) an audio tape of broadcast news icon/sailor Walter Cronkite guiding you around. Annapolis is a delight from the water. **Chesapeake Marine Tours and Charters** (410-268-7600) at City Dock offers an array of boat tours, from headboats to simple taxis, lasting less than an hour to a full day. The 40-minute harbor and Spa Creek tours are a deal at $6 for adults, $3 for 11 and under. **Discover Annapolis** minibus tours cram centuries of information into an hour-long ride that's $10 for adults, $3 for 3-12, free for 2 and under (410-626-6000). The **Naval Academy Museum** (410-293-2108) is not to be missed by maritime history buffs. For guided tours of the **Naval Academy** itself, call 410-263-6933 for the seasonally complicated schedule ♿.

Besides shops and historic houses on many streets, other notable sites include the **William Paca House** (186 Prince George St., 410-263-5553), the Georgian manse of the Declaration of Independence signer, with its colonial-era exhibits and a boxwood garden hidden out back. **Banneker-Douglass Museum** (84 Franklin St., 410-974-2893; closed Mondays ♿) testifies to the historic role of Annapolis' still-sizable African American community, including an exhibit of slave artifacts and religious items unearthed at the Carroll House, a four-story plantation manse on Spa Creek. Over in Eastport, the **Barge House Museum** (133 Bay Shore Dr., 410-268-1802; open Saturdays 11 to 4 and by appointment) offers a glimpse of a more recent but all but extinct Annapolis maritime culture: that of the waterman. (While you're there, pick up the Historic Eastport Walking Tour brochure and explore the peninsula at your own pace.)

GETTING THERE: Annapolis is 45 minutes from Beltway Exit 7. Take U.S. 50 to Exit 24 (Rowe Blvd.). For a more scenic (but less rapid) trip, try Route 450, which winds through woods and wetlands north of U.S. 50.

WHERE TO STAY: Historic Inns of Annapolis (410-263-2641) operates four moderate-to-expensive renovated properties in town, including the triangular, 222-year-old **Maryland Inn**, (doubles start at $175, suites at $200 ♿). There's also a noted in-house restaurant and adjacent **King of France Tavern**, the place to hear live jazz in close quarters (five nights a week in season, weekends otherwise). A block from City Dock but more moderate are **Gibson's Lodgings** (410-268-5555; doubles $68-$125, including a large breakfast). These three buildings house 19 rooms and two ⬚ private baths, no phones or TVs) with access to a particular yard and oasis-like lounge. The renovated **Loews Annapolis** doubles $109-$209 ♿) has 217 rooms and 23 suites ne plus one of the most highly rated restaurants in town, the ticularly noted for its prime rib and crab cakes. Less distinctive but with the best location and harbor view is the full-service **Annapolis Marriott Waterfront** (800-336-0072; doubles $179-$249 ♿).

A **Holiday Inn** and **Comfort Inn,** both well run, are out in shopping-strip territory. Beyond that, we've heard good things about the **Chesapeake Bay Lighthouse Bed & Breakfast** (410-757-0248; doubles $125-$220). It's a three-room inn carved out of a working, full-scale lighthouse replica on Sharps Point (and much easier to find by boat than car). It has peerless water views on an isolated stretch of bay shore. Two boat-and-breakfast pioneers also operate here: **Harborview Boat & Breakfast** (800-877-9330; doubles start at $230) and **Schooner Woodwind** (410-263-8619; doubles start at $200). For other options, check with **Annapolis Accommodations** (800-715-1000) and the Annapolis-based **B&Bs of Maryland** (800-736-4667).

WHERE TO EAT: The crab bisque and crepe Annapolis at **Cafe Normandie** (410-263-3382 ♿) add a pleasantly French coastal flavor to a visit. If you'd rather eat on the run, or on the walk, grab a bite to go at **Market House** (410-269-0941 ♿). It's got a raw bar, a sandwich stand, deli, a Baskin-Robbins, a bakery and more, and there are tables and park benches outside. **Pusser's Landing** (in the Marriott Waterfront) serves nicely prepared specials in a dining room right on the harbor. In Eastport, there's nouvelle cuisine and an ageless view of the Spa Creek bridge and boat traffic at **Carrol's Creek** (410-269-1406 ♿). **McNasby's** (410-280-2722 ♿), on Back Creek, established in 1886 and now under city ownership but private operation, survives as both a retail fish outlet and a spot to buy lunch. "The home of the $2.99 crab cake sandwich" is not exactly a restaurant, but there are four booths inside, plus an outside deck with tables by the water and a loudspeaker that lets you know when your order is ready. For traditional Chesapeake Bay fare, Annapolitans know to head just outside town, to **Cantler's Riverside Inn** (410-757-1467 ♿) on Mill Creek in St. Margaret's, or to **Mike's Restaurant & Crab House** (410-956-2784 ♿) on the South River (southern shore) and Riva Road (northbound) at Riva. Cantler's is known for catching its own crabs in season. Mike's is another classic hard-shell-crabs-and-beer kind of place with indoor and outdoor tables and a small marina where sailboats and powerboats coexist in adjoining slips.

For a reminder that this is often unlovely but lovable Maryland, stop at **Chick & Ruth's Delly** on Main St. (410-269-6737 ♿), run by the same Levitt family for 33 years (Chick and Ruth have turned things over to son Ted). Open all night, the place is painted neon-yellow inside with 7-Eleven orange accents, plus faded photos and ceiling fans. The food is reasonable, the service fast and friendly. The clientele runs from hotshot lobbyist to unemployed sailboat crews.

CHESAPEAKE BEACH

Long ago, Chesapeake Beach was the dream of one man, Otto Mears, a Russian orphan. He accumulated a fortune before indulging an appetite for railroad construction and building a turn-of-the-century resort here. The railroad took Washingtonians and Baltimoreans straight to the town's boardwalk, dance pavilion, German beer garden, Victorian hotel and huge wooden roller coaster. When the railroad opened on June 9, 1900, about 5,000 visitors were greeted at the station by waltzing bears, high-wire performers, a marching band, balloonists, a gypsy fortune-teller and others. At the tiny **Chesapeake Beach Railway Museum** (410-257-3892), in the original train station, you still can see remnants of Mears' dream in an extensive photo collection. While no train comes here any more, the beach and a small boardwalk remain, as do 15 million-year-old fossils that wash up every day, plus a handful of no-frills seafood restaurants and a healthy charter-fishing trade. Next to the museum, the **Rod 'N Reel** restaurant (410-257-2735 ⓖ) offers head boats at $30 a person for a 7-hour bay trip. Charter boats start at about $280 for six people at the Rod 'N Reel or at **Seaside Charters** (301-855-4665), tackle and bait included. There's a beach near the Rod 'N Reel and a small boardwalk and beach up the road at **North Beach**. An especially nice spot called **Brownie's Beach**, off Rt. 261, is about a mile outside town. Nearby attractions: the dark waters and evocative bald cypress "knees" of **Battle Creek Cypress Swamp** in Prince Frederick (410-535-5327), a 100-acre nature center offering field trips and exhibits year round; **Flag Ponds Nature Park** in Lusby (410-586-1477 ⓖ), its upland forest trails leading to a small beach below the cliffs that's said to be great for fossil hunting; and St. Leonard's **Jefferson Patterson Park and Museum** (410-586-8501 ⓖ), whose 512 acres of pastures, woodlands and shoreline include an archaeological museum and trail covering Maryland history and prehistory.

GETTING THERE: Chesapeake Beach is about 30 miles from the Beltway. Take Exit 11 to Route 4 south to Calvert County. Go left on Route 260 to town.

WHERE TO STAY: Tidewater Treasures (410-257-0785) has four rooms (and five animals) and doubles from $94 to $115, including breakfast, in a tranquil hilltop house overlooking the bay.

WHERE TO EAT: Abner's Seaside Crab House (410-257-3689 ⓖ) serves soft-shell crab, crab cakes and other local specialties in a Formica setting with a view out back of Fishing Creek marsh, complete with wading birds and swaying grasses. **Italia by the Bay** (410-257-1601 ⓖ) has homemade pasta and pizzas from a wood-burning oven. We've also heard good things about **Lagoon's Island Grille** (410-257-7091 ⓖ) and, in North Beach, the exceptional mussels at **Neptune's Seafood Pub** (410-257-7899 ⓖ).

FOR MORE INFORMATION: The **Calvert County Department of Economic Development** (phone numbers and web site on Page 143).

SOLOMONS ISLAND

Solomons Island is where lots of people traveling south from Annapolis are heading, and for good reasons. Not least are the memorable sunsets viewed from Solomons' unrivaled "Riverwalk" boardwalk, which at any time of day offers exceptional vistas back across the Patuxent River. A small, hook-shaped sliver of land that doesn't quite obstruct the mouth of the Patuxent, Solomons Island was a sleepy watermen's town until the yachting folks discovered its sheltered-harbor charms. The marinas and charter fleets followed, along with upscale restaurants and inns. All of us city folks seeking romance and tranquility were not far behind. Naval consolidations have increased the presence of dress whites at the Naval Air Test Center just across the Patuxent bridge in Lexington, and some weekdays it's impossible to find a room anywhere between here and the Beltway. (On sunny weekends, it's a strictly out-of-uniform crowd, and there's usually no problem finding a place to stay.)

The **Calvert Marine Museum** (410-326-2042; open daily 🔁) displays life-sized exhibits on bay and river life from the Miocene Epoch to the skipjack age. One part of the museum, the **Drum Point Lighthouse**, built in 1883, offers daily guided tours. Other museum attractions include the **Wm. B. Tennison**, a historic Chesapeake Bay bugeye, which provides hour-long Patuxent River tours Wednesday-Sunday at 2 from May to October; and the **J.C. Lore Oyster House**, with its hands-on learning about the life and times of local watermen. For a more romantic time, Patrick Derry offers charters (most evenings and on weekends, May-October) on his 50-foot cutter-rigged ketch, *Seanchai,* from the **Solomons Island Yacht Club** (410-326-4700). Two-hour evening charters are $200; a full weekend day, 9 to 5, goes for $600 for up to six people.

GETTING THERE: From Beltway Exit 11, follow Route 4 south for 1.5 hours.

WHERE TO STAY: Back Creek Inn (410-326-2022; doubles $95-$145, including breakfast) was built by a waterman a century ago and is now owned by two women, one a painter, the other a gardener. All seven rooms with private baths, like the common patio and hot tub, are nestled in a lush garden with a lawn that slopes to the water's edge; each room is impeccably furnished. Other choices include **Solomons Victorian Inn** (410-326-4811; doubles $90-$175 ⓑ), with six rooms on the harbor; **Webster House** (410-326-0454; doubles $85-$110), a self-described "Christian bed & breakfast" with four comfortable rooms, three with private bath, plus a garden and a hot tub; and the three-room, Victorian **By-the-Bay Bed & Breakfast** (410-326-3428, doubles $90-$125) on the waterfront. There's also a huge **Holiday Inn**, with its own marina and a large pool (800-356-2009; doubles start at $104); pets are allowed—but, inexplicably, only in smoking rooms. Next door is a **Comfort Inn** (doubles start at $87; 410-326-6303 ⓑ) with punier rooms but a better situated and friendlier restaurant. For nearby lodging options, also see Calvert Cliffs lodgings (Page 143) and Chesapeake Beach (Page 146).

WHERE TO EAT: Solomons is awash in restaurants. For breakfast, the local legend is **Edith's Place** (410-326-1036). It opens early, has low prices and is not known to have ever let a customer go hungry. For lunch, the bright, light-filled **C.D. Cafe** (410-326-3877 ⓑ) in the Avondale Center on Solomons Island Road (the main street) has a creative cuisine, espresso drinks, terrific pastries and a peerless view of the graceful Gov. Thomas Johnson Bridge. For dinner, the **Dry Dock Restaurant** (410-326-4817) and **Lighthouse Inn** (410-326-2444 ⓑ) are both virtually glass-walled and thus suited to viewing sunsets. The Dry Dock is small and cozy, while the Lighthouse is spacious, high ceilinged and quietly bustling.

FOR MORE INFORMATION: The **Solomons Information Center** at 410-326-6027 or the **Calvert County Department of Economic Development** (numbers and web site on Page 143).

St. Mary's City

The site of Maryland's first capital is now known as the site of **Historic St. Mary's City** (301-862-0990 or 800-762-1634; admission $7.50, $3.50 6-12 ⓑ), which is almost the same thing. It's an 800-acre outdoor museum and active archeological dig, the fruits of which are displayed in the visitors' center (Wednesday-Sunday 10-5, year round). The outdoor exhibits (Wednesday-Sunday, April through November) of this likable mini-Williamsburg are populated by interpreters in period dress. The exhibits themselves include a replica of the square-rigged *Maryland Dove* (one of the two ships that carried the first settlers here from England in 1634), a working tobacco plantation and the reconstructed 1676 State House. Digs have revealed the foundation of the first Catholic church built in the colonies, a hint of the early tolerance, religious and otherwise, that distinguished what was to become the state of Maryland. Among the original mavericks who came to St. Mary's were Margaret Brent, who asked for the right of women to vote more than 350 years ago, and Mathias de Sousa, the nation's first black man to join a legislative body. The first print shop in a southern colony also operated here.

To get to lush, evocative and wonderful-for-biking St. Mary's County from Beltway territory, you pass through Amish country and much else out of the past. If that doesn't persuade you that you've entered a time warp, ask your innkeeper about the last time a guest saw a ghost. It's not unusual here to encounter straight-faced reports of spirits—perhaps of early settlers or native tribe members or the 3,300 Rebel prisoners who died at the Union prison in what is now POINT LOOKOUT STATE PARK (see following section).

For a look at what is still perhaps the least changed watermen's village along the bay, take Route 249 to mile-long **St. George's Island** on the Potomac. On the way, you can stop at **Piney Point Lighthouse Museum & Park** (301-994-1471; weekends noon-5, May through October &). From the tip of the island, **Capt. Jack Russell** (301-994-2245) takes out school and environmental on his working skipjack, the *Dee of St. Mary's*, and pre-arranged groups of 30 or more on a two-hour dinner cruise up the St. Mary's River, for about $35 per person.

GETTING THERE: St. Mary's City is about two hours from Beltway Exit 7. Head south on Route 5 all the way to St. Mary's City. A slightly faster alternative is to get on Route 235 south after passing Mechanicsville.

WHERE TO STAY: St. Michael's Manor (301-872-4025; doubles $65-$70, including full breakfast) has four air-conditioned rooms in a 200-year-old home overlooking Long Neck Creek in nearby Scotland, with boating, swimming, biking and wine tastings available. In Ridge, **Scheible's Motel and Fishing Center** (doubles $42, 301-872-5185) has waterfront rooms with TVs, a restaurant, charter fishing, a crab dock and a gift shop. On St. George's Island, **Swann's Hotel** (301-994-0774; doubles $80 &) in Piney Point has basic, clean rooms adjacent to its general store and restaurant/bar (closed December through February), where breakfasts and dinners are good home cooking and reasonably priced. Also on St. George's, **Camp Merryelande** ($65-$125; 800-382-1073 &) has reasonable, well-equipped cottages and about 30 tent sites on 25 wooded, waterfront acres. For camping at POINT LOOKOUT STATE PARK, see following section.

WHERE TO EAT: Down at Point Lookout Marina, home-grown chef John Spinicchia has successfully married haute cuisine and Southern Maryland fare at **Spinnakers** (301-872-4340 &). In St. Mary's City, the **Broome-Howard House** (301-866-0656, open Thursday-Sunday &) has been impressing city slickers and locals alike with its creative regional American fare. For a more casual menu of fresh-caught seafood (the owner is a waterman), try **Courtney's** (301-872-4403) in Ridge.

FOR MORE INFORMATION: The **St. Mary's County Division of Tourism** in Leonardtown at 800-327-9023 or 301-475-4411.

POINT LOOKOUT STATE PARK

Well known to sport fishermen and Civil War buffs, the picturesque peninsula separating the Chesapeake and the Potomac also is one of Maryland's most underrated state parks. It has three miles of beaches, about 150 campsites (a fifth with full hookup facilities), rental facilities for boats and flat-water canoes, a fishing pier, a pet trail and hiking and biking trails. Open year round, 8 a.m. to sunset, the park also offers a museum and lectures on the area's Civil War history. The only federal monument to Rebel soldiers is here, a small obelisk honoring the 3,300 Confederate prisoners who died in Point Lookout's stockades, which housed more than 20,000 prisoners of war. Admission is $3 per person on weekends only, May through September. Otherwise it's free. Call 301-872-5688.

Also, June through Labor Day, the **Captain Tyler**, a 150-passenger ferry cruiser, leaves Point Lookout for the one-hour, 40-minute passage to **SMITH ISLAND** (see Page 162), the Chesapeake island some claim was named for explorer Capt. John Smith. The boat, which returns from Smith Island at 2 p.m., has restrooms and a snack bar; call **Tyler's Cruises** in Ewell at 410-425-2771. Cost: $30 for adults, $15 for children 6 to 11.

Tilghman Island Surprises

By Roger Piantadosi

I COULD tell you about the sunsets and skipjacks and uncomplicated charms, and I will, but a better reason to like Tilghman Island, Md., has to do with the young guy who mooned us from the top of the old Knapps Narrows drawbridge on our first visit. God knows the Eastern Shore tourism people, much less the sheriff, wouldn't approve, but it made me feel, well, welcome.

The day's crabbing done, the tanned and shirtless twentysomething and his two companions apparently had spent too much of a summer Saturday afternoon with brother Budweiser. The mooning done, he ran and jumped a good 30 feet into the Narrows. Then he climbed back ashore, walked stiffly back to his friends' table at the bar/restaurant next to the bridge and sat quietly. Such a stupid stunt easily could have ended in disaster, but it didn't—and it said something about Tilghman that the brochures, especially the glossy ones for new luxury homes, don't mention.

More than any town I've seen along the Chesapeake, Tilghman Island remains unpredictable and independent-minded—independence being the quality every waterman mentions first when you ask about job benefits. Tilghman, a waterman's town very much in transition, retains its essential quirkiness in the face of the powerful forces, natural and otherwise, that are slowly transforming so much of the Eastern Shore.

Out here along the Chesapeake, unpredictable is what you want to be, have to be, because the bay is the ultimate in unpredictable. It is flat, calm and balmy one October moment, covered in fog, a stinging wind and four-foot swells 20 minutes later. It yielded a bounty of oysters for generations of families, but now those who start plying the creeks and flats every October have no choice but to work harder and worry about those truckloads of Oregon oysters arriving sooner at the wholesaler's.

Maybe being fond of the quirky and unpredictable is just my reaction to the alarming number of people in this world who are, at this moment, wearing little McDonald's hats and greeting customers in the monotones of many languages. In any case, there is no McDonald's on Tilghman Island. Yet.

What you'll encounter here, if you drive the extra dozen miles past the better known and more often repainted St. Michaels, is one of the state's busiest drawbridges (over the Narrows, the aptly named boater's shortcut from Annapolis and Kent Island down to the Choptank River and Oxford). Beyond that are a couple of family-owned country stores, a bait and tackle shop, some lovingly tended book and collectibles shops, some decoy carvers and wooden-boat builders, a half-dozen inns and B&Bs, ranging from simple to spectacular, and the Harrison family's famous sport fishing-seafood-sleepover empire. You'll also find, rocking in the gentle swells at Dogwood Harbor, one of the country's last commercial sailing fleets—a few proud, aging skip-jacks whose captains not only dredge the bay for oysters in fall and winter but, more often nowadays, take tourists on day trips.

On one visit to Tilghman, my wife, Charmaine, and I took one of Ed Farley's half-day sails aboard his skipjack *H.M. Krentz*. The bay's wild beauty seemed somehow more real when met from the rail of a heaving old wooden sailing boat. Farley's demonstration of oyster-dredging was both intriguing and heart wrenching. He culled by rote a few puny keepers from the dredge's mud, talking quietly about seeding projects and the disease that has decimated the bay's oyster population.

On our most recent day trip to Tilghman, we spent a couple of memorable late-afternoon hours on the Choptank with Randolph Murphy, 42-year-old son of Capt. Dan and Miss Edwina Murphy, as they are known, elders of the oldest clans of watermen here. In his hand-built, diesel-powered workboat, Randy Murphy makes his living on the water pretty much year round—fishing and crabbing when it's warm, oystering and guiding hunting parties when it's not. He has an easy laugh, a permanent wind- and sun-resistant reddish-brown glow, and that Eastern Shore knack for saying more by saying less.

"Oh, it's definitely not for the security," he says of why he remains a waterman. "Yep, making $2,000 one week and $200 the next is not what you'd call security." He leaves you to see that it has to do with being out here between the endless sky and the brownish-blue waters, applying skill and spirit to the waterman's tasks, as his forefathers did before him.

As he's setting out his 4,700-foot crabbing trotline, a 40-foot pleasure sailboat running on diesel crosses it. He gently but precisely slackens the line. Murphy smiles. "You know, we have a saying about sailboaters. The sailboater arrives on Friday with a crisp white shirt and a crisp dollar bill. And he leaves on Sunday without having changed either one of 'em."

Our friends Jerry and Maura bought a small place in Tilghman almost a decade ago and now hardly ever spend time around their native Washington. They first introduced us to the island. Most afternoons, they take their 22-foot Seahawk onto the bay just to be out there when the sun sets, and every time Maura talks about her adopted town, she paints from a similarly warm palette.

"The people on the island are always friendly," she says, "but they are also very spontaneous and straightforward. They all have a wonderful way of saying something incisive, of putting their finger right on the point and saying something just . . . as it is."

The Maritime Museum in St. Michaels gives you an excellent idea of how things *were* on the Eastern Shore. The way things are, on the other hand, changes daily. But you can count on some things, particularly meeting independent and often surprising people with an uncanny ability to sense a school of fish or a storm ahead.

GETTING THERE: Tilghman Island is about two hours from the Beltway. At Exit 7, take U.S. 50 east across the Bay Bridge. Before Easton, turn right on Route 322 and right again on Route 33 east, which ends in Tilghman.

BEING THERE: If you're after sport fishing, start at **Harrison's**, where the fleet (at last count 14 boats and rising) and fish-finders are hard to beat (410-886-2121). **Dockside Express** (410-886-2083) offers morning eco-tours and sunset champagne tours, each $20 per person. Or take a walk down Mission Road (third left from the drawbridge) to the Choptank. Along the way you'll likely find **Dan Vaughan** (410-886-2083) among the aromatic cedar shavings of his decoy workshop and Maynard Lowery just up the street building his trademark squat and graceful wooden boats. Two-hour-to-all-day sails can be had on the skipjacks **H.M. Krentz** (410-745-6080 ♿) and Wade Murphy's **Rebecca T. Ruark** (410-886-2176), the bugeye **Mamie M. Mister** (410-886-2703) and the restored 1931 pleasure yacht **Lady Patty** (800-690-5080).

WHERE TO STAY: At the warm and central **Sinclair House** (888-859-2147 or 410-886-2147), a room and breakfast is $75-$110 a night. At the island's far tip, it's $150 for the 4-person Cove Cottage on the 57-acre wildlife-refuge grounds of the **Black Walnut Point Inn** (410-886-2452). And there are ever more options in between: the elegant Victorian **Chesapeake Wood Duck Inn** (800-956-2070 or 410-886-2070), where rates (starting at $139) include a gourmet breakfast; the four-room **Lazyjack Inn** B&B (800-690-5080), also known for its breakfasts ($130-$230); the quiet and homey harborside efficiencies at **Norma's Guest House** ($75-$85; 410-886-2395); a two-night weekend package for two, including Saturday dinner and Sunday brunch, for $370 at the **Tilghman Island Inn** (800-866-2141 or 410-886-2141 ♿); or the $209 room/meals/fishing package at **Harrison's Chesapeake House** (room only: $110-$125; 410-886-2121).

WHERE TO EAT: Choices in Tilghman itself include the traditional seafood specialties of **Harrison's** plus the prettier (especially at sunset) **Tilghman Island Inn**, and the outdoor patio on the Narrows or upstairs observation deck of the casual and friendly **Osprey** (410-886-2330 ♿). Directly opposite the Narrows from the Osprey is the newer **Pescado's** (410-886-2126 ♿), where fresh local seafood is married to a modern Mexican-Southwestern menu. For more nearby options, see St. Michaels (Page 157).

FOR MORE INFORMATION: Call 410-822-4606 for the **Talbot County Office of Tourism**, or look up the web site at *www.talbotcounty.md*.

CHESTERTOWN, MD.

Founded on the banks of the Chester River in 1706 and once a prosperous port, Chestertown is now often overlooked by tourists but sought after as an idealized small-town home by escaped city dwellers. Every May, Chestertown celebrates its last big crime wave: On May 13, 1774, six months after the more famous Boston protest against a new British tea tax, locals dumped 342 chests of tea into the river. Today, the Chestertown Tea Party is celebrated with a reenactment, boat races, crafts fairs and a parade. But this storybook town has romantic and historic high points year round. Among the latter are the **Geddes-Piper House** (410-778-3499), open for tours from 1 to 4 p.m. May-October, and there are almost as many elegantly restored Georgian, Federal and Queen Anne's-style homes here as there are in archeology-minded Annapolis. There also are restaurants, craft and antique shops, pubs and the unique shoe store **Scotties** (410-778-4944 ♿)—which also doubles as a newsstand and unofficial community center—scattered throughout the riverfront area. As in much of the gently rolling Eastern Shore, biking is a popular pastime here; if you don't have your own, **Bikeworks** (410-778-6940) will rent you one. **Historic Chestertown & Kent County Tours** conducts walking tours by appointment at 410-778-2829. Finally, there are two nearby wildlife sanctuaries. One is the 2,300-acre **Eastern Neck National Wildlife Refuge** (410-639-7056 ♿) on Route 445, with good trails, an observation tower with a seemingly endless view of what most of the Eastern Shore looked like before macadam roads and, in winter, thousands of geese, tundra swans and ducks. The other is **Chesapeake Farms** (formerly Remington Farms), off Route 20 north of Rock Hall, a privately owned, 3,000-acre, wildlife research area with a self-guided driving tour.

GETTING THERE: From Beltway Exit 7, this is about a two-hour drive. Take U.S. Route 50/301 east over the Bay Bridge and then head north on 301, exiting at Route 213 north toward Centreville; 17 miles later, cross the Chester River into town.

WHERE TO STAY: In the thick of the historic district, the **White Swan Tavern** (410-778-2300 ♿), which toiled for two centuries as a saloon, is now a pristinely restored B&B (rates are $100 to $150, including breakfast). Just down High Street, the full-service Victorian confection **Imperial Hotel** (410-778-5000; $100 to $200 ♿) has both rooms and suites and a pricey, formal restaurant. About a mile south of town is the 135-year-old former plantation house that is now **Brampton Bed & Breakfast Inn** (410-778-1860; $125 to $215, including a full breakfast ♿). Rising regally from a hilltop amid huge trees, it offers six bedrooms and two suites—some with canopy beds, all with down comforters, high ceilings and tall windows. About 1.5 miles from downtown is a clean and friendly **Comfort Suites** (410-810-0555; $90 to $140 ♿). A bit farther—eight miles northwest, but right on the Chesapeake, and next door to golf, tennis and swimming—is **Great Oak Manor** (410-778-

5943: $124-$235), a 25-room, 200-year-old converted mansion.

WHERE TO EAT: For an ambitious meal, try the **Blue Heron Cafe** (410-778-0188 &), or go about eight miles north of town to the remote but rewarding **Kennedyville Inn** (410-348-2400 &), where co-owner/chef Kevin McKinney is earning an excellent reputation for blending Maryland home

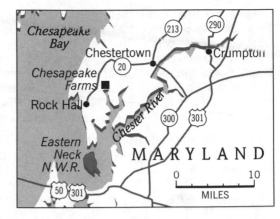

cooking with haute cuisine. Chestertown proper—often a bit too proper—also benefits from a funky coffee shop in **Play It Again Sam** (410-778-2688), with a diverse selection of teas and homemade desserts. If it's lunchtime Tuesday through Saturday, try **Feast of Reason** (410-778-3828), an upscale new age deli/cafe/bakery—and whine, as many do, that it's closed for dinner. If you prefer dining where someone creatively books bluegrass and roots rock and acoustic folk into a big living-room-looking place with a fireplace and folding chairs, head to the back room at one of the Eastern Shore's most affable saloons, **Andy's** (410-778-6779; open Monday-Saturday at 4 p.m.)

FOR MORE INFORMATION: Contact the **Kent County Chamber of Commerce** at 410-778-0416 or *www.chestertown.com* or the **Historical Society of Kent County** at 410-778-3490.

ROCK HALL, MD.

Rock Hall is a former ferry port and waterman's town that's been undergoing a condo-intensive transformation into a boaters' and artists' retreat. It's worth a side trip (it's 13 miles west of Chestertown) for its lack of crowds and its eclectic restaurants, interesting inns and slower pace. It still has a few vital remnants of its earlier life, including the informal **Rock Hall Museum** in the Municipal Building on S. Main Street, 2 to 4 Wednesday through Friday. Also, the **Mainstay** (410-639-7361), a center for visual and performing arts in Rock Hall, offers bluegrass, folk and jazz on weekend evenings.

GETTING THERE: Follow the directions to Chestertown, where you'll pick up Route 20 west to Rock Hall.

WHERE TO STAY: Huntingfield Manor (410-639-7779; doubles $100 to $150 &), is a five-room B&B on a 70-acre farm on the water (one room is a family- and dog-friendly cottage). Other good bets include the **Inn at Osprey Point** (410-639-2194, $135 to $170) and **Moonlight Bay** (410-639-2660, $98 to $134 &). The **Mariner's Motel** (410-639-2291 &) has basic rooms on Rock Hall's harbor that start at $65.

WHERE TO EAT: Every place in Rock Hall serves fresh local seafood. The **America's Cup Cafe** (410-639-7361) is a bookstore, coffee shop and unofficial community center. The **Bay Wolf** (410-639-2000 ⌷) has a bar and smoking and non-smoking dining rooms, and it serves Austrian cuisine as well. **Swan Point Inn** (410-639-2500 ⌷) offers seafood, veal and prime rib and is open shorter hours in winter, longer in warmer months. If you want something a littler simpler, try Rock Hall's **Pasta Plus** (410-639-7916 ⌷), which serves pizza, pasta and several meat dishes.

FOR MORE INFORMATION: Contact the **Kent County Office of Tourism** (410-778-0416) for a free visitors guide or check their web site at *www.kentcounty.com.*

EASTON, MD.

The county and cultural seat of Talbot and the Eastern Shore's wealthiest county, Easton is also the upper peninsula's commercial hub and unofficial capital. Most visitors have good reasons to be here. The attractions include Easton's two championship golf courses, its antiques, galleries and boutiques and such annual events as June's **Eastern Shore Chamber Music Festival** (410-819-0380) and mid-November's **Waterfowl Festival** (410-822-4567), when some 20,000 visitors celebrate, as fine art, the once utilitarian craft of making decoys. (Most people who live in Easton also have good reasons for being here: A national magazine named it one of "America's Top 100 Small Towns," praising its health care industry, its restaurants, arts, airport and historic preservation efforts).

For visitors, downtown Easton's orderly mix of colonial, Federal and Victorian shops, professional buildings and homes invites strolling. For a look at how simple life used to be here, you might start with the **Historical Society of Talbot County's** (410-822-0773 ⌷) small museum and complex of 18th and 19th Century buildings and a typically shaded, spare private garden at 25 Washington Street. Or you may prefer the nearby **Third Haven Meeting House** (410-822-0293 ⌷). Built by Quakers in 1682, it is still in use on Sundays but is otherwise open to visitors. Easton also shares with neighboring St. Michaels one of the most active after-dark scenes outside of the Shore's ocean resorts. Check out the smoky singles scene at **Washington Street Pub** (410-822-9011 ⌷) or the eclectic mix of music and dance performances and cultural events at the fetchingly restored, vaudeville-era **Avalon Theatre** (410-822-0345, or *www.avalontheatre.com* ⌷).

GETTING THERE: Easton is about a 90-minute drive from the Beltway. At Exit 7, take U.S. 50 east across the Bay Bridge and follow it to Route 322 south to a left on Marborough Ave.

WHERE TO STAY: Expect to pay the highest rates for rooms in Easton from Labor Day through the end of the year. The elegant and imposing **Tidewater Inn** right in town (800-237-8775 ⌷) has rooms for $100 to $250, with package deals often available. The **Bishop's House Bed & Breakfast** (800-223-7290) is a comfortable and romantic 1880 Victorian on a residential street a few blocks from the town center, with golf and biking packages and six rooms (three with fireplaces, two with hot tubs). Cost: $110 to $120 ($150 for any two nights Sunday-Thursday). Out on Route 50, an **EconoLodge** (410-820-5555) has rooms for $60 to $100.

WHERE TO EAT: Peach Blossoms (410-822-5220 ♿), with its wall-to-wall peach-tree murals and central location on the courthouse square, serves consistently good and creative food to a mix of locals and visitors. The **Rustic Inn** (410-820-8212 ♿) has an atmosphere of intimacy and a menu of seafood and steaks. For fresh California and Tuscany fare and hearth-oven dishes, try the new **Out of the Fire Cafe** (410-770-4777 ♿). If you're a pushover for espresso drinks and homemade muffins, be sure to stop in early and meet the locals at **Coffee East** (410-819-6711).

FOR MORE INFORMATION: Call the **Talbot County Office of Tourism** (phone numbers and web site on Page 154).

St. Michaels, Md.

St. Michaels is a great place to anchor for an expansive (or just expensive) dinner, or to spend a romantic weekend at an inn amid antique sideboards, silver tea service or uniformed porters. But you don't have to get pricey lodgings to have a good time at St. Michaels, with its quaint shops, cafes and B&Bs. You should expect it to take a little longer, however, to find a parking space than in other Eastern Shore villages.

Spread across a series of coves on the Miles River, St. Michaels began as an important port in the early 1700s. By the mid-1900s it had dwindled to a waterman's hamlet and a hunt-country hub, and in the past 30 years or so it has become a realtor's paradise. But its waterfront remains its heart and soul. For an exceptional window on the rise and fall of the Maryland waterman's culture, don't miss the exhibits and open-air wonders of the **Chesapeake Bay Maritime Museum** (410-745-2916; open daily ♿). The museum offers many programs to get participants into the bay, literally and otherwise, including classes in sailing, ecology and decoy-making, crabbing trips and ship-fixing demonstrations. A small but impressive fleet of historic watercraft is moored at its wharf, with a restored 19th Century "screwpile" lighthouse—one of the last "cottage" lighthouses in the world—as its centerpiece. While you're down on the water, you can rent a boat at **Town Dock Marina** (410-745-2400), which also rents bicycles by the hour ($4) or day ($16). April through October, you can take a narrated, 60-minute cruise on the Miles River at **Patriot Cruises** (410-745-3100 ♿), right next to the museum's wharf.

GETTING THERE: St. Michaels is not quite two hours from the Beltway. At Exit 7, take U.S. 50 east across the Bay Bridge. Before Easton, turn right on Route 322 and right again on Route 33 east. In about 15 minutes it becomes Talbot St., St. Michaels' main drag.

WHERE TO STAY: St. Michaels has an array of lodgings, from the **Best Western Motor Inn** (800-528-1234; doubles $98 to 130 ♿) to the pricey **Inn at Perry Cabin** (800-722-2949; doubles $275 to $695, including breakfast and afternoon tea ⓐ); the inn has an indoor pool, croquet, boating, bicycling and access to nearby golf and tennis. In between are: **Barrett's Bed & Breakfast** (410-745-3322; doubles $160-$260, including full breakfast), with nine rooms in the heart of town, five with queen beds and double Jacuzzis in front of a fireplace; **Harbourtown Golf Resort** (800-446-9066; doubles $189, suites $259 ⓐ); and **Dr. Dodson House** (410-745-3691, doubles $170-$180, including full breakfast), two rooms with private baths in a restored former tavern. Five miles west of town is the hidden-away **Wades Point Inn** (410-745-2500; doubles $115-$235 ⓐ), a former manor house on a 120-acre riverfront farm.

WHERE TO EAT: Next door to the maritime museum, the **Crab Claw** (410-745-2900 ⓐ), overlooking the harbor, is a good seafood place that's had the same owners for about 35 years. **Town Dock Restaurant** (410-745-5577 ⓐ) is another casual and often crowded place with a seafood bent and a pleasant harborside deck. Among the best New American restaurants on the Eastern Shore, **208 Talbot** (410-745-3838) offers innovative entrees for $24 to $30. Just across Talbot Street, you might try **Poppi's** (410-745-3158) for breakfast or a burger, and you'll definitely want to stop there for hand-dipped ice cream. For a midday break or a midnight snack, the central **Carpenter St. Saloon** (410-745-5111) is often the most happening spot in town.

FOR MORE INFORMATION: Call the **Talbot County Office of Tourism** (phone numbers and web site on Page 154).

OXFORD, MD.

Oxford is a nice place to both visit and live—except that you'd be a couple of centuries late for most of the best real estate. The oldest well-to-do homes are up on the Strand, the hillock overlooking the Choptank River. They originally were bankrolled by the early tobacco trade dating to Oxford's heyday as a pre-Revolutionary port or by the brisk oyster trade that kept the port going a century or so later. You can view such spreads best from the ferry (see below) or from a rented day sailer (check with **Maryland Yachts** at 410-226-5571). But the quaint, historic and still relatively quiet town of Oxford itself is best enjoyed on foot or on a bike (you can rent those at **Oxford Mews,** 410-820-8222, for $7 for two hours or $14 for the day).

GETTING THERE: From Easton, take Route 322 to Route 333 south; it dead-ends about 20 minutes later at the Tred Avon River in Oxford. Or take the 10-minute **Oxford-Bellevue Ferry** (410-745-9023; daily, year round). Begun in 1683, it is the oldest continuously operating free ferry in the nation. (The northern terminus at Bellevue is a seven-mile drive or cycle from St. Michaels.)

WHERE TO STAY: A fetching three-story clapboard house at the edge of town, the **Oxford Inn** (410-226-5220; doubles $90 to $150) has 11 rooms, many with window seats and private baths, and a wide porch, all a short walk from the historic district. Opposite the ferry is the venerable **Robert Morris Inn** (410-226-5111; doubles $130-$290, open weekends only December-March ⓐ). Named for local hero and Revolutionary War financier Robert Morris Sr., the mansion's original owner, it offers 35 authentically furnished rooms in three buildings.

WHERE TO EAT: Locals tend to recommend **Latitude 38** (410-226-5303 ♿), the most consistent and least hidebound (or, rather, scale-bound) restaurant in town, where the crab cakes also are fabulous. Of course, the **Robert Morris Inn** advertises *its* crab cakes as having been chosen "the best" on the Eastern Shore by the late James Michener, the author of "Chesapeake" and many other works who was a local icon. **Le Zinc** (410-226-5776 ♿) offers creative country French lunches and dinners, plus an espresso bar and a good bunch of microbrews. **Oxford Market** (410-226-0015 ♿) is a good place for sandwiches

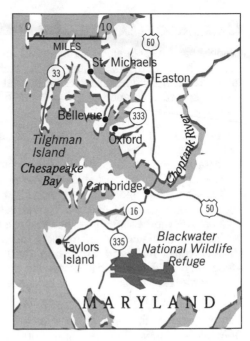

or picnic provisions, and **Schooner Landing** (410-226-0160 ♿), with its deck at the foot of Tilghman Street, is the place to find low-tariff local seafood and live music and dancing on weekends in season.

FOR MORE INFORMATION: Call the **Talbot County Office of Tourism** (phone numbers and web site on Page 154).

BLACKWATER NATIONAL WILDLIFE REFUGE

This "Everglades of the north" covers 17,121 acres, set aside in 1933 as a duck refuge and now a winter layover as well for tens of thousands of swans and Canada geese at the November peak of their flight south. Besides seasonally harboring the endangered peregrine falcon, the refuge, 20 miles south of Easton, is a year-round home to the endangered bald eagle and Delmarva fox squirrel and many families of otters and muskrats. The best time to visit is late October through March, when you will avoid the summertime hordes—of mosquitoes, that is, and biting flies. Pick up a brochure in the visitor center (open daily). The refuge itself is open daily, sunrise to sunset. Entry is $3 a car ($1 per bicyclist or pedestrian). For more information, call 410-228-2677.

GETTING THERE: At Beltway Exit 7, take U.S. 50 east across the bay and south through Easton to Cambridge. Turn right onto Route 16 west and follow the signs to the refuge. The drive is about 2.5 hours.

WHERE TO STAY AND EAT: See CAMBRIDGE/TAYLOR'S ISLAND next.

CAMBRIDGE/TAYLORS ISLAND, MD.

"People have disappeared into these wooded swamps and vast wet savannas, never to be seen again," Eastern Shore author Helen Chappell says. She often takes "road trips" through this sparsely settled corner of the Eastern Shore—always, she says, in appreciation of a personal hero, anti-slavery activist Harriet Tubman.

Tubman was born here in Dorchester County in the early 1820s, escaping her own chains with the help of the "underground railroad," as the network of slave-saving activists became known, and returning repeatedly to help lead an estimated 300 others to freedom. "The places where Harriet hid more than a century-and-a-half ago have not changed all that much," Chappell writes. "Coming into the marshes, I can feel Harriet listening for the baying of the bloodhounds over the beating of her heart, moving by night, taking the North Star as her guide." In addition to information and a video about Tubman, Cambridge's **Underground Railroad Gift Shop** (410-228-0401; closed Sundays) offers African and African American crafts and art. A two-hour guided driving tour can be prearranged for groups, and individuals often can persuade one of the bright guide-interpreters to shepherd them about for a modest fee.

Cambridge is worth a visit for other reasons (if you're not birding or biking at the BLACKWATER NATIONAL WILDLIFE REFUGE or hunting or fishing in the wilds nearby). For local history and maritime lore, see **Spocott Windmill** (410-228-7090), a reproduced working post windmill with a miller's house and restored schoolhouse; the **Brannock Maritime Museum** (410-228-6938 ♿); the **Jim Richardson Maritime Museum** (410-221-1871 ♿), and **Meredith House/ Nield Museum** (410-228-7953 ♿).

GETTING THERE: From Beltway Exit 7, Take U.S. 50 east across the bay and south past Easton. Bucktown Road, which will wind through many of Harriet Tubman's old stomping grounds before reaching Taylor's Island, is the last light past Cambridge; turn right. (An alternate and better-marked road to Taylor's Island is Route 16, which also intersects Route 50 in Cambridge.)

WHERE TO STAY: The 1760 plantation house that is now the **Glasgow Inn** (410-228-0575, 888-373-7890) has seven comfortable, antique- and re-production-filled rooms for $100 to $150 on the west end of Cambridge. **Wingate Manor** (410-397-8717; doubles $80-$115) in Wingate is especially heedful of the needs of bicyclists, offering self-guided tour maps, "biker's breakfasts" and a bike-repair facility. **Loblolly Landings & Lodge** (410-397-3033; $80, including breakfast ♿) is on Liners Road just south of the wildlife refuge. For camping, there's **Taylors Island Family Campground** (410-397-3275), right on the Chesapeake and **Tideland Park** (410-397-3473) on Slaughter Creek.

WHERE TO EAT: If you don't want to make the trip to the homey crab cake restaurant/bar at **Taylors Island General Store** (410-221-2911), try the **Cambridge Diner** (410-228-8898 ♿), which offers great home cooking (try the specials) and homemade desserts.

160

OUT STANDING IN ITS FIELD

IT IS KNOWN simply as "Crumpton" by hundreds of antiques dealers and collectible sellers, rank amateurs and veteran pickers. They can be found here, rain or shine, from 9 to 6 every Wednesday (except between Christmas and New Year's). Technically, it is a country estate auction by **Dixon's Furniture** (410-928-3006) in four open fields and a barn in the tiny crossroads town of Crumpton. And, as *Post* columnist Anne Groer discovered not long ago, it also is not for the faint of heart.

The auctioneer drives a golf cart from pile to pile; at just one five-minute stop, she says, there were 16 transactions totaling $1,480 for items ranging from a $15 birdhouse to a $300 dry sink. Then there was the South Carolina man who loaded up an empty tractor-trailer to conduct his own auction back home, and the New Yorker who paid $40 for a 1930s bed frame, vanity and bench, nightstand, bureau and two mirrors to resell for $600 to a Soho shop (which might charge $1,200 to $3,000 for the suite).

Indoor sellers lay wares on tables and indoor buyers, unlike those who bid on lots and boxes outside, often isolate single items: $100 for a 1927 "Welcome Lindbergh" flag and $900 for an ordinary-looking Chinese vase. A Virginia dealer paid $30 for a 1940s Silex Flamingo Percolator in its original box. "Omigod," she said, you're not going to write about Crumpton so all my customers will know how cheap I get this stuff?"

Another dealer told her, straight-faced, that the weirdest of all Crumpton's weirdness was "the old guy who died on a couch in the third field. He got sick and lay down in the morning, passed away in the afternoon, but nobody knew. The golf cart came, they poked him and he didn't move. So they just put him on the ground, sold the couch and then called the rescue squad."

Groer's advice for normal folks looking for a find: Take cash, drive a van or get a roof rack and rope to lash that adorable moose head to your vehicle. Pack foul weather gear (cleats when it sleets, parasols in August). Don't take very young kids—they risk getting run over by the auctioneer, and they certainly won't grasp why those antique toy soldiers or original Jetsons lunch box they so badly want cost $500."

GETTING THERE: It's about two hours. From the Bay Bridge, follow U.S. 301 north to Route 290 north until you see Dixon's and truck-filled parking lots.

FOR MORE INFORMATION: Dorchester County Tourism Office, 800-522-8687 or *shorenet.net/tourism*.

CRISFIELD AND SMITH ISLAND, MD.

In Crisfield, the **J. Millard Tawes Museum** (410-968-0673; $2.50, open daily mid-May through mid-October, weekdays otherwise ♿) is devoted to the area's fishing history and to the life of its namesake, the former Maryland governor and Crisfield native. In early September, Crisfield also hosts the annual **Hard Crab Derby & Fair** (800-782-3913). Beyond that and its superb seafood, Crisfield has **Somers Cove Marina** (410-968-0925), the state's largest marina and a jumping-off point to Smith Island, 12 miles west and the only populated island in Maryland reached solely by boat. There are also seasonal ferries to Smith from Maryland's Western Shore (see POINT LOOKOUT STATE PARK, Page 149) and from Virginia's Northern Neck (see the NORTHERN NECK, Page 180).

Smith Island actually is an eight-mile archipelago, erosion and storms having altered the original crest of sand discovered by Capt. John Smith. Three villages eventually grew and endured there, populated largely by those who ever-tenuously make their living off the bay. As on Tilghman Island, the villagers are routinely friendly and speak with a similar Eastern-Shore-by-way-of-Elizabeth I brogue. What Smith Island offers is access to lonely and beautiful marshes and deserted islets. These are best explored by canoe, or kayak, though a skiff captained by a local guide will transport you around just as handily.

GETTING THERE: From the Beltway, it's about four hours to Crisfield. Take Exit 7 to U.S. 50 east to Salisbury. There, take Route 13 south to Route 413, which runs into downtown Crisfield. There is year-round ferry service (410-425-4471 or 410-425-5931) to Smith from Crisfield's City Dock, at the foot of Main St.. In winter, service can be sporadic, so call ahead. Departures daily at 12:30; tickets $15 roundtrip ($20 if you spend the night).

WHERE TO STAY: In Crisfield, the **Pines Motel** (410-968-0900) on Somerset Ave. is simple and friendly, offering in-season doubles at $75 a night. On Smith, the **Ewell Tide Inn** (410-425-2141) has doubles for $40-$65 a night, and the **Inn of Silent Music** (410-425-3541) in Tylerton, Smith's most isolated village, has four wonderfully decorated rooms from $75 double, one with private bath, including breakfast. (Home-cooked dinners also are available for $12 on the inn's porch overlooking the bay.) Smith Islander **Janice Marshall** (410-425-3701) offers accommodations and meals in her home for $60 a person, including dinner.

WHERE TO EAT: On Smith, the **Bayside Inn** in Ewell (410-425-2771 ♿) offers crab cakes and other seafood specialties for about $30 for two. In Crisfield, *Washington Post* writer Gary Lee dined heartily at the **Waterman's Inn** (901 W. Main St.; 410-968-2119 ♿), where he found the crab cakes as tasty as the Maryland clam chowder and freshly baked carrot cake, with a tab for two coming to about $50, including a couple of microbrews.

FOR MORE INFORMATION: The **Somerset County Tourism Office** can be contacted by phone at 800-521-9189 or 410-651-2968 and on the web at *skipjack.net/leshore/visitsomerset*. For the **Crisfield Chamber of Commerce & Visitors Center**, call 410-968-2500.

Ocean City in the Off-Season

By Jeannette Belliveau

Recreational forecasts, Maryland beaches: Today, partly sunny, flurries. High 38-46. Wind west 11-22 mph. Ocean temperature 40-43.

A PERFECT FORECAST for a weekend at the beach. That is, if you want a good look at Ocean City's nine miles of off-season sand with about 300,000 fewer partiers than usual.

Before driving east on an unclogged U.S. 50, I canvassed people for suggestions of things to do. "Sleep," my neighbor Rich offered. "I pack sweats, knitting and a book—then wonder if it's too much," said my sister Sharon. "A lot of books are read," said Martha Clements of the Ocean City Visitors and Convention Bureau. The advice boiled down to: Take walks. Eat. Read. Blob. Repeat.

The beauty of Ocean City anytime is that there are plenty of activities yet no must-sees. Especially in the off-season, this is one escape where you don't have to rush at all.

A simple pleasure: strolling beaches as deserted as Western Australia's, yet lined with enough condos behind the dune grass to house the entire population of Norfolk or Tampa.

Sharon jogged ahead, logging her standard three miles. I walked behind, with my Shetland sheep dog, Beau. I counted a total of eight people in either direction, as far as the eye could see. At the high-water mark lay scoured seashells and carcasses of horseshoe and blue crabs, but no human litter. Gull congregations gaggled at the water's edge like penguins. It was the first time I'd seen these magnificent beaches virtually empty, and I felt like an explorer stumbling on a secret hideaway. Maryland's boom resort seemed deserted and wild, more like the rocky Caribbean edge of Cozumel off the coast of Mexico.

A stiff west wind, crashing surf and big cloudless sky sent Beau into crazed raptures. He barked maniacally, attacked my shoelaces, snatched my glove and pranced off. Mind reading his little dog thoughts was easy: Cold weather! An environment like my ancestral home! Another best day of my life!

Later on the boardwalk, Beau greeted his mirror image, Saber the Sheltie, part of a mini-throng lending a hint of summertime liveliness to Ocean City's main drag.

Strollers bundled in parkas and scarves ambled past open game arcades and shuttered eateries. Vendors passed buckets of Fisher's caramel popcorn directly onto the boardwalk, through a window somewhat protected from the cold by hanging plastic sheets. T-shirt shops threw their doors open to the elements. A man added more layers of glitter and tackiness to the exterior of the Ocean Gallery. A policeman on horseback purchased funnel cakes.

A trio of Washington experts on the off-season—Angie, Richard and Rob— met us for delicious pancakes and home fries at Rayne's, in a 1926 building near the base of the boardwalk. Wooden floors, flowery curtains, a 1950s green Hamilton Beach shake blender and loads of philodendrons reminded Sharon of our grandmother's house.

Three local young people looking a bit worse for the wear took the next table. "Mountain Dew is good for hangovers," the waitress counseled. Angie, Richard and Rob shared their insiders' secrets on things to do in the off season: "Sleep late. Get up, read the paper, and sometimes not speak until noon. Swim in the condo's pool. We rode the tram behind Northside Mall to look at the Winterfest Lights, but we nearly froze." Mainly they go almost daily to Assateague Island National Seashore, a nature reserve that acts as both Ocean City's polar opposite and perfect complement.

Angie led us for our first visit to the Life of the Marsh nature walk. Two marsh deer peered at our quintet of wind-lashed humans tromping along, studying placards about palmyra grass and ditches once intended to get rid of mosquitoes (they didn't work).

Assateague's wild ponies proved about as elusive as K St. squirrels. Squadrons of them surrounded autos on the roads and in the parking lots, smearing car windows with their noses, begging for food like Yellowstone bears in the '60s. The ponies looked particularly rugged and healthy with their woolly winter coats. A long wild forelock curled across the eyes of a piebald stallion, while a dark chocolate mare had a copper-blond mane and tail, an eye-catching photo-negative effect.

Let us not give a wrong impression of ourselves as highbrows who only take nature walks. Something about the very atmosphere of Ocean City permits grown adults to savor without guilt:

1. Reading People magazine for content.

2. Watching the Beavis and Butt-head "Moron-a-thon" on MTV.

3. Blowing $20 of quarters on Terminator 2 and arcade football.

"I started at Ocean City, went up to Dewey, then up to Rehoboth, and now I'm back at Ocean City," said Sharon. "If you're really sophisticated, you reach the stage of, I don't care, I don't have to go to the right places." That's how everyone's favorite summer beach at 16 becomes a winter favorite at 40.

GETTING THERE: In the off-season, Ocean City is about a three-hour drive from the Beltway. At Exit 7, take U.S. 50 east across the Bay Bridge. It ends in Ocean City.

BEING THERE: Ocean City hosts 8.1 million visitors a year at 35,000 hotels, rental houses, apartments and high-rise beachfront condos. It has suffered hurricanes, beach erosion and massive condo overbuilding at its north end, but, well, it's got character. Even in the off-season, Ocean City's heart remains its boardwalk, which is equal parts scruffy, tacky and electric. At Third St. you hit "downtown," and in mid-season the noise level rises, with pinball, Skee Ball and video games drawing crowds and lots of families, couples and 16-year-olds on the prowl. **Trimper's** amusement park rides have changed very little in 40, perhaps 50 years: The Himalaya, the Matterhorn, the Hurricane, the old-time carousel are all still here. For some quieter, off-the-beach or off-season pursuits, head to **Old Pro Golf** (6801 Coastal Highway; 410-524-2645), with its year-round indoor miniature golf with a dinosaur theme and arcade games, or to **Northside Park**, a local favorite on the bay at 125th St. featuring a marsh walk. (Dogs are permitted on the Ocean City beaches anytime in the off-season.) For more things to do nearby, see BERLIN/SNOW HILL (Page 172), ASSATEAGUE ISLAND (Page 174) and CHINCOTEAGUE (Page 175).

WHERE TO STAY: For visitors seeking bay views and a bit of luxury, there are two hotels in the Fager's Island neighborhood, 59th St. at the Bay. One is the **Coconut Malorie** (410 723-6100 or 800-767-6060; doubles $118-$379 &), a newish Caribbean-style resort with romantic four-poster beds, original Haitian art and slow-turning mahogany ceiling fans. The smaller **Lighthouse** (888-371-5400) has winter rates that range from $149 to $269. Memorial Day through September, the **Atlantic Hotel** (800-328-5268), at the boardwalk and Wicomico St., isn't fancy but sits right in the heart of the busiest part of Ocean City, and rates are $125-$150 double with a free parking space. Don't confuse it with **Atlantic House** (410-289-2333, winter doubles $65-$110), a B&B in the center of town that's certifiably fancy but in a homey way. Some guests compare it to staying with Grandma. If your dog loves the beach as much as you do, try the **Fenwick Inn** on 138th Street (410-250-1100 or 800-492-1873 &), with winter rates starting at $49 (pets allowed October-March), or the **Sheraton** on 101st Street (800-638-2100), with winter rates starting at $85 & (pets permitted year round, with a $20 nightly surcharge).

WHERE TO EAT: At **Fager's Island Restaurant** (410-524-5500 &), those seated comfortably before dusk are in for a special treat: Sunsets are accompanied by a rendition of the 1812 Overture. And the food's not bad, either. **B.J.'s on the Water** (410-524-7575 &) offers an alternative venue for the same lovely bay sunset, good steaks and plenty of TVs for sports fans. At **Captain's Galley** (410-213-2525 &) you can have two tennis ball-sized crab cakes, with almost no filler, for $20. **Talbot Street Cafe** (410-289-

3806) is friendly and funky, a block from the downtown boardwalk, with live but not-too-loud music weekend nights and sturdy, home-cooked fare.

FOR MORE INFORMATION: Contact the **Ocean City Visitors Center** at 800-626-2326 or *www.ocean-city.com*.

LEWES, DEL.

The northernmost Delaware resort town is the state's oldest (settled in 1631 by Dutch colonists, who were massacred by the local Lenni Lenape tribe). It also is the most historic (filled with restored 17th, 18th and 19th Century structures) and the quietest and most charming (how can you not love a beach town that refuses to have a boardwalk and once was known as "Whorekill?"). Perched on the yawning lower jaw of the Delaware Bay's mouth, Lewes first found prosperity as a home for pilots guiding ships on their way to Philadelphia past shoals with names like the Shears, Old Bare Shoal and Hens and Chickens Shoal. Many pilots became wealthy, building fine homes here. Blessed with an excellent harbor, Lewes remains a seafaring town, home to marinas for pleasure boats, a fleet of charter fishing boats and the Delaware Bay and River Pilots Association. (The shoals, after all, are as dangerous as ever.) And, for a town of 2,300, Lewes also offers a lot of diversion.

A self-guided walking tour of Victorian houses is available from the Chamber of Commerce. The **Lewes Historical Society** (302-645-7670) maintains a half-dozen old houses at Shipcarpenter and Third Streets, including a one-room cabin built before 1700. Finally, perhaps the best reason to spend a few days in Lewes—especially in the fall and early spring—is its proximity to the beaches of **Cape Henlopen State Park** (302-645-8983; for guided walks and special programs, call 302-645-6852). A less-crowded and more natural alternative to the ocean resorts further south, Cape Henlopen has both gentle and rough beaches—it separates the Atlantic Ocean and Delaware Bay—and is open 8 to sunset year round. Its 4,000 acres include nature trails, bike paths, maritime forest and the highest sand dune between the capes of Hatteras and Cod. Lewes' **Zwaanendael Museum** (302-645-1148; free, closed Mondays and holidays [&]), modeled after the town hall at Hoorn in the Netherlands, exhibits military and maritime artifacts from 1631 to the War of 1812. Don't miss the half fish-half monkey, a curiosity from the mid-19th Century, when people were just beginning to dope out the idea of evolution and sailors had a lot of free time. For day trips into quaint, Victorian and restaurant-thick Cape May, N.J. (or on to not-so-Victorian Atlantic City), the **Cape May-Lewes Ferry** (800-643-3779) runs daily from 8:40 to 5 year round. One-way tickets are $18 a car, including the driver, plus $4.50 for each additional adult passenger and $2.25 for children aged 6 to 12.

GETTING THERE: Lewes is about a three-hour drive from the Beltway (on a summer weekend, closer to 4 hours). At Exit 7, take U.S. 50 east over the Bay Bridge, continuing about 25 miles until you see signs for Route 404 east. Take 404 to Business Route 9 into Lewes.

WHERE TO STAY: In the heart of "downtown" Lewes, the **Zwaanendael Inn**

(800-824-8754; in-season doubles $130-$225, including continental breakfast ♿) has 24 rooms and two suites furnished with antiques and private baths and without TVs. The **Wild Swan Inn** (302-645-8550; doubles $85-$135, including a full breakfast) is a three-room B&B in a restored Queen Anne-style Victorian lightship captain's house. It has a very private pool in a side yard, ringed by a patio and a flower-filled garden. The town center is about a 10-minute stroll away,

and the inn provides bicycles for the four-mile ride to Cape Henlopen. **Blue Water House** (302-645-7832 or 800-493-2080; doubles $85-$165, including continental breakfast), offers six rooms on the bay and an attic-level sunroom/study. The **Savannah Inn** (302-645-5592, doubles $50-$80) has seven no-frills rooms (read: not air-conditioned) right in town and is known for its plentiful vegetarian breakfasts.

WHERE TO EAT: Three good bets are **La Rosa Negra** (302-645-1980; Italian ♿); the **Buttery** (302-645-7755; New American cuisine, in the same building as the New Devon Inn) and the **Rose and Crown** (302-645-2373; English pub atmosphere, three dining areas, from loud to cozy ♿). All are on the same block of Second Street.

FOR MORE INFORMATION: Contact the **Lewes Chamber of Commerce and Visitors Bureau** at 302-645-8073 or *www.leweschamber.com* or *www.lewestown.com*.

REHOBOTH/DEWEY BEACH, DEL.

Rehoboth Beach, Del., somehow manages to retain its small-town identity despite the development boom of the past three decades. This may be because the city's Route 9 and Route 1 corridors, with their fast-food barns and outlet malls (including the sprawling **Rehoboth Outlet Centers,** 888-746-7333 or 302-226-9223) are far enough from the beachfront that most people don't connect them. Every summer "downtown" Rehoboth's small boardwalk tries, and fails, to be garish. Rehoboth Ave., the main drag, is still a shoulder-to-shoulder gauntlet of pizza, T-shirts, ice cream and other beach debris, but on Baltimore and Philadelphia Avenues, which parallel Rehoboth Ave., and the mini-alleyways between are numerous fine (and ever more funky) shops, galleries and restaurants. The beach crowd is a mix of families, young adults and the largest gay resort crowd between Fire Island and Key West. Just south of Rehoboth, Dewey Beach is younger and still a bit more raucous (despite a decade of local ordinances meant to alter its reputation as a party town).

South of Dewey is an oasis of calm: the **Delaware Seashore State Park** (302-227-2800). This seven-mile strip has parking, boating (with a 300-slip marina on the bay side), camping (145 sites with full hookups, 133 without), picnicking facilities and some less crowded, almost-natural beaches, should you tire of all those sandcastle-building contests in Rehoboth or Bethany. If you tire of the beach in general, nearby sights include the **Nanticoke Indian Museum** in Millsboro (302-945-7022; summer hours: 9-4 Tuesday-Friday, 10-4 Saturday and noon-4 Sunday 🚹), about 12 miles west of Rehoboth. The Nanticoke Nation, Delaware's last remaining indigenous tribe, runs this small museum in a former schoolhouse.

GETTING THERE: Rehoboth is a little more than three hours from the Beltway (or, on a summer weekend, closer to four hours). At Exit 7, take U.S. 50 east over the Bay Bridge, continuing about 25 miles until you see signs for Route 404 east. Follow 404 to Business Route 9 into Rehoboth.

WHERE TO STAY: For peacefulness and character (but less than two blocks from the boardwalk), try the **Sea Voice Inn and Retreat House** (302-226-9435 or 800-637-2862; doubles $75-$120). If you're willing to trade off the short walk to the beach for unusual peace (and memorable sunsets over Rehoboth Bay), **Barry's Gull Bed and Breakfast** (302-227-7000; doubles $120-$180) has a handful of wicker-filled, wood-paneled rooms in a quiet residential area of Dewey Beach. In Milford, Del., about a half-hour's drive from Rehoboth and Dewey, there's a particularly well restored Victorian confection known as **The Towers** (302-422-3814; doubles $95-$135, including breakfast). It has a formal garden, a swimming pool and its own restaurant (the **Banking House Inn**) across the street.

WHERE TO EAT: The choices—after you've had your fill of **Grotto Pizza** and **Thrasher's Fries**, that is—are many. **Beach House** (302-227-4227 🚹) has something for everyone, from meatloaf with mashed potatoes to caramelized shrimp with ginger risotto. **Big Fish Grill** (302-227-9007 🚹) is a cheerful take on resort surf-and-turf, with a light hand on the saucepan. The Delmarva's only real sushi bar, **Cultured Pearl** (302-227-8493 🚹), is in Rehoboth, and it recently doubled its space by adding a "garden room" including rock fountain walls and a little stream zigzagging among the tables. **Blue Moon** (302-227-6515) usually is packed, and its creative, seafood-leaning menu is not quite as pricey as the Asian-influenced American fare at award-winning **La La Land** (302-227-3887), where the food is outdone only by the over-the-top faerie-dust decor. On the other hand, the shocking-purple exterior of **Planet X** (302-226-1928) only hints at the multicultural, imaginatively beyond-healthy entrees within.

170

Bethany Beach/Fenwick Island, Del.

The "Quiet Resorts" are so called mostly for their lack of mechanized amusements and their collective emphasis not on the Single but the Single Family, as in dwellings. Some of Washington's best middle-class neighborhoods seem to come with two weeks in **Bethany Beach**. Bethany's high-rise Sea Colony dominates an otherwise low-rise town, which offers a bit of shopping and dining along its main drag, Garfield Parkway. For a weekend visit, the beaches are best just south of town in **Fenwick Island State Park** (302-539-9060 or 302-539-1055 &), which has no high-rises or boardwalk. South of the park is the small town of Fenwick Island, stretching from the bay across the coastal highway to the surf. Once the quietest town on the Delaware/Maryland shore, it is an ever more popular place for dining, shopping and time-tested amusements. These include, not surprisingly, no less than three miniature golf courses plus the **Fenwick Water Park** (302-539-4027), with its steep and relatively cheap waterslide. You'll also encounter such unexpected finds as Dale Clifton's **DiscoverSea Shipwreck Museum** (302-539-9366). Above Sea Shell City on Route 1, the museum displays cannons, daggers, coins, emeralds and gold jewelry dating from 1541 to 1860, much of it collected by Clifton over the past 20 years or so from shipwrecks along the Delmarva coast (he still organizes dives and expeditions).

In Bethany in season, news junkies will appreciate **Rhodes 5 and 10** (302-539-9191 &), where you can get about every major East Coast newspaper by 7:30 a.m. daily. **Bethany Rental Service** (302-539-6244) rents everything (including household items), particularly bikes and in-line skates for all sizes. You can bike to a locals' favorite, **Holt's Landing State Park**, on Indian River Bay, with its beach, playground, picnic tables, ballfield, boat ramp and access to shallow waters teeming with clams. Out-of-staters pay $5 a car. Also close by is **Assawoman Wildlife Refuge** (302-539-9820), a 1,000-acre park popular with birders and canoeists. In nearby Ocean View, Md., **Iron Age Antiques** (302-539-5344) offers books, knick-knacks and furniture restored by owner Bob Svenson, whose octogenarian associate Bill Gichner is a working blacksmith, the shop's other specialty. Iron Age is one of 10 antique stores on or just off Route 26, the road to and from Bethany.

GETTING THERE: Bethany, Del., is about a three-hour drive from Beltway Exit 7: U.S. 50 east, Bay Bridge, Route 404 east to 113 south to 26 east.

WHERE TO STAY: While most visitors rent homes here for extended family vacations, for shorter stays or off-season visits the **Addy Sea Bed and Breakfast** (302-539-3707; in-season doubles $155-$225) is the only oceanfront B&B between New Jersey and North Carolina. It has a lovely tin-roofed parlor, a big rocking-chair porch on the Atlantic and a less crowded beach. Other options include **Bethany Arms** (302-539-9603 &), with oceanfront apartments starting at $145 a night; and **Westward Pines** (302-539-7426 &), a five-minute drive from the beach, with 14 rooms ($80-$100 per night), some with Jacuzzis and fireplaces, nestled amid the pines (to some a particularly peaceful, low-cost winter retreat).

WHERE TO EAT: Bethany's **Sedona** (302-539-1200) is a hip Southwestern restaurant that 's usually packed. Way back on the bay in Fenwick Island, **Bay Cafe** (302-436-3622 ♿) is a vast (525-seat) theme park/restaurant complex with a fun "Key West atmosphere" and big sandwiches, fresh fish, pasta and state-of-the-art stir-fry entrees. **Tom and Terry's** (302-436-4161 ♿), also on Fenwick, is the classic, casual, beach surf-and-turf restaurant, with an interior almost as inviting as the sunsets diners can watch over the Assawoman Bay marshes.

FOR MORE INFORMATION: Contact the **Bethany-Fenwick Area Chamber of Commerce** at 800-962-7873 or *www.bethany-fenwick.org*.

BERLIN/SNOW HILL, MD.

Amid the beach season crush, these two rejuvenated, Victorian-era Maryland towns pride themselves on being nice places to come home to, even if it's just a home for the weekend. Berlin's charms await you just 10 miles west of Ocean City, on the way to Assateague; Snow Hill is about 20 miles southwest, a bit closer to Chincoteague and Virginia's Eastern Shore.

In Berlin, as Post staff writer K.C. Summers discovered recently, streets are lined with antique stores, cafes and charming, low-key shops, set against a backdrop of towering trees, tidy flower gardens and a dazzling array of Victorian and Federal-era houses—the perfect yin to Ocean City's yang. Highlights include the magnificent **Atlantic Hotel** (see WHERE TO STAY) and, around the corner, the **Globe Theatre** (410-641-0784 ♿), which has been transformed into a mini-mall that provides every necessity known to yuppies: coffee, upscale carryout food, books, art, whimsical clothes and cool jewelry. Just across Main St., **Town Center Antiques** (410-629-1895 ♿) has kitschy, oddball collectibles, including an assortment of vintage Pez dispensers. Another antique store, **Findings** (410-641-2666), has gorgeous mantels and other salvaged architectural details. If shopping's not your bag, grab a walking tour map and check out the architecture: 47 structures in Berlin are in the National Register of Historic Places.

A decade ago in Snow Hill, Worcester County's equally fetching, 300-year-old county seat, a couple of part-time antique dealers had the town to themselves. Now, with 90 dealers set up in four emporiums, Snow Hill calls itself the "Antique Capital of the Shore." The town's most enduring charm and the reason it came to be back in 1642, however, is its access to the lovely Pocomoke River. If you do nothing else here, take a walk beneath the oaks in **Sturgis Park** on the riverfront. If you have an hour or two, take the self-guided walking tour of the mostly 100-year old homes (an 1893 fire erased much of the original town center). And make time to browse the 60-year-old **Pusey's Country Store** and sample Cindy Pusey's oatmeal cookies. Also in Snow Hill, **Furnace Town** (410-632-2032, open April-October ♿) is the site of one of the oldest blast furnaces in existence as well as of other historic buildings, archaeological digs and a museum.

For inexpensive canoe and kayak rentals, or for guide services and group trips around the deep wilds down river, check with the **Pocomoke River Canoe Co.** (410-632-3971 ♿), next to the River House Inn. Among year-round stopovers down river well liked by hikers, birdwatchers, campers, canoeists and fishermen is **Pocomoke River State Forest and Park** (410-632-2566), the largest section of which, **Shad Landing**, comprises almost 15,000 wooded acres between Snow Hill and Pocomoke City. It is renowned for, among other things, its loblolly pine, white dogwood and pink laurel in spring, cypress swamps, river otters and bald eagles.

GETTING THERE: Berlin and Snow Hill are both about three hours from Beltway Exit 7. For Berlin, take U.S. 50 east and south through Salisbury. Before reaching the bridge to Ocean City, turn south on U.S. 113; Berlin is a few minutes ahead. For Snow Hill, at Salisbury take the U.S. 13 bypass south. About 2.5 miles ahead, take Route 12 about 16 miles into town.

WHERE TO STAY: To those who enjoy days on the relatively uncrowded beaches or trails of Assateague, Berlin provides several clearly more comfortable but pricey nighttime alternatives to camping out amid the island's untamed wildness (which intensifies after sunset—often, in mosquito season, to biblical proportions). On Route 113 outside Berlin, **Merry Sherwood Plantation** (800-660-0358; doubles $95-$175) is a gorgeously restored plantation house with wonderfully furnished bedrooms and public rooms. The eight guest rooms on the second and third floors include a two-level honeymoon suite with Jacuzzi. In Berlin proper, the landmark **Atlantic Hotel** on Main St. (800-814-7672; doubles $85-$150) was established in 1895 and is still holding its own quite nicely, thank you. Rocking chairs beckon on the front porch; inside, the 16 guest rooms are furnished with period antiques, and there's an elegant dining room (reservations suggested) and sunny cafe. The **River House Inn** (410-632-2722; doubles $140-$220 ♿) is in a faithfully restored 1895 Victorian in Snow Hill, also with 16 rooms, all with private baths and TVs, and a wide lawn sweeping dramatically down to the Pocomoke. River House and five other inns participate in a highly recommended "Canoeing Inn-to-Inn" program with the Pocomoke River Canoe Co.; rates start with a two-night package for two at $600, including all meals, portages and transfers. Other participating inns: **Hayman House B&B** (410-651-2753) and **Waterloo Country Inn** (410-651-0883 ♿), an elegantly restored 1750s waterfront estate, both in appealingly out-of-the-way Princess Anne, Md.; **Holland House** (410-641-1956) and the **Atlantic Hotel** in Berlin; and the **Garden and the Sea Inn** (see CHINCOTEAGUE, VA., Page 175) in tiny New Church, Va.

WHERE TO EAT: In Berlin, the best restaurant in town probably is the Atlantic Hotel's dining room (see above). The **King's Pub** (410-641-3506 ♿) has decent food and a small-town tavern feel. For lunch or breakfast in Berlin, try the cafe at the **Globe Theatre** mini-mall (410-641-0784 ♿) or **Sassafras Station** (410-641-0979). In Snow Hill, for lunch there's **Judge's Bench** (410-632-1900 ♿) and **Bailey's** deli (410-632-3704) and, for dinner the **Snow Hill Inn & Restaurant** (410-632-2102), which also rents three second-floor rooms for $50 to $75 double, including wine.

FOR MORE INFORMATION: Contact the **Snow Hill Chamber of Commerce**

at 410-632-0809. For other details on dining and lodging as well as on birding, hiking, canoeing and cycling, contact **Worcester County Tourism** at 800-852-0335.

ASSATEAGUE ISLAND, MD.

Assateague is an undeveloped, federally managed barrier island with some 37 miles of pristine beach and an inland pine forest and salt marsh, stretching into Virginia. It's popular with anglers, birdwatchers, campers, hikers and the RV crowd—as well as with a couple of herds of wild horses. Assateague's uncrowded beach does have its drawbacks: Only about five miles of it are accessible by car, so you have to hike or boat your way into the more isolated sands. But for some that's what makes them so wonderful, as only a few make the effort. Visitors can access the island's beaches on the north at Maryland's **Assateague State Park**, which has parking areas, a visitors' center, full-hookup camping areas and concessions, and at the adjacent and vaster **Assateague Island National Seashore**, which has a more rustic campground and a 4.5-mile road that takes you south along the island and to two parking areas for the beach.

If you really seek privacy, park in the national seashore area and walk south along the sand. After 100 to 200 yards, you'll be almost alone. If you continue south, most likely aboard a boat or four-wheel drive vehicle (permits required for the latter), you'll eventually come to a high fence at the Virginia-Maryland state line. It's there largely to separate the two herds of wild horses, all of which are believed to be descended from domesticated stock owned by 17th Century Eastern Shore planters seeking relief from mainland taxes by sneaking some livestock out here. For more about the horses (including the famous Virginia ponies that are persuaded to swim to a village auction every year by the volunteer fire company that owns them) see the CHINCOTEAGUE section on page 175.

Assateague's national seashore area also offers three trails. Two—the Marsh Trail and the Forest Trail—follow well-marked, half-mile boardwalks. Both are places to run into the island's wealth of resident birds, including red-winged blackbirds, yellow warblers, boat-tailed grackles and (especially) great egrets, and to look for the harder-to-spot, forest-bound mammal population, from the ponies to the shier white-tailed deer and their tiny cousins, the sika. For details and maps, stop on your way in at the Barrier Island Visitor Center. Though a popular camping spot, especially in warmer months, Assateague doesn't welcome inexperienced campers. If you want to stay on the island, you ought to know how to protect your food from roaming ponies, pitch a wind-resistant tent and avoid mosquitoes (including the easy method of limiting your visits to October through mid-May). For other nearby places to stay and eat, see OCEAN CITY lodgings, Page 167; BERLIN/SNOW HILL, MD. on Page 172, and CHINCOTEAGUE on Page 175.)

GETTING THERE: From the Bay Bridge, Take U.S. 50 east, following signs for Ocean City. A few miles outside Ocean City, turn right on Route 611 to the Barrier Island Visitor Center.

FOR MORE INFORMATION: Contact **Assateague State Park** (410-641-2120) or **Assateague Island National Seashore** (410-641-1441 or www.nps.gov/asis). To reserve May-October campsites, call 800-365-2267.

CHINCOTEAGUE, VA.

The Virginia end of Assateague Island is widely associated with its feral herd of about 150 ponies owned by the Chincoteague Volunteer Fire Company and rounded up at the end of every July for a swim across Assateague Channel and a population-stabilizing foal auction. The ritual has assumed semi-legendary dimensions thanks largely to Marguerite Henry's 1947 children's tale "Misty of Chincoteague." (The book also helped popularize the notion that Assateague's ponies weren't descended from the offshore stock of colonial tax-evaders but from animals swept ashore here in the shipwreck of a Spanish galleon.) The pony auction brings but a fraction of the dollars dropped that week in this otherwise sleepy fishing village by tourists who enjoy the carnival and related events as well. For the rest of the year, Chincoteague is a low-key, family-friendly place for sport fishing, seafood eating and marine eco-tourism—the latter due largely to its proximity to **Chincoteague National Wildlife Refuge**. The refuge has several extensive nature trails, de-

serted and walkable beaches and, at last count, some 300 species of birds, both resident and migratory, including osprey, peregrine falcon, bittern, tern and horned lark. **Assateague Island Tours** (757-336-6154) offers daily narrated tram tours of the refuge's nature trails and 90-minute, narrated eco-cruises aboard its 42-foot pontoon boat. (To make things more confusing: The wildlife refuge, though named Chincoteague, is on Assateague Island. You have to go through the town—and island—of Chincoteague to get there.) The many other recreational pastimes on Assateague and Chincoteague include, of course, bicycling, canoeing, fishing and rugged beach hiking. (Note: In summer on the islands, essential gear includes insect repellent, sunscreen and drinking water. And, cute as the ponies are, every time you feed one you encourage them to hang out near paved roads, a potentially lethal habit; every year, moreover, at least a few people who ignore the signs and pet the horses are also bitten or kicked.) Other places worth visiting hereabouts, especially if kids are with you, include the **Oyster & Maritime Museum** (757-336-6117; closed November-April &), with its impressive displays of live sea creatures and historical exhibits on the Eastern Shore seafood industry; the **Refuge Waterfowl Museum** (757-336-5800 ⓖ), which has carved decoys, paintings and crafts; and, six miles west on Route 175, the **NASA Visitor Center** at Wallops Island (757-824-1344; closed December-February ⓖ), which has full-scale models of rockets and airplanes, scale models of X-15 and other experimental aircraft, videos on scientific experiments in space and more. All three are free.

GETTING THERE: Chincoteague, Va., is about a 3.5-hour drive from Beltway Exit 7. Take U.S. 50 east across the Bay Bridge and south to Salisbury, pick up U.S. 13 south and then Route 175 east to the island.

WHERE TO STAY: In a motel- and campground-dominated area, the **Refuge Motor Inn** (800-544-8469; doubles $90-$105 ⓖ) stands out as a comfortable, friendly place, with cottages, a gift shop and an indoor/outdoor pool. Other choices include **Miss Molly's Inn** (800-249-0818; doubles $69-$155), where Marguerite Henry stayed; **Island Manor House** (757-336-5436; doubles $85-$130), built in 1848 by a doctor who treated Union troops there during the Civil War; and the **Inn at Poplar Corner** (757-336-6115; doubles $99-$159), a place of Victorian gingerbread charm. In New Church, Va., the **Garden and the Sea Inn** (800-824-0672; doubles $85-$165, including breakfast ⓖ) offers six elegant rooms and a fine restaurant with French country cuisine. The inn is open late March through Thanksgiving.

WHERE TO EAT: Village Restaurant (757-336-5120 ⓖ) is a local favorite. The **Castaways** (757-336-5781 ⓖ) wins points for its kiddie cocktails.

FOR MORE INFORMATION: Contact the **Chincoteague Chamber of Commerce** (757-336-6161 or *www.chincoteaguechamber.com)* or the **Chincoteague National Wildlife Refuge** (757-336-6122).

Norfolk Tugs an Ex-Salt's Heart

By Jerry Haines

PLEASE, LORD," I'm thinking as I return the young ensign's salute," don't let me geez." It's 28 years since I've been aboard a Navy ship, and for the past few hours I've been rehearsing my reactions to the anticipated highlights of the tour I'm about to take. Something between "Well, sonny, back in the real Navy . . ." and "Wow! That is, like, so totally cool."

The USS Laboon is totally cool. A new destroyer, she is the ship designated for public tours on the weekend we visit the Norfolk Navy base. She was commissioned only in 1995, and her rakish anti-radar design makes her look like the new Acura. She's powered by four gas turbine engines, while my old ship had eight leaky, oil-fired boilers that . . . *Bwaah! Geez alarm! Geez alarm! Geezer in Sector 7!* Ahem, and the Laboon's crew is 340 young women and men, all recruited by Central Casting with the specification of "clean-cut American."

My wife, Janice, and I drove from Washington on a Friday night with the intention of seeing as much of Norfolk as we could in a weekend. On Saturday we learned Norfolk Visitor Tip No. 1: Sleep late; have a big breakfast. Nothing much opens before 10 a.m., but once it does, there's so much to see that you may not have time for lunch.

Norfolk exists for the sea and seafaring. We started at Nauticus, the National Maritime Center, at the edge of the waterside downtown area. Nauticus combines traditional museum-type attractions with interactive simulators and large-screen theaters. It has an extensive exhibit on the Civil War ironclads Monitor and Merrimac and the Battle of Hampton Roads.

Although some of the video terminals seem a bit primitive, I spent several minutes at one, piloting my virtual ship out to sea (and running her aground on virtual islands). But my favorite exhibit was the first one. At the top of the escalator was a sign advertising "Sailor Language." I wondered if children should be allowed in, but the coarsest thing we found was "B is for Butthead"—which refers not to "frigate captain who has just pulled in front of you at the channel entrance" but to a type of square-ended boat.

Tied up to the dock outside Nauticus is what must be Norfolk's smallest museum. The Tug Huntington was built in 1933 and made the transitions from steam to diesel to diesel-electric power. Now she's a tugboat museum.

On board I confirmed what I'd always guessed: A tug is basically an engine, with just enough boat around it to keep it afloat. "Little Toot," I remarked to Janice, remembering the children's book about the heroic harbor tug. Sure enough, the gift shop was selling copies of "Little Toot."

Nearly every sailor in the Atlantic fleet at one time or another goes through Norfolk—if not the big Naval Operating Base, then the Portsmouth Naval Hospital, or Oceana, the huge naval air station in Virginia Beach, or the amphibious base at Little Creek.

None of these may seem likely to inspire a sentimental journey. But that's the sweet perversity of it. For every sailor who complained incessantly during his entire enlistment, there's a veteran whose pulse quickens at the smell of red lead and Brasso and who gets misty hearing the Navy hymn. Actually, they're the same person.

Your guide on the bus tour of the Norfolk Navy Base will have a handy command of the base's impressive statistics, but they quickly overwhelm you. The oddest things caught my attention instead: Street signs that are only three feet high (so airplanes can be towed down the street); big steam pipes snaking above ground (there's no zoning, so why not?); and the fact that today, in place of barracks, there are dormitories, where sailors can obtain maid service for an extra charge. Maid service! Why, when I was . . . *Bwaah!* Sorry.

And we saw the ships: carriers, looking like nuclear-powered icebergs, and cruisers, oilers, tenders and replenishment ships. There was a floating drydock with a submarine cradled inside, resembling an oversize breadbasket holding a baguette. And, in the middle of all this immensity, a line of little gray tugs— the Navy's own Little Toots—just waiting for the chance to be heroic.

But now it's time for the tour we came here for. We motor right up to Laboon's pier. (It's an open base, and you can drive onto and through it without challenge.) We are met by two enlisted sailors (one of each sex) who guide us around the upper decks and onto the bridge, proudly noting the sophisticated weapons systems and navigation equipment. "Was I ever that earnest?" I whisper to Janice. "Were you ever that young?" she whispers back.

Notwithstanding all the technology, there are still many remnants of the real, black-shoe Navy. The anchor still looks like an anchor, they still use paper charts (though supplemented by computer) for navigating, and you can still bang your head on the deck as you scramble down a ladder.

We descend to "combat," the only place where photographs are not permitted. The darkened compartment is filled with video terminals and reminds me of an arcade at the mall—except that these terminals are connected to real missiles and torpedoes.

We squint in the sun when we return to the quarterdeck. We salute the officer of the deck again and head back downtown for a visit to St. Paul's Episcopal church, the sole original building in Norfolk to survive British destruction of the city in 1776. I am reminded that we are in the South. The courtly gentleman inside apologizes that he is unable to show us the British cannonball embedded in the exterior wall, as he is not permitted to leave a lady unaccompanied in the church. The lady in question, who has come to tend the altar, is utterly astonished by this pronouncement and scoffs at the very idea.

We finish our Norfolk weekend with a harbor sail on the American Rover, a schooner. It's like visiting the brontosaurus section of Jurassic Park—enormous cranes are loading containers onto ships at the rate of one every two minutes. "Containers," mind you, are essentially semi-trailers, minus the wheels. Over at the Norfolk Southern coal terminal, another benign giant takes two rail cars at a time, rolls them over and empties them, then gives them a little pat on the behind and scoots them up a siding.

It's hard not to be impressed by Norfolk and equally difficult to figure out why it took me so long to come back. Why, the last time I was here I . . . oh, never mind.

GETTING THERE: Norfolk is a three-hour drive from the Beltway via I-95, I-295 (bypassing Richmond) and I-64 east. Then take I-564 west to the Norfolk Naval Base or I-264 west to Norfolk's downtown

BEING THERE: Besides its seafaring emphasis, Norfolk offers a variety of other attractions. The **Chrysler Museum of Art's** impressive collections include extensive displays of Tiffany glass (757-664-6200; $4 admission, $2 students and seniors; closed Mondays &). The **Douglas MacArthur Memorial** has the Old Soldier's corncob pipe and World War II memorabilia (757-441-2965 &). **St. Paul's Church**, built in 1739, is still in use and can be toured Tuesday through Friday (757-627-4353). **Norfolk Naval Base** bus tours leave from the base's tour office (9079 Hampton Blvd.; 757-444-7955 &) and cost $5 ($2.50 ages 3-11). **Navy ship tours** (they're free but not part of the bus tour) are available on weekends. **Nauticus** (800-664-1080; $7.50, $5 ages 6-17) and the **Tug Huntington** (757-627-4884; $2, $1 11 and under &) are at Norfolk's waterfront, off Boush St.. Right off Route 44, the **Boathouse** (757-622-6395), tucked behind Norfolk's Harbor Park baseball stadium, is a cavernous concert hall by the Elizabeth River. The rustic, shed-style hall, which hosts a plethora of national acts, remains a favorite with both its party-loving patrons and the performers, despite echoing acoustics and limited seating.

WHERE TO STAY: Page House Inn (800-599-7659; rates from $125-$220 double) is in Norfolk's Ghent historical district, close to the Chrysler Museum. While this 1899 Georgian mansion looks like a B&B, it was rebuilt in the 1990s to local hotel and restaurant code and thus lacks the creature discomforts (cranky radiators, bathroom down the hall) one often accepts philosophically for the sake of authenticity. All the upscale chains are represented in downtown Norfolk, and there are many inexpensive chain motels near the naval base.

WHERE TO EAT: Freemason Abbey (757-622-3966 ⓖ), a renovated church, is a neat place for Sunday brunch. **Todd Jurich's Bistro** (757-622-3210 ⓖ), which some local critics consider the best restaurant in South Hampton Roads, has an agreeable fusion cuisine. **Baker's Crust** (757-625-3600 ⓖ) is an informal bakery and sandwich-and-soupery in the Palace Shops on West 21st St. Also worth trying are the Italian favorites and brick-oven pizza of **Aldo's** (757-491-1151 ⓖ) and the eclectic American fare and wine list of **501 City Grill** (757-425-7195 ⓖ).

FOR MORE INFORMATION: Contact the **Norfolk Convention and Visitors Bureau** at 800-368-3097 or 757-664-6620 or *www.norfolk.va.us.*

THE NORTHERN NECK

A broad swath of rural country between the Potomac and Rappahannock rivers and the Chesapeake, Virginia's Northern Neck region may lack the drama of the state's better-known western mountains, but it's an excellent (and less crowded) area for hiking, biking, antique hunting and much else. True to its agricultural past, the region often seems suspended in time—whether it's the 1950s small-town atmosphere of downtown Montross, the tidy expanse of a restored 200-year-old plantation, or the prehistoric feel along the densely wooded banks of the Potomac at Westmoreland Park. Most highways here trace old tribal trails and Colonial roads, and there are said to be only six stoplights in the Neck's four counties. With its wealth of both saltwater and freshwater tributaries, this also is a fisherman's and boater's paradise. For a weekend visit, consider basing yourself in Montross, in the center of the Neck, or out in turn-of-the-century Reedville, on the bay at Cockrell's Creek. Each offers the most lodgings and eateries in their areas, and Reedville is the site of the worthwhile **Reedville Fishermen's Museum** (804-453-6529; open daily May-October ⓖ). It's also another launching point for boat trips to Smith Island, Md. (see CRISFIELD AND SMITH ISLAND, Page 162) with **Smith Island & Chesapeake Bay Cruises** (804-453-3430 ⓖ) and to Virginia's Tangier Island or up the Rappahannock River with **Tangier Island & Rappahannock River Cruises** (804-453-2628 or 800-598-2628).

The Northern Neck provides clues to the plantation-centered early lives of two famous forefathers. **George Washington Birthplace National Monument** (804-224-1732 ⓖ), a restored 18th Century Virginia tobacco farm where young George indeed slept every night, is a 530-acre park open daily in Oak Grove. Robert E. Lee's birthplace, the 1,600-acre **Stratford Hall Plantation,** a 1738 working farm with nature trails and a warm-weather, log-cabin luncheon room on the Potomac at Route 214 (804-493-8038 ⓖ), is likewise open daily. At **Westmoreland Berry Farm**, west of Oak Grove on Route 634, you can pick your own fruits and vegetables throughout the harvest season (800-997-2377 or 804-224-9171), and if you just want to walk, the adjacent Voorhees Preserve, owned by the Nature Conservancy, has nature trails on 800 acres along the Rappahannock. **Ingleside Plantation Vineyards**, south of Oak Grove on Route 638 (804-224-8687), has daily tours and tastings, plus a picnic area and a small museum. For antique hunting, try **Elderly Treasures**, Route 3 between Oak Grove and Montross (804-224-8895; 10-5, Thursday-Sunday).

If you hanker to kayak these generally calm and bird-rich waters, check with either **Atlantic Canoe & Kayak** in Alexandria (800-297-0066 or 703-838-9072), whose annual tour schedule includes a few trips to the Northern Neck, or **RiverRats** in Ophelia (804-453-3064), which offers continuous warm-weather classes, sea kayak rentals ($35 a day) and kayak tours on the Wicomico and Potomac, including several among the salt marshes and 140-foot dolomite cliffs around **Westmoreland State Park** (804-493-9191). Westmoreland park, just north of Montross, is itself a delightfully low-key, 1,300-acre place that draws everyone from hardcore sun worshipers to fishermen to the salt-water squeamish, who can swim in the Olympic-sized pool at one of end of its beach. Six miles of trails lead from the river to the 115 campsites and rental cabins inland, and high on a bluff behind the beach, next to a camp store, is another picnic area and playground overlooking the river.

GETTING THERE: Montross, Va., is about a 90-minute drive from the Beltway. Follow I-95 south to Fredericksburg, then Route 3 east to Montross. You also can take the older and more interesting route: through southern Maryland on U.S. 301, across the Potomac, then up Route 3 east.

WHERE TO STAY: Probably the Northern Neck's best known lodging, and certainly its priciest, is Irvington's genteel and renovated **Tides Inn** (800-843-3746; doubles start at $320, including breakfast and dinner). Less famous but run by the same family (now in its third generation) is the adjacent **Tides Lodge Resort** (804-438-6000; doubles $145 and up &), whose Binnacle restaurant serves excellent crab cakes. Either Tides stay makes available golf at one of three courses (the "Golden Eagle" often is ranked among Virginia's top 10), tennis, nature trails, two pools (one with saltwater), boats (paddle, sail, motor) and daily river cruises aboard the resort's own yacht. Evening events in clude music, movies and dancing, and a daily kids program offers daytime or evening activities and babysitting. The Inn's lovely dining room is not to be missed, but opt for breakfast or lunch if your budget is limited. Other less expensive lodgings on the Neck include the **Inn at Montross** (see WHERE TO EAT below), the **Mt. Holly Steamboat Inn** (804-472-3336; doubles $75 and up, including breakfast); **Linden House Bed & Breakfast** in Champlain (804-443-1170 or 800-622-1202; doubles $85-$135); **Greenwood Bed and Breakfast** in Warsaw (804-333-4353; doubles $50); and the **Washington & Lee Motel** in Montross (804-493-8093; doubles $45 and up). There's also camping near the river at **Westmoreland State Park** (804-493-8821), camping adjacent to the 115-slip marina and restaurant at **Coles Point Plantation** (804-472-3955 &) and campsites, furnished four-person cottages ($75), a pool and hiking trails at the 243-acre **Heritage Park Resort** in Warsaw (800-335-5564).

WHERE TO EAT: The **Inn at Montross** (804-493-0573) has a highly rated restaurant—and also rents rooms ($110)—although a faster way to get to know the town is lunch on a round stool at the **Peoples Drug Store** soda fountain (804-493-9505 ♿). The rustic **Stratford Hall Plantation Dining Room** (804-493-9696) serves breakfast and plantation lunches ($8 adults, $4 12 and under) from May through October. For a memorable brush with both locals and local seafood, try **McPatty's** in Kilmarnock (804-435-2290).

FOR MORE INFORMATION: Contact the **Northern Neck Visitor Information Service** (800-453-6167) or the **Westmoreland County Visitor Center** in Montross (804-493-8440).

VIRGINIA BEACH

This city, Virginia's largest, puts up more than 2.2 million visitors a year in over 11,000 aggressively generic rental units. This vacationing public—a broad mix of races, ages and beliefs—proceeds to clam up, for the most part happily. Maybe this is some natural consequence of all those military aircraft in the skies over Virginia Beach or, more likely, of the city elders' preemptive legislative strike against public revelry after 1989's student-led riots. Whatever the case, Virginia Beach's tendency toward beigeness is kind of a nice contrast to Ocean City, Md., where so many summer fun-seekers seem unable to express their truest feelings unless there's a good chance of a crowd forming.

Virginia Beach's actual beach is of record-setting length (28 miles) and a disappointing width, making it often quite crowded in July and August—except north of town (in the cottage-dominant residential areas, where outlanders should know that they also might have trouble parking legally) and south of town, especially in the lesser-known ocean community of Sandbridge. Virginia Beach also offers a three-mile, smooth-concrete "boardwalk," a fishing pier, all-day cycling or in-line skating (on a path parallel to the boardwalk) and a plethora of summer concerts. Hotels are primarily low-rise but packed close to the beach, creating intimacy—and a 3 o'clock shadow that hides the sun. As the largest city in the Commonwealth, Virginia Beach offers enough amenities and nearby historical, cultural and natural attractions to make rainy days, or non-beach months, more appealing. These riches include the **Virginia Marine Science Museum** (757-425-3474 ♿), whose $35 million makeover added a 300,000-gallon open-ocean aquarium filled with stingrays, sea turtles and sea bass, a river otter habitat and a six-story Family Channel IMAX 3D Theater. The museum also organizes boat trips to watch whales in winter and dolphins in summer. The **Contemporary Art Center of Virginia** (757-425-0000 ♿) is an eight-minute walk from the boardwalk. The 20,000-seat **Virginia Beach Amphitheater** (757-368-3000 ♿) in Princess Park, less than 10 miles southwest of the city's resort area, draws the top names on the summer concert circuit. (When it opened in May 1996, it was christened with a performance by Tidewater native Bruce Hornsby.)

Fifteen miles south of town is an eco-tourist's haven: the dunes, woodland, marsh and fields of **Back Bay National Wildlife Refuge** (757-721-2412 ♿), its 7,700 acres of undeveloped barrier-peninsula offering year-round habitat to hundreds of bird species and such mammals as otters, deer, mink, nutria and the elusive gray fox. On a recent springtime trek down the Dune Trail boardwalk, one of a web of nature walks in the refuge, *Post* reporter Gary Lee found himself winding through fern-covered paddies to a freshwater cove "as still and blue as an eye. We found enough flora and fauna to populate a minor but nonetheless wondrous rain forest," he says. "Here was a red-winged black-bird spreading jet-colored wings to reveal the shock of scarlet and snow-white feathers underneath. There was a tiger's swallowtail, a yellowish-green butterfly, fluttering lazily

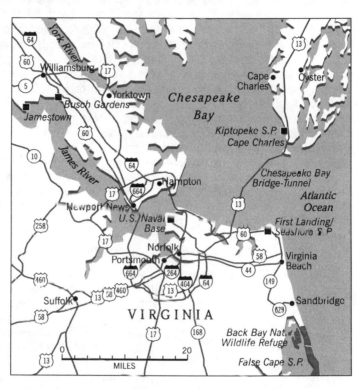

tering lazily through the breeze. And everywhere were coniferous trees, lime-green reeds and tall grass the color of light brown sugar. After a few hours of hiking, we found the special allure of a getaway to Virginia Beach to be as clear as crystal. Although the beach itself is hardly distinguishable from other popular stretches of sand in the Delmarva triangle, the surrounding area has far more ecological appeal than most other seaside retreats in the region."

Those looking for a total-immersion ecological escape in the Virginia Beach area also should consider hiking the four-mile-long trail through the Back Bay refuge to adjacent **False Cape State Park**. Accessible only by foot, bicycle or a new eco-friendly tram service, it provides as rustic and serene a wildlife environment as you can hope for. Campsites are available, but you'll have to bring your own binoculars and bug spray.

GETTING THERE: Virginia Beach is a little more than 4¼ hours, from the Beltway. Take I-95 south to I-295 east to I-64 east through Norfolk to Route 44 east (the Virginia Beach-Norfolk Expressway).

WHERE TO STAY: The resort area has 6,500 hotel and motel rooms. For oceanfront and ocean-block hotel and motel rooms, expect to pay daily rates of $90 to $200; check with **City of Virginia Beach Reservations** (800-822-3224) and **Virginia Beach Central Reservations** (800-828-7477). An unassuming but adequate choice right on the beach is the **Belvedere Motel** at 36th and Atlantic (800-425-0612; doubles $50 to $104). A kid-friendly oceanfront hotel, **Dunes Family Lodge** (757-428-7757, doubles start at $98, including two kids) has a games room, a children's host and a separate pool for youngsters, and guests can use the laundry facilities at the adjacent Dunes Motor Inn. Outside town, on its own 25-acre estate of English gardens and a lake, is the self-contained city (restaurants, a fitness center and tennis-racquetball courts, indoor-outdoor pools and a dinner theater) otherwise known as the imposing **Founders Inn and Conference Center** (757-424-5511; doubles $89-$159 ♿). **Barclay Cottage Bed and Breakfast** (757-422-1956; doubles $65-$90, closed November-March) has five rooms in a restored historic house. And north of town, **First Landing/Seashore State Park** (757-481-2131 ♿) offers beach access only to its campsite customers, of which there can be only 150 at a time. This is Virginia's most visited park, largely because of its boat launch facilities and its 19 miles of hiking and biking trails through genuinely otherworldly cypress swamps.

WHERE TO EAT: The fruits of the sea get top billing on most menus, but the same old show is produced here in increasingly varied ways. At **Timbuktu** (757-491-1800 ♿), you'll find no fried seafood platters but the most innovative and elaborate food at the oceanfront. Barbecue reigns at the **Beach Bully** (757-422-4222 ♿), and **Waterman's** (757-428-3644 ♿) offers a good mix of scallops, fresh fish, shellfish and vegetables at reasonable prices. **Mahi-Mah's** (757-437-8030 ♿) is popular for its ocean view, extended menu for the whole family, sushi bar, microbrew selection and cheery staff. Visitors often miss outstanding food in neighborhoods away from the boardwalk. The **Coastal Grill** (757-496-3348 ♿), nearer the Chesapeake than the Atlantic, is a much-lauded neighborhood restaurant serving some of the finest seafood in town, including soft-shell crabs and a range of all-American specialties like bistro chicken, roast lamb and steak. Locals are partial to a row of restaurants along the Lynnhaven Inlet off Shore Drive, known for their steamed crabs and shrimp, fish specials and outdoor seating. These include **Chick's Oyster Bar and Marina** (757-481-5757 ♿), **Bubba's Crabhouse** (757-481-0907 ♿) and the **Dockside Inn** (757-481-7211 ♿). Similarly, for after dinner, the natives lovingly refer to a section of Atlantic Ave. as "the Block"; notable residents include the mini-but-mighty **Chicho's** (757-422-6011 ♿), a tiny, crowded pub with adventuresome media masters behind the bar spinning a mix of alternative rock and rockabilly to action-packed surf footage—plus some pretty good pizza by the slice. Further up the Block,

Abbey Road (757-425-0330 ♿) is a must for the acoustically inclined, featuring fine acoustic rock and folk from local and regional artists most nights. The atmosphere's low-key at this congenial tavern, and there's even a patio for alfresco refreshment. Another favorite of both beach veterans and visitors, the **Jewish Mother** (757-422-5430 ♿), just north of the Block, offers a globe-trotting array of beers, yummy deli fare and a near-nightly schedule of blues, acoustic and easy-listening rock from local and regional artists. The decor is well-worn deco; dress is casual. And, should you be thinking everyone in Virginia Beach is just too well-behaved, find your way (it isn't easy) to the cutting-edge techno/alternative rock danceteria **Abyss** (757-422-0748 or 757-422-0486), a hulking, throbbing place of no-frills steel pipe, chain link and concrete with a large sunken dance pit and a monster-decibel sound system. A rear gangway serves as an elevated stage for a roster of underground and other acts.

FOR MORE INFORMATION: Contact the **City of Virginia Beach** at 757-437-4888 or 800-446-8038 or *www.vabeach.com.* (Staff who answer the phones for the City of Virginia Beach, by the way, can actually make your room reservations, and—because they're required to tour every hotel they represent—can offer valuable information as well).

WILLIAMSBURG/COLONIAL VIRGINIA

It can be hard to get a sense of Williamsburg in broad daylight, when the restored colonial capital is clogged with strollers, camcorders and late 20th Century fashions. "So I found myself enjoying Williamsburg the most at night, and in the rain," Post contributor Daphne White reports. "One evening," she says, "we joined a musical tour, 20th Century voyeurs observing the 18th Century nightlife. We were not to talk to the 'personages,' merely observe them as they entertained each other in period style. As we entered the first house at twilight, a mother was playing the spinet and teaching her teenage daughters the fine points of the minuet. At the more aristocratic Wythe House, we watched two portly, middle-aged men in ruffled shirts playing a string duet, their bearing very restrained. But then, just as my son began squirming with boredom, Mr. Wythe reached over to turn the page—and tipped over one of the candles on the music stand. Wax began dripping on his viola da gamba, and he quickly extinguished the flame. 'To tell you the truth, that was not the first time I've done that, and I suspect it won't be the last,' he confided to his friend. 'Maybe it would be better if I dipped the entire instrument in hot wax!' " While there are lots of historical facts to be absorbed at Williamsburg, "what I remember best are these unexpected moments, when the present slipped away and the past was momentarily revealed: the danger of fires, the fragility of life."

That said, there is still much to do around Virginia's "historic triangle"—in which the 23-mile Colonial Parkway connects points defining colonial America's beginning, middle and end: **Jamestown**, site of the first English settlement in the New World, **Williamsburg**, first capital of the newly independent Commonwealth of Virginia, and **Yorktown Battlefield**, where the British surrender ended the Revolutionary War in 1781. Contact **Colonial National His-**

torical Park (757-898-3400, or *www.nps.gov/colo*), which has visitors centers at both the Jamestown and Yorktown ends of the parkway, for information on biking, walking tours, self-guided battlefield drives, reenactments and other activities.

If you start feeling like a fifth-grader on a field trip, there's also much else to do hereabouts, without even venturing to nearby Newport News, Hampton or Norfolk. You could merely cool your heels at the **Abby Aldrich Rockefeller Folk Art Center** (757-220-7698; $10, $6.50 ages 6-12) or a Patriot Pass gets you in &), one of the largest showcases of American folk art, or head out to Route 60 for outlet mall shopping (including at the sprawling shops of **Williamsburg Pottery Factory**, 757-564-3326 &), or just browse the shops and cafes of Merchants Square, up at the College of William and Mary end of town.

If you're hot and with the kids, there's **Water Country USA**, which is open daily Memorial Day through Labor Day and on weekends in May and September (regularly $25.50, $17.95 for ages 3-6) as well as **Busch Gardens**, with a similar schedule, except it's open later. (Both can be reached at 800-343-7946 or 757-253-3350.) It may be hard for grownups to decide if long waits for popular rides or slides are worth the regular $33 Busch Garden admission ("only" $26 for ages 3 through 6), but for most kids the call is easy: This is a cool place. Discount coupons are widely available, and both theme parks also offer late-day specials. Call for details.

GETTING THERE: Most of Colonial Virginia can be reached by car in four hours, longer if you're leaving on a summer Friday afternoon and coming back Sunday. Take I-95 south to I-295 south to I-64 east to Exit 238 (Williamsburg-Camp Peary) and follow the signs. You can avoid a lot of beach-season traffic by passing up the I-64 exit off I-295 and instead following the slower-paced and more scenic U.S. 60 east.)

WHERE TO STAY: Colonial Williamsburg itself offers many vacation packages (800-447-8679), including lodging at one of four hotels, food and admission tickets. Weekend packages for couples begin at about $425 and vary by season and hotel; nightly room-only rates for fall and spring begin at $115 at the **Williamsburg Woodlands**. The **Williamsburg Hotel/Motel Association** (800-446-9244) handles reservations for more than 70 locations. **Kingsmill** (800-932-2892 &), a 3,000-acre country club-style resort on the James River three miles from Williamsburg and next door to Busch Gardens, is pricey but offers relatively reasonable packages, particularly for families. Guests can golf free at Kingsmill's nine-holer or pay $45 to $105 for a round at any of its three renowned 18-hole courses. Then there's the Spa at Kingsmill, with packages from $75 (manicure/pedicure) to $329 (the works). A clean, reasonable place with a great breakfast buffet, **Courtyard by Marriott** is just east of town on U.S. 60E (757-221-0700; doubles from $99 off-season, $135 in summer &). The Williamsburg area now has more than 20 B&Bs, many along Jamestown and Richmond roads on the western edge of town. Among these, the **Cedars** (800-296-3591; doubles $95 and up) probably is the largest and most professionally run. A 10-room Georgian-style brick structure, the inn is elegantly furnished in a Williamsburg motif, with breakfast served on a flower-filled sun porch. **Liberty Rose** (800-545-1825; doubles $135-$195) has four whimsically furnished Victorian rooms with all the amenities that a romantic, respite-seeking soul could want. **The Legacy of Williamsburg Tavern** (800-962-4722; doubles $135-$185) is a lovely replica of an early American tavern, with two rooms and two suites filled with antiques that are offered for sale. The neighboring **Williamsburg Sampler** (800-722-1169; doubles $100 and up) is a six-room, colonial-style brick home with a more eclectic assortment of antiques.

Around Jamestown, you can camp year round among the 600 sites at **Jamestown Beach Campsites** (757-229-7609 &). The **Best Western West Park** (757-229-1134), six miles from the settlement, one of the closest motels to the historic area. Adjacent to Yorktown Battlefield, **Newport News Park** (757-888-3333 &) has camping year round, and the **Duke of York Motor Hotel** (757-898-3232 &) offers great views of the York River, a mile from the Colonial Parkway's Yorktown terminus.

WHERE TO EAT: Within Colonial Williamsburg, dining reservations can be made before arrival by calling their 800-447-8679 number. If you have time for just one tavern meal, make it **Chowning's Tavern**, meant to replicate Josiah Chowning's 1766 tavern, with wait staff in period dress, reasonable prices on authentic colonial fare (Welsh rarebit, meat pies, Brunswick stew) and nightly gambols—colonial-style music, games and other "diversions." There are family gambols early in the evening, but the songs get bawdier as the evening wears on.

For a reasonable buffet outside the colonial compound, try **Country Harvest** (757-229-2698 &); for deli and great soup, **Beethoven's Inn** (757-229-7069 &). For a special dinner, make a reservation—they're recommended year round—at **Trellis** (757-229-8610 &), widely acclaimed as one of the area's best restaurants, in the tony Merchants Square center west of the historic district. In the small town of Yorktown, the **Yorktown Pub** (757-898-8793) is a cool and friendly spot, with decent food, to rest between battles. And **Le Yaca** (757-220-3616 &), in the Village Shops at Kingsmill, is an airy and creative French restaurant whose appetizers, salads and desserts alone can be worth the (moderately high) cost.

FOR MORE INFORMATION: For information about and reservations in **Colonial Williamsburg**, call 800-447-8679 or visit *www.history.org*. A Patriot's Pass (good for a year) costs $34 for adults, $19 for ages 6-12. The Basic Admission Ticket (good for one day only, and not including all attractions and tours) is $26 for adults, $15 for children. You'll find that Williamsburg offers a dizzying array of programs and attractions, most of which are included in a Patriot's Pass, but others require extra fees, or just early reservations. For information about specific programs, tours and tickets, call 757-220-7645. And when you arrive, pick up a copy of the Visitor's Companion, which provides a complete calendar of events. For general information on eating, staying and sightseeing in the area, contact the **Williamsburg Convention and Visitors Bureau** at 800-368-6511.

Cross-Preferences

ANTIQUES

Following are specific antique stores and fairs that are cited in the text, followed by other towns and roadsides that have plentiful antique shopping.

a. Stores

b. Towns and Roadsides

ARTS

BARGAIN STORES, OUTLET CENTERS

BIKING

BIRDING

CAMPING/CABINS

CANOEING, KAYAKING AND RAFTING

CHEAP EATS/LOCAL HANGOUTS

FAMILY FRIENDLY

The following are in addition to the numerous beach resorts in the book.

FISHING

Index

A

Abbey Road (R), Virginia Beach, Va. 185
Abner's (R), Chesapeake Beach, Md. 146
Academy of Natural Sciences, Phila. 62
Access Atlantic City (N.J.) 80
Adam's Place for Ribs, Pr. Frederick, Md. 143
Adamstown 66
Addy Sea Bed and Breakfast, Bethany, Del. 171
Admiral Fell Inn, Baltimore 57
Adolpho's (R), Westminster, Md. 72
Adrian's Book Café, Baltimore 55
Afton Mountain Vineyard (Va.) 16
Albert Music Hall, Waretown, N.J. 81
Alden House (H), Lititz, Pa. 66
Aldie, Va. 98
Aldo's (R), Norfolk, Va. 180
Allegheny Adventures, Cumberland, Md. 131
Allegheny County, Md. 130
Allegheny Expeditions, Cumberland, Md. 131
Allenberry Resort, Boiling Springs, Pa. 70
American Pie (S), Manayunk, Pa. 61
America's Cup Cafe, Rock Hall, Md. 156
Amsterdam Court (H), New York 53
Andy's (R), Chestertown, Md. 155
Angel of the Sea (H), Cape May, N.J. 77
Ann Street B&B, Baltimore 57
Annapolis (Md.) Accommodations 145
Annapolis, Md. 143–146
Antietam National Battlefield (Md.) 108–109
Antique Emporium, Pt. Pleasant Bch., N.J. 88
Antrim 1844 (H), Taneytown, Md. 72
Apollo Civic Theater, Martinsburg, W.Va. 107
Appalachian Trail 70, 112
Appetite Repair Shop (R), Sperryville, Va. 34
April Cornell (S), New York 53
Aquatic Center, Oakland, Md. 128
Ark (R), Pt. Pleasant Bch., N.J. 89
Artists at Work Gallery, Elkins, W.Va. 120
Ash Lawn-Highland (A), Charlottesville, Va. 14
Ashby Inn (H,R), Paris, Va. 36
Assateague Island 174–175 See also Berlin/
    Snow Hill, Md.
Assateague Island Tours, Chincoteague, Va. 175
Assawoman Wildlife Refuge (Del.) 171
Atlantic Canoe & Kayak, Alexandria, Va. 181
Atlantic City, N.J. 78–80
Atlantic Hotel, Berlin, Md. 173
Atlantic Hotel, Ocean City, Md. 167

Atlantic House (H), Ocean City, Md. 167
Audrey Claire (R), Philadelphia 61
Augusta Festival/Workshops, Elkins, W.Va. 120
Avalon Theatre, Easton, Md. 156

B

B&B of Maryland 145
B&O Railroad Museum, Baltimore 56
B.J.'s on the Water (R), Ocean City, Md. 167
Back Bay National Wildlife Refuge (Va.) 183
Back Creek Inn, Solomons, Md. 147
Bailey's deli, Snow Hill, Md. 173
Baker's Crust (R), Norfolk, Va. 180
Baldwin's Book Barn, West Chester, Pa. 68
Baltimore, Md. 54–58
Baltimore Tickets 55
Baltimore Zoo 56
Bankhouse (H), West Chester, Pa. 69
Banking House Inn Restaurant, Milford, Del.
    170
Banneker-Douglass Museum, Annapolis, Md.
    144
Barbara Fritchie House (A), Frederick, Md. 96
Barboursville Vineyards (Va.) 14
Barclay Cottage B&B, Virginia Beach 184
Barge House Museum, Annapolis, Md. 144
Barrett's B&B, St. Michaels, Md. 158
Barry's Gull B&B, Rehoboth, Del. 170
Basil T's (R), Red Bank, N.J. 85
Bass River State Forest (N.J.) 81
Bath House, Berkeley Springs, W.Va. 105
Batona Trail (N.J.) 81
Batsto, N.J. 80
Battle Creek Cypress Swamp, Prince Frederick,
    Md. 146
Battlefield B&B, Gettysburg, Pa. 101
Baugher's (R), Westminster, Md. 72
Bavarian Inn (H,R), Shepherdstown, W.Va. 111
Bay Cafe, Fenwick, Del. 172
Bay Head (N.J.) Windsurfing 88
Bay Head, N.J. See Point Pleasant Beach, N.J.
Bay Wolf (R), Rock Hall, Md. 156
Bayside Inn, Smith Island, Md. 162
Beach Bully (R), Virginia Beach, Va. 184
Beach House (R), Rehoboth, Del. 170
Bear Branch Nature Center, Westminster, Md.
    71
Bear Run Nature Reserve, Ohiopyle, Pa. 136

A=attraction H=hotel/place to stay R=restaurant S=shop   199

A=attraction H=hotel/place to stay R=restaurant S=shop

D

Daily Grind (R), Baltimore 55
Deep Creek (Md.) Outfitters 128
Deep Creek Lake, Md. 127–128
Deep Creek Lake State Park (Md.) 128
Deer Park Inn (R), Oakland, Md. 130
Deerlane Cottages, Luray, Va. 27
Delaplane (Va.) Store & Antiques Ctr. 35
Delaware Seashore State Park 170
Dewey Beach, Del. 169
DiBruno Bros. (R), Philadelphia 60
DiscoverSea Shipwreck Museum, Fenwick, Del. 171
Dixon's Furniture, Crumpton, Md. 161
Dobbin House (R), Gettysburg, Pa. 101
Dock's Oyster House, Atlantic City, N.J. 80
Dockside Express, Tilghman, Md. 153
Dockside Inn (R), Virginia Beach, Va. 184
Dolly Sods Wilderness (W.Va.) 116, 118
Douglas MacArthur Memorial, Norfolk, Va. 179
Douthat State Park (Va.) 39
Downriver Canoe Co., Front Royal, Va. 28
Dr. Dodson House, St. Michaels, Md. 158
Drip (R), New York 53
Dry Dock Restaurant, Solomons, Md. 148
Duke of York Motor Hotel, Yorktown, Va. 187
Dunes Family Lodge, Virginia Beach, Va.. 184

E

Earthly Paradise (R), Warrenton, Va. 36
Eastern Neck National Wildlife Refuge (Md.) 154
Eastern Shore Chamber Music Festival (Md.) 156
Easton, Md. 156–157
Ebbit Room (R), Cape May, N.J. 77
Edgar Allan Poe Museum, Richmond 21
Edith's Place (R), Solomons, Md. 148
Eisenhower National Historic Site (Md.) 100
Elderly Treasures, Oak Grove, Va. 181
Elk River (W.Va.) Touring Center 121
Elkins, W.Va. 120–123
Embassy Suites Hotel, Philadelphia 62
Emlen Physick Estate (A), Cape May, N.J. 75
Endless Caverns, New Market, Va. 26
Endless Mtn. Retreat Ctr., Hightown, Va. 42
English Inn, Charlottesville, Va. 15
Ernie's Texas Cafe, Gettysburg, Pa. 101

Ewell Tide Inn, Smith Island, Md. 162
Expressions (S), Elkins, W.Va. 120

F

Fager's Island (R), Ocean City, Md. 167
Fairville Inn, Chadds Ford, Pa. 69
Fallingwater (A), Ohiopyle, Pa. 136
False Cape State Park, Va. 183
Famous 4th Street Delicatessen, Phila. 61
Fan district, Richmond 21
Fantastico's (R), Warrenton, Va. 36
Farnsworth House Inn (H,R), Gettysburg, Pa. 101
Fauquier County, Va. 34–36
Feast of Reason (R), Chestertown, Md. 155
Fells Point See Baltimore, Md.
Fenwick (Del.) Water Park 171
Fenwick Inn, Ocean City, Md. 167
Fenwick Island (Del.) State Park 171
Fenwick Island, Del. See Bethany Beach/ Fenwick Island, Del.
Findings Antiques, Berlin, Md. 172
First Landing/Seashore State Park 184
501 City Grill, Norfolk, Va. 180
Five Spot (R), Philadelphia 60
Flag Ponds Nature Park, Lusby, Md. 146
Fleetwood Farm B&B, Leesburg, Va. 99
Flint Hill (Va.) Public House 34
Flying Circus (A), Bealeton, Va. 34
Forsythe National Wildlife Refuge (N.J.) 79
Fort Lewis Lodge, Bath County, Va. 40
Fort McHenry, Baltimore 55
Founders Inn, Virginia Beach, Va. 184
Four and Twenty Blackbirds (R), Flint Hill, Va. 34
4-U Restaurant, Seneca Rocks, W.Va. 117
Fox Diner, Front Royal, Va. 29
Franklin (Pa.) Mint Museum 68
Franklin Institute, Philadelphia 62
Fran's Place, Purcellville, Va. 102
Frederick, Md. 96
Fredericksburg (Va.) Natl. Military Park 19
Fredericksburg, Va. 18–20
Freemason Abbey (R), Norfolk, Va. 180
Frick Collection, New York 52
Friends of Rappahannock, Fredricksburg, Va. 19
Frog and the Redneck (R), Richmond 22
Front Porch (R), Seneca Rocks, W.Va. 117
Front Royal (Va.) Canoe Co. 28

A=attraction H=hotel/place to stay R=restaurant S=shop

L

L. Sarcone & Sons (R), Philadelphia 60
La Fonte (R), Berkeley Springs, W.Va.. 106
La La Land (R), Rehoboth, Del. 170
La Petit Auberge (R), Fredericksburg, Va. 20
La Rosa Negra (R), Lewes, Del. 169
Lagoon's Island Grille, Chesapeake Beach, Md. 146
Lake Moomaw (Va.) 39
Lake Pointe Inn, Deep Creek Lake, Md. 129
Lancaster County, Pa. 63–66
Land of Little Horses, Gettysburg, Pa. 100
Landis Valley Museum (A), Lancaster, Pa. 66
Lansdowne Conference Resort, Leesburg, Va. 100
Latin Quarter (R), New York 54
Latitude 38 (R), Oxford, Md. 159
L'Auberge Provençale (H,R), White Post, Va. 29
Laurel Caverns, Chalk Hill, Pa. 136
Laurel Highlands, Pa. 136–138
Laurel Highlands River Tours (Pa.) 128, 136
Laurel Mills Farm (H), Castleton, Va. 34
Lazyjack Inn, Tilghman Island, Md. 153
Le Bernardin (R), New York 53
Le Yaca (R), Williamsburg, Va. 187
Le Zinc (R), Oxford, Md. 159
Leesburg, Va. 97–102
Legacy of Williamsburg (Va.) Tavern (H) 187
Les Celebrités (R), New York 54
Lewes, Del. 168–169
Lewis Mountain Cabins, Shenandoah National Park 32
Liberty Rose (H), Williamsburg, Va. 187
Lighthouse (H), Ocean City, Md. 167
Lighthouse Inn (R), Solomons, Md. 148
Limberlost Trail, Shenandoah National Park 30
Lincoln Train Museum, Gettysburg, Pa. 100
Linden House B&B, Champlain, Va. 181
Linden vineyards (Va.) 29, 35
Lista's (R), Baltimore 58
L'Italia (R), Staunton, Va. 45
Little Inn, Shepherdstown, W.Va. 111
Little Kraut (R), Red Bank, N.J. 85
Loblolly Landings & Lodge, Cambridge, Md. 160
Lobster House, Cape May, N.J. 78
Lodge at Chalk Hill (Pa.) 138

Loews Annapolis (H), Md. 145
Loft Mountain Campgrounds, Shenandoah National Park, Va. 32
Longwood Gardens, Kennett Square, Pa. 68
Longwood Inn (R), Kennett Square, Pa. 69
Looking Glass House (H), Afton, Va. 18
Lost Dog (R), Shepherdstown, W.Va. 110
Loudoun County, Va. 97–102
Loudoun Museum, Leesburg, Va. 98
Luray (Va.) Caverns 26
Luray (Va.) Caverns Motel East 27
Luray (Va.) Reptile Center & Dinosaur Park 26
Luray, Va. 23–27
Lutece, New York 53
Luv N' Oven (R), Scottsville, Va. 15

M

Ma Jolie (S), Manayunk, Pa. 61
Mad Batter (R), Cape May, N.J. 78
Maggie L. Walker National Historic Site, Richmond 22
Maharaja (R), Charlottesville, Va. 15
Mahi-Mah's (R), Virginia Beach, Va. 184
Main Stay B&B, Medford, N.J. 81
Mainstay (A), Rock Hall, Md. 155
Manassas (Va.) National Battlefield Park 36
Manayunk, Pa 61
Manheim, Pa. 65
Manor Inn, Berkeley Springs, W.Va. 106
Maple Festival, Highland County, Va. 41
Marietta, Pa. 65
Marine Mammal Stranding Center, Brigantine, N.J. 79
Mariner's Motel, Rock Hall, Md. 155
Mario's (R), Red Bank, N.J. 85
Mario's Italian Food, Purcellville, Va. 102
Market House, Annapolis, Md. 145
Marriott Ranch (H,A), Hume, Va. 35
Marriott Waterfront, Annapolis, Md. 145
Martell's (R), Pt. Pleasant Bch., N.J. 88
Martinsburg, W.Va. 106–110
Mary Washington House, Fredericksburg, Va. 18
Maryland Inn (H), Annapolis, Md. 144
Maryland Yachts, Oxford, Md. 158
Matoaka Beach Cabins, St. Leonard, Md. 143
Maxilla & Mandible (S), New York 52
Mayflower Hotel, New York 53
McClive's (R), McHenry, Md. 130

N

A=attraction H=hotel/place to stay R=restaurant S=shop

O

Oasis Vineyards (Va.) 29, 35
Oatlands Plantation (A), Leesburg, Va. 98
Obrycki's (R), Baltimore 58
Ocean City, Md. 165–168
Ohiopyle State Park (Pa.) 136
O'Hurley's General Store, Shepherdstown, W.Va. 110
Old Dominion Brewpub, Leesburg, Va. 101
Old Jail Museum, Warrenton, Va. 35
Old Mill Inn (R), Spring Lake Heights, N.J. 87
Old Pharmacy Cafe, Shepherdstown, W.Va. 111
Old Pro Golf, Ocean City, Md. 167
Old Town Cafe, Warrenton, Va. 36
Olde Kilbourn Mill (S), Martinsburg, W.Va. 107
Olde Mudd Tavern, Thornburg, Va. 20
Ole Mink Farm (H), Thurmont, Md. 96
Oriskany Inn (R), Canaan, W.Va. 120
Orpheum theater, Baltimore 55
Out of the Fire Cafe (R), Easton, Md. 157
Outpost outfitters, Hot Springs, Va. 40
Overall Run, Shenandoah National Park 30
Oxford (Md.) Inn 158
Oxford (Md.) Market 159
Oxford, Md. 158–159
Oxford-Bellevue Ferry (Md.) 158
Oyster & Maritime Museum, Chincoteague, Va. 175
Oyster Point Hotel, Red Bank, N.J. 85

P

Page House Inn, Norfolk, Va. 179
Palais Royal (S), Manayunk, Pa. 61
Pampered Palate, Staunton, Va. 45
Panorama Steak House, Berkeley Springs, W.Va. 106
Paramount's King's Dominion, Doswell, Va. 19
Park Hyatt at the Bellevue, Philadelphia 62
Park-n-Dine, Hancock, Md. 133
Parkhurst (R), Luray, Va. 27
Pasta Plus, Rock Hall, Md. 156
Patriot Cruises, St. Michaels, Md. 157
Pat's King of Steaks, Philadelphia 61
Paw Paw Tunnel (Md.) 133
Peach Blossoms (R), Easton, Md. 157
Peaches at Sunset (R), Cape May, N.J. 78
Penn Alps (R), Grantsville, Md. 130
Pennmerryl Farm (H), Staunton, Va. 44

Penn's View Hotel, Philadelphia 61
Peoples Drug Store 182
People's Place (A), Intercourse, Pa. 66
Peppermill Gourmet Grille, Martinsburg, W.Va. 110
Pescado's, Tilghman Island, Md. 153
Philadelphia 58–62
Phillips Mushroom Museum, Kennett Sq., Pa. 68
Physick House (A), Philadelphia 59
Piccolo's Fells Point (R), Baltimore 58
Piedmont Vineyards & Winery (Va.) 35
Pierpont (R), Baltimore 58
Pinelands (N.J.) Preservation Alliance 81
Pines Motel, Crisfield, Md. 162
Piney Point Lighthouse Museum & Park, Md. 149
Piper House B&B, Sharpsburg, Md. 111
Plain & Fancy Farm (A), Intercourse, Pa. 66
Planet Wayside (R), Hamilton, Va. 102
Planet X (R), Rehoboth, Del. 170
Play It Again Sam (R), Chestertown, Md. 155
Please Touch Museum, Philadelphia 62
Pocomoke River Canoe Co., Snow Hill, Md. 173
Pocomoke River State Forest and Park (Md.) 173
Point Lookout State Park (Md.) 149–150
Point Pleasant Beach, N.J. 87–89
Popover Cafe, New York 53
Poppi's (R), St. Michaels, Md. 158
Potomac Appalachian Trail Club 32, 43
Potomac Eagle (A), Romney, W.Va. 132
Powel House (A), Philadelphia 59
Precision Rafting (Md./Pa.) 128
Prospect Hill (H), Charlottesville, Va. 15
Prospect Peak (A), Berkeley Springs, W.Va. 106
Pullman (R), Staunton, Va. 45
Pulpit & Palette B&B, Martinsburg, W.Va. 109
Purcellville (Va.) Inn (R) 102
Pusey's Country Store, Snow Hill, Md. 172
Pusser's Landing (R), Annapolis, Md. 145

Q

Quick Book 53

R

Radisson Empire, New York 53

A=attraction H=hotel/place to stay R=restaurant S=shop

Y

Z

ACKNOWLEDGEMENTS

For making *Escape Plans* possible, thanks are owed to many people. Among *Post* staff members and contributors whose writing and editing found their way into these pages, much credit goes to Eric Brace, Carolyn Spencer Brown, John Deiner, Larry Fox, Anne Groer, John F. Kelly, Gary Lee, Kathy Legg, Nancy Lewis, Jeanne Maglaty, M.J. McAteer, Eugene Meyer, Peat O'Neil, Lois Romano, Lloyd Rose, Carol Sottili, Craig Stoltz, K.C. Summers, Linton Weeks, James Yenckel, Eve Zibart and, especially, frequent *Escapes* contributors Jerry Haines, Bill Heavey, Patrick Symmes, Amy Brecount White and Daphne White. No less crucial were the freelance contributions of Jeannette Belliveau, Barry Berkey, Lisa Bregman, Helen Chappell, Patricia Dempsey, Margaret Engel, Susan Glick, JoAnn Greco, Steve Hendrix, Donavan Kelly, Dana Lemaster, John Luck, Jay Mallin, Stephanie Mansfield, Cathleen McCarthy, Anne McKeithen, Barbara Morris, Mariah Nelson, Christine H. O'Toole, Todd Pitock, Adam Seussel, Jeff Stein and Linda Turbyville.

For his nearly two decades of encouragement and support, *Post* executive editor Len Downie has my deepest appreciation, as does former *Post* managing editor Bob Kaiser, the forward thinker who took the first steps to make this book happen. Without the advice, friendship and occasional armed interventions of the founding editor of *Weekend*, the late Dan Griffin, and former *Travel* editor Linda Halsey, this book might have indeed happened—but surely without me. Without the encouragement, creative counsel and patience of former *Travel* editor Craig Stoltz, it might not have happened at all.

Working with the team that put this book together has been both exhiliarating and humbling, starting with designer Bob Barkin and illustrator-like-no-other Susan Davis, and continuing with graphics whiz Kathy Myrick, the *Post's* own world-class cartographer Dick Furno and Herculean researcher Susan Breitkopf (who provided a sharp editing eye as well). Most heartfelt thanks go to *Escape Plans'* multi-talented editor-publisher, Noel Epstein, who put that team together.

Last and about as far from least as you can get, words can't describe how grateful I am to my wife, Charmaine, stepson Luke and the rest of my family for their unshakable love and support.

—RP